INSIDE THE
BELTWAY

A Guide to
Washington Reporting

Second Edition

INSIDE THE BELTWAY

A Guide to Washington Reporting

Second Edition

Don Campbell

Wendell Cochran

Iowa State Press
A Blackwell Publishing Company

Don Campbell, currently a lecturer and freelance writer, has more than 35 years journalistic experience as a reporter, editor, political analyst, author, educator, researcher, syndicate manager and newsroom consultant. He served as Gannett News Service managing editor, as Washington editor of USA Today, and as Gannett's White House correspondent, national political writer, political editor and congressional correspondent.

Wendell Cochran is an associate professor and journalism division director at American University in Washington, D.C. He has more than 25 years in daily newspaper journalism, including experience as a Gannett regional and national correspondent based in Washington, D.C.

©1991 Iowa State University Press

©2003 Iowa State Press
A Blackwell Publishing Company
All rights reserved

Iowa State Press
2121 State Avenue, Ames, Iowa 50014

Orders:	1-800-862-6657
Office:	1-515-292-0140
Fax:	1-515-292-3348
Web site:	www.iowastatepress.com

Authorization to photocopy items for internal or personal use, or the internal or personal use of specific clients, is granted by Iowa State Press, provided that the base fee of $.10 per copy is paid directly to the Copyright Clearance Center, 222 Rosewood Drive, Danvers, MA 01923. For those organizations that have been granted a photocopy license by CCC, a separate system of payments has been arranged. The fee code for users of the Transactional Reporting Service is 0-8138-1494-4/2003 $.10.

♾ Printed on acid-free paper in the United States of America

First edition, ©1991, Iowa State University Press
Second edition, ©2003, Iowa State Press

Library of Congress Cataloging-in-Publication Data

Campbell, Don, 1948–
     Inside the beltway: a guide to Washington reporting/Don Campbell, Wendell Cochran.—
     2nd ed.
       p. cm.
     Includes bibliographic references and index. ISBN 0-8138-1494-4 (alk paper)
     1. Journalism—Political aspects—United States. 2. Reporters and reporting—
Washington (D.C.). 3. Press and politics—Washington (D.C.). I. Cochran, Wendell. II. Title.
PN4899.W29C36 2003
071'.53—dc21

                                                        2002155859

The last digit is the print number: 9 8 7 6 5 4 3 2 1

DEDICATION

To Emmaline, Eden and Julia

and

To Mom and Dad (you make it easy to "honor thy father and mother").
To Susanne (who had given up hope). And especially to
Faye (you truly are "my soul and my heart's inspiration").

CONTENTS

PREFACE

This book, like the first edition published in 1991, attempts to shed some light on how Washington works, or at least to explain the workaday and rarely glamorous world of some of the best reporters who cover the place. Along with updating the first book throughout, this edition includes three new chapters. The new first chapter suggests that the historical model for Washington journalism—a codependency that connects government and reporters—no longer serves the government, journalism or the public well. It also explores ways journalists might update their approach to Washington reporting. It is based on a survey and on discussions with leading journalists and media watchers. The other two new chapters cover regional reporting as a specialty and the challenges facing foreign correspondents in Washington.

Although the authors between them have observed Washington up close for 40 years, the conclusions and advice rendered herein are drawn heavily from the observations of others.

ACKNOWLEDGMENTS

No book is done by the authors alone and we owe great debts to:

Our friends and colleagues in the Washington press corps who willingly lent their time and insights to both the first and the current edition of "Inside the Beltway."

The staff at American University, including Maralee Csellar, who generated the lists of journalists included in the survey described in Chapter 1; Myle Luong, who handled the computer work necessary to distribute and analyze the survey results; and Rose Ann Robertson, the best editor we've ever known.

The students in Wendell's Seminar in Journalism class at American University in the spring semester of 2002: Gihane Askar, Benjamin Duncan, Pichaya Fitts, Debbie Hodges, Toni Johnson, Brent Kendall, Timur Loynab, Yasmin Sati and Rachel Zoberman. This book, literally, could not have been done without them. Their long hours of research, interviewing and transcribing made it possible for us to cover a lot of ground in a little time. Their work produced information and material that added immeasurably to the book. Write down their names, you will hear more from them in the future.

Tony Mauro and Jerry Moskal, who helped refresh our understanding of the intricacies of the U.S. Supreme Court and the U.S. Tax Court.

Our families, especially our wives: Julia Wallace and Faye Cochran.

Finally, Wendell wants to thank Don for letting me "move in" on his project.

Don Campbell
Wendell Cochran
March, 2003

INSIDE THE
BELTWAY

A Guide to
Washington Reporting

Second Edition

1 THE UNEASY ALLIANCE

A great deal has changed in Washington and in journalism in the dozen years since the first edition of *Inside the Beltway* was published in 1991. The end of the Cold War and the collapse of the Soviet Union, leaving the United States as the sole superpower in the world, put even more focus on Washington as the predominant world capital. The 1994 Republican takeover of the House of Representatives after 40 years of Democratic control—and the GOP's ability to sustain its House majority for a decade—sent shockwaves through Washington as old leaders faded away (or got pushed aside) and new power bases were established. Each of the presidential and congressional elections from 1992 through 2002 has exposed a deeply divided electorate that appears unwilling to give a significant advantage to either major political party. One result of this political split has been, in the eyes of most observers, an increase in partisan wrangling as the Republicans and Democrats try to find issues to help them break the political logjam and emerge with a clear majority that will give them a mandate for governing the nation.

For most of the 1990s the nation enjoyed the longest economic boom in American history, one that promised the possibility of eliminating the huge federal budget deficit built up during the Cold War and the post-World War II expansion of social programs. But a downturn in the economy as the new century began once again brought the nation face to face with questions about whether it has the resources to deal with such major issues as the need to strengthen Social Security before it is overwhelmed by baby boom retirees over the next couple of decades.

Even more dramatically, the terrorist attacks of Sept. 11, 2001, demonstrated that the nation's security is not assured simply because no other nation has the power, at present, to challenge American might. The ensuing "war on terror" has forced the United States and its government to rethink military strategy and tactics, to be sure, and to shift significant resources back to the Defense Department after a decade of mostly stable or declining military expenditures as a share of the federal budget. Additionally, and perhaps more important, it has caused Americans to confront the trade-offs that might exist between having an open society and having domestic security. Finding that balance in a nation governed by a Constitution that guarantees the primacy of individual liberties—including freedom of expression—over the interests of the central government, and in a nation so accustomed to "domestic tranquility," will test virtually every institution, including journalism.

For Washington-based reporters and editors, these political, economic and cultural upheavals have meant the need to learn to tell old stories from new perspectives and to confront a set of issues that, if not entirely novel, had been given scant attention in the past. Many Washington reporters, accustomed to mostly dealing with a congressional leadership dominated by Democrats, have struggled to develop new sources and to understand the ways in which issues are being framed by the newly ascendant leaders. Of course, covering Washington has never been easy, but the current challenges seem to present especially thorny questions for the profession. In particular, will journalists in Washington be up to the task of putting these political, economic and cultural changes into context? Will they be willing to take the risks associated with examining the government's performance in the war on terror? Will they vigorously root out and challenge government intrusions into privacy? If the Washington press is to live up to these challenges, it will have to do so against a discouraging backdrop of citizen disinterest in major issues, corporate and competitive business pressures, changes inside journalism that seem to devalue public affairs reporting, and a lack of public credibility that makes it easier for government officials to dismiss aggressive reporting as meddling at best or unpatriotic at worst.

Nearly every reporter or editor would tell you that journalism serves democracy by giving citizens access to information to help them make better decisions about important issues in their lives. The evidence, unfortunately, is that much of the public doesn't seem attuned to that argument. Despite the historic occurrences of the past few years, Washington news is not in great demand from readers and viewers across the nation, according to surveys done for the Pew Research Center for the People and the Press. In 2002, in the wake of the terror attacks, only about one in five Americans said they "follow news about Washington closely." The 2002 figure was a little higher, but still in line with previous Pew surveys: In 2000 the comparable number was 17 percent; in 1998, it was about 19 percent. Additionally, journalists need to ask whether some of this lack of interest stems from the way the public perceives the profession. A great deal has been written about bias in the press, but whatever journalists feel about the merits of those arguments, they should understand, as Washington Post political reporter Thomas B. Edsall wrote in 2001 in Public Perspectives, a magazine published by the Roper Center for Public Opinion Research: There is a "public perception that the press, in terms of beliefs, ideas, and political values, stands apart from the rest of the citizenry. . . . Journalists are substantially more cynical about the motives of politicians than either the public or policy elites. . . . And perhaps most significantly, the media diverge from both the public and from the policymaking community in terms of partisanship and ideology" (Edsall, 1).

And the nation's editors seem to be responding to the public with an indifference of their own toward Washington news. In an unpublished study of more than 4,200 American newspaper front pages taken from the first 100 days of 2000, co-author Wendell Cochran found that just a third of the pages even mentioned the president or the White House; about 30 percent mentioned Congress. While no similar study has been conducted since Sept. 11, 2001, intuition says that the war on terror and subsequent developments—including a massive reorganization under way to create a new Department of Homeland Security—have produced a larger front-page focus on stories based in Washington. Yet Columbia Journalism Review reported in 2002 that many newspapers have closed or reduced their presence in Washington, while a study by American Journalism Review showed that coverage of many federal agencies declined after Sept. 11.

External factors are not the only forces at work in journalism, however; the world of news also has been shaken internally in the past dozen years. About 120 newspapers have disappeared from American cities since 1991, according to the Newspaper Association of America, as the trend toward consolidation of newspaper ownership proceeded apace. Daily newspaper readership fell from about 60 percent of the population in 1991 to about 52 percent in 2001. In 1991 two-thirds of all American newspapers were published in the afternoon, by 2001 it was less than half; in 1991 afternoon newspapers accounted for 31 percent of circulation, by 2001 it was under 16 percent. Television became even more dominant as a news source for most Americans over the past decade, but even there the story was mixed. Ratings of three network evening news shows have fallen dramatically, replaced in some cases by competing cable news channels, in some cases by prime-time "magazine" shows produced by the networks' own news departments. While it may be difficult to remember how recently it occurred, the emergence of cable television as a prominent source of news also is a key feature of the past dozen years. The Gulf War of 1990 and early 1991 was the real coming-out party for Cable News Network. MSNBC and the Fox News Channel didn't exist until 1996. These channels were spawned at least partly in response to dramatic growth in the number of cable television subscribers, from about 54 percent of U.S. households at the beginning of the 1990s to about 68 percent at the end.

For those in areas of the country where cable still isn't available, satellite systems gave millions more television viewers access to the channels first developed for cable distribution. C-SPAN, one of the first cable channels to make a real impact on Washington journalism, estimates that 85 million households have access to its offerings, the centerpiece of which is gavel-to-gavel coverage of the House of Representatives and the Senate. The network estimates that more than 20 million people tune in each week. It is hard to measure C-SPAN's effect in newsrooms and offices around Washington. When Congress is in session, nearly every newsroom has a television tuned to C-SPAN, and for some reporters, much of their congressional coverage consists of watching TV. The same is true of congressional offices, where staff members can monitor floor developments as they happen.

Certainly, members of the House and Senate are aware that when they are speaking, the camera is on them, and they know that their constituents might be watching. The rules of Congress are that members are not supposed to play to the galleries; but the reality of C-SPAN is that it gives politicians (and others) a direct link to voters, and a chance to bypass the press. The 24-hour schedules of the cable networks have created a new form of "wall-to-wall" news, in which one story, covered from many different angles, takes over the airwaves for hours or days at a time. Some of the more memorable ones: the O.J. Simpson trial, the Clinton scandals, the Chandra Levy disappearance, the aftermath of election 2000. The 24-hour channels also have given rise to a variety of Washington-based talk shows, such as CNN's "Crossfire" and MSNBC's "Hardball with Chris Matthews," which demand instant analysis and commentary, usually spiced up with a bit of shouting on the part of the hosts or the guests or both. Often these shows feature print and broadcast journalists as guests, making them into celebrities and calling into question the traditional line between news and opinion. But they also provide platforms for politicians and activists, who use them to deliver their messages directly to the people.

Unquestionably, however, the most important media development of the 1990s was the creation of the World Wide Web. The Web's birth helped fuel the massive stock market run-up of the mid-to-late 1990s and spawned hundreds of "new media" start-up companies, most of which crashed and burned in the subsequent stock market collapse. More significant is the fact that mainstream news organizations—at first defensively, but later affirmatively—embraced the Web, both as a news-gathering tool and also as a news delivery device. The Web has given newspapers a medium that allows them to replace afternoon editions and also to compete in "real time" with broadcast outlets. Additionally, and potentially more revolutionary as far as journalism is concerned, is the ability that the Web affords to politicians, government agencies, corporations, labor unions and almost anyone with $1,000 and some free time to communicate directly with their audiences.

It is against this backdrop of momentous world events and upheavals in media and communication techniques that the relationship between the press, especially Washington journalists, and the politicians and officials they cover should be considered.

THE NOTION OF PARTNERSHIP

Over the years it has been fashionable, perhaps even trite, to refer to the relationship between the press and American government as a "partnership." In the 1950s, Douglass Cater, himself a longtime and well-respected Washington correspondent, wrote a book about the Washington press corps under the title "The Fourth Branch of Government." Journalism scholar and educator William O. Rivers followed in the mid-1970s with "The Other Government." Donald Ritchie, in his extensive history of the development of the Washington press corps, went so far as to say that, "A 'symbiotic' partnership has existed . . ."(Ritchie, 1). In other words, it would be difficult to imagine one institution existing without the other; at the least each institution would be vastly different if the other did not exist.

It is easy to understand how the notion of a press-government partnership developed. After all, the theories of American government emerged largely out of the concept of a Lockeian contract between the government and people. Additionally, of course, the Bill of Rights explicitly protects freedom of expression and freedom of the press, the better to enhance political discourse. Unquestionably, in a democratic republic, such as governs the United States, political leaders must be able to achieve and maintain the consent of the people. From the earliest days after the Revolution, correspondents were assigned (or took it upon themselves) to cover the political, bureaucratic and social goings-on in the capital. As Leo Rosten, one of the best-known scholars on the subject of Washington journalism, writes in his classic book "The Washington Correspondents": "The agencies of the federal government cooperate with them, with varying degrees of efficiency and ingenuousness, in the process of informing the United States about what is going on in its capital" (Rosten, 4). To do that, politicians and government officials require access to means of communication, which until very recently were controlled by those who own newspapers, magazines and broadcast stations. Thus, the government officials had no choice except to use the press, imperfect as the relationship might have been on both sides.

Obviously, the relationship between journalist and government officials, at any level, often has been marked by tension, distrust and suspicion. Journalists believe, too often rightly, that politicians engage in "spin" designed to cover up any mistakes, withhold vital facts and insights and only are interested in favorable coverage. For their part, the politicians believe, too often correctly, that reporters only want "the dirt," are biased and won't let the facts get in the way of a good story.

Still, it seems there was a time when the relationship between Washington reporters and politicians was not quite so contentious. Consider this story from the late 1800s, as relayed by a correspondent of the era, E.J. Gibson. Gibson, covering a tariff bill, discovered a provision under consideration by a secret conference committee that would impact readers in his part of the country. ". . . I summoned a cab (which would have meant a horse and carriage) and drove to the residence of one of (the senators). He was in bed, but the butler consented to awaken him, and my card with a few words on it brought me to his bedchamber" (Gibson, 716). Gibson also declares: "The leading newspapers keep up expensive and finely furnished offices in Washington, which are daily visited by members of Congress. . . . Newspaper correspondents who have the time to accept invitations are welcome guests in the houses of public men" (Gibson, 719). Almost no journalist working in Washington today could imagine accosting a senator in his bedroom—few (except perhaps the best-known columnists and highly recognizable television pundits) are visited in their offices by elected officials. In fact, it seems, few reporters even regularly visit members of Congress in their Capitol Hill offices today. And not many working journalists in Washington socialize frequently with the people they cover.

Certainly, Washington has changed a great deal over the past century, as the nation emerged to take its place at the center of the world stage and as the role and scope of the federal government expanded exponentially. It is hard to remember, but at the turn of the 20th century, there was no federal income tax, no Social Security, no Department of Housing and Urban Development or Department of Health and Human Services (or several other cabinet agencies), no Federal Reserve Board or Securities and Exchange Commission or FBI or CIA. Newspapers were just becoming large enough to be considered mass media. The telegraph had transformed journalism by giving reporters (and the government) the ability to instantly communicate messages across the country, but radio was still more than a decade away and television wouldn't make its mark until after World War II. The White House didn't get its first pressroom until 1931 (Rosten, 21). Additionally, the enormous explosion in the numbers of journalists who cover the city has made it impractical for as much socializing and face-to-face contact between journalists and politicians and bureaucrats as once occurred. Writing in The Cosmopolitan in 1892, Washington reporter T.C. Crawford said there were about 160 correspondents accredited to Capitol Hill (Crawford, 356); by the time Rosten wrote his book in 1937, he counted 504 "accredited newspaper and magazine correspondents in the capital" (Rosten, 3). Today, nearly 7,000 reporters, photographers and technicians hold Capitol Hill credentials, and despite consolidation of ownership of news organizations, the number seems to rise inexorably.

But this is not just about who comes to whose office or who gets invited to cocktail parties and dinner parties. Instead, it is about whether the relationship is one that serves both sides, and more importantly, the American people, who, after all, still need to know what is going on in Washington. Ultimately, they need that information delivered by an independent source that has sufficient contacts and access to those in power. And if democracy is to be served, the politicians deserve a platform that will give them the opportunity to make their views heard.

Inside government and the Washington journalism establishment, many disagree with the conclusion that the partnership is in trouble. In a survey of nearly 300 Washington-based journalists done for this edition of *Inside the Beltway*, the respondents were nearly evenly split on whether covering the city has become easier or more difficult since they came to the capital. James Thurber, head of the Center for Congressional and Presidential Studies at American University, says that to politicians, the press is "still an important part" of the communications mix. Thurber says the nature of the relationship varies depending on the type of issue that is involved. The Brookings Institution's Stephen Hess, a leading observer of the Washington press scene, says that reporters for the specialty press and regional reporters "still have a pretty comfortable relationship." In those cases, he says, reporters and politicians "still need each other." And Ron Nessen, head of public affairs at Brookings, says he thinks the problems may have been overstated. "Whatever you think of the media, it is the primary way you get your message out," Nessen says. However, in the past three decades, the stresses and strains have created fissures that call into question the fundamental notion of a press-government partnership. In the wake of Vietnam and Watergate, many journalists began to speak openly, and even to praise, the idea of an "adversarial relationship" with government. Of the survey respondents more than a third said they thought that the relationship with government sources is either "somewhat more adversarial" or "much more adversarial" than when they began their Washington assignment. Less than 10 percent said relations today are "somewhat friendlier" or "much friendlier." Although nearly everyone would agree there needs to be an arms-length relationship between the two sides, it seems illogical to expect anyone (in this case political and governmental officials) to stay in a partnership with someone who has declared himself or herself to be the adversary of the other partner. When this happens in marriage, the next step usually is to call in the lawyers and divide the property. The stark reality for Washington correspondents in particular is that while they still need the government, many in the government have moved on. Mike Mills, the daily editor of Congressional Quarterly, says many politicians have decided, "They need the press less and less to push their agenda out."

So how did this occur? Technology has given politicians and government officials more direct access to their audiences. Political advertising was one of the first real manifestations of this phenomenon. In closely contested races a potential voter is much more likely to see advertising rather than news stories about the candidates, especially if that voter relies on television for most of his or her news. And the political consultants, the corporate PR types, the activists and lobbyists for every cause under the sun have become more sophisticated. They see the press as just one part of the communication mix (what reporters provide is "free media," in this lexicon). They have become more adept at creating events and stories. They have learned to form coalitions with grassroots organizations (or to create the organizations if they don't already exist) to promote their causes. Both houses of Congress have created their own television studios, and several think tanks and others have followed suit. The Brookings Institution, for example, spent more than $800,000 on a television facility. Ron Nessen, now head of public affairs at Brookings, served as press secretary for President Gerald Ford, the last working reporter to hold such a position. When he looks back on his time in the White House, the former NBC correspondent says: "We were really amateurs . . . incredibly naive," in getting out the story. Now, he says "they've learned . . . how to overcome some of the folkways of the press corps." Nessen adds, "The techniques of the government are much more sophisticated today." In particular, there is a focus on images that will be appealing on television. When the president speaks before a large audience (usually enough in itself to get at least partial coverage from the cable news channels), there almost always is a carefully designed banner summing up the day's message in a pithy phrase, and around the president will be arrayed a virtual "rainbow coalition," usually including photogenic children. These are the "eyewash" images you see on the evening news, usually accompanied by an anchor or reporter's short voice-over summarizing the president's point. Additionally, it seems to many journalists that their access to Washington sources has *become* more problematical; sometimes just getting a telephone call returned can be difficult. Many agencies and Hill offices have put everyone except press secretaries and public affairs officers off limits. One result of this is an increased use of nongovernmental sources in stories, according to the survey conducted for this book. Meanwhile, the respondents said they are relying less on elected or appointed public officials as sources. Some of that no doubt comes because reporters simply find it easier to get interest group representatives, think-tank analysts and other nongovernment sources to agree to be quoted. In the survey, two-thirds of the respondents said getting nongovernment sources to speak on the record was "not difficult at all"; only four in 10 said it was "not difficult" to get elected or appointed officials on the record; and only one in 10 said it was "not difficult" to get other officials to speak on the record.

Meanwhile, the press has done its share to contribute to the dissolution of the relationship. Most press offices know that television cameras will rarely cover the routine happenings on Capitol Hill or anywhere inside the vast bureaucracy. News releases about bill introductions routinely are scrapped in Washington bureaus (although they might get used by small newspapers in the district). And political scientists and others have lamented the tone of much Washington coverage. Mark Rozell writes in his 1996 book "In Contempt of Congress":

The trend in congressional coverage has been toward an increasingly negative view of the institution. . . . Whereas Congress used to receive press criticism for not conforming to an idealistic press view of how the legislative process should work, much of the recent coverage can be described simply as "Congress bashing." It is one thing to portray that institution as inefficient and incapable of leadership. It is something else to portray its members as venal and corrupt.

Politicians also complain that they have trouble getting the press to focus on their activities and arguments. Shortly after the 2002 mid-term elections, a CNN interviewer challenged former Senate Minority Leader Tom Daschle, D-S.D., on whether the Democrats had a message. Daschle's quick, ungentle response: "We had one, you just didn't cover it."

WHAT IS NEWS?

We first need to dispense with the notion that "news" is, in and of itself, a tangible commodity, one that can be readily identified and quantified. In this traditional view, "news" merely is a set of naturally occurring events, and journalists are observers, in something of the way that an anthropologist might observe a colony of gophers. Thus, it is "sources" or "events" that make news and it is not the role of journalists to "make news." However, as sociologist Gaye Tuchman wrote, "the act of making news is the act of constructing reality rather than a picture of reality. . . . Newswork transforms occurrences into news events" (Tuchman, 12). In this sense, because it is journalists who do "newswork," only journalists "make news," because it is journalists who select the occurrences that will be transformed, and journalists who do the transformation.

Of course, when journalists "make" news, they follow a set of practices and cultural conventions. Among those, at least in modern American journalism, is that reporters and editors should seek fairness and balance in their stories. Often, journalists and others speak of "getting both sides of the story." Unfortunately, it seems that many news stories are framed in this bilateral fashion. Perhaps this is inevitable, given the considerable influence that television has over the shape of news. Television is, by its nature, a dramatic medium, which requires easily expressed conflict (usually between a protagonist and an antagonist) to engage viewers. Complexity is the first casualty in this construction, and nuance dies along with it. Thus, the mid-1990s debate over health care reform became not a debate over conflicting ideas but a contest between President Clinton and Newt Gingrich. But the two-sided conflict is much too simplistic a formulation when it comes to dealing with the array of opinion, views and facts attached to such issues as providing prescription drug benefits or reforming Social Security or dealing with the war on terror. Not only does this type of coverage fail to serve the public but it also puts off sources. Nessen of the Brookings Institution says: "Things look very simple for a journalist. Things are far more complicated." Chet Lunner, a newspaper reporter for more than 20 years, including several years spent covering Washington for Gannett News Service, and who served as chief spokesman for the Transportation Department, says he has lost some of his respect for journalists. Lunner says:

> Frankly, the view has changed because the reporters are generally ignorant about how the national government operates at this level. As a reporter, I did not have a lot of opportunities to hear the other side in the crush of the daily grind. . . . I understand it, from this perspective now, that it's real stuff that we're dealing with and real bad guys and real lives that are at stake.

How, then, do journalists break out of the model that produces simplistic coverage of complex, nuanced issues? How can the methods and cultures of "newswork" be altered to guarantee that reporters meet the goal of fully and fairly reflecting the range of views that exist on any given topic? To help achieve this outcome, consider the following matrix.

A Matrix of Sources for Washington Reporting

	Congress	Executive	Nongovernment
Support			
Neutral			
Oppose			

To be certain, this matrix fails to describe the full scope of the problem of finding a wide enough range of sources to provide complete, fair and balanced stories. However, if reporters filled in most of these boxes on every story they write or broadcast, it is likely they would come closer to the goal of fully and fairly reflecting the range of views that exist on most issues. It also reflects the reality, which might surprise some, that there are diverse views about most subjects inside the executive branch, where, ostensibly at least, everyone works for the same person—the president. Notice the matrix does not use partisan labels (though that is one shortcut often taken) to identify positions. However, the matrix purposely does not completely remove the tension (the "two sides" approach) that is a natural part of the debates over serious issues. Public policy matters are the subject of much contention, and there often are strongly reasoned and strongly held views in competition. "Politics ain't beanbag," as the saying goes. However, the matrix also tries to encourage reporters to try to find sources who do not have a high personal or political stake in the outcome, and who, therefore, can provide a more analytical point of view.

Obviously, this approach would put less emphasis on spot or breaking news stories, although they, too, would be better if reporters took the time to reach out to more sources. Certainly, it depends less on officials and their "spokespeople" as sources. It could well reduce the greatly lamented "herd journalism" that characterizes so much of what passes for reporting in Washington. Indeed, watching the Washington press corps at work often resembles nothing so much as watching 5-year-olds play soccer: There is a great cloud of dust around the ball, and no one is paying any attention to the rest of the field. Instead of waiting for the government and politicians to put the ball in play, journalists should take on more of the burden of defining news. And journalists should not shrink from that role, even though it is not the traditional approach. In fact, they should embrace it, as it would liberate them to develop innovative approaches to reporting and telling stories. What it should do is to free reporters to do systematic coverage of issues, instead of the day-by-day, episodic journalism that often characterizes Washington news. There would be less emphasis on process, on the blow-by-blow coverage of legislation, and more reporting on the potential impact of proposed new laws and regulations. Washington-based reporters and editors would put more focus on what happens after a bill is signed into law and become more aggressive in the oversight or "watchdog" role, asking whether programs and policies are failing or succeeding, rather than waiting for a study from a congressional investigations committee or the General Accounting Office. Some research suggests there might be an appetite for this type of Washington journalism. The Pew Center for the Press and People found in 2002 that: "Though the public has much lower regard for the media's values, most Americans continue to favor the watchdog role performed by news organizations. . . . Six-in-ten Americans (59%) say press criticism keeps political leaders from doing things that should not be done, while just 26% believe it prevents politicians from doing their jobs."

Charlie Peters, the longtime editor of the iconoclastic Washington Monthly (and one of the best developers of young reporters in the city) wrote in Columbia Journalism Review, "The (Washington) press needs an anthropological approach . . ." By that, he means that journalists need to understand the cultures of the city and its institutions, and that they must let those cultural factors inform and become part of their stories. Peters says reporters can get this knowledge by spending some time working in government, an idea that he acknowledges holds little appeal for most journalists. Or, he says, "Another way for reporters to acquire this understanding is through reporting in depth. Every time reporters take the time to go into a story thoroughly, they are increasing their intellectual capital, their understanding of how Washington really works. And, if they continue to do these kinds of stories on government, they will gradually learn what the insiders know and the public needs to find out."

Perhaps it is through this type of committed, public service journalism that Washington reporters can rebuild their standing with the public and, simultaneously, forge stronger relationships with their sources both within and outside government. The intent of the rest of this book is to show you ways you can do that kind of journalism.

REFERENCES

Crawford, T.C., "The Special Correspondents at Washington," *The Cosmopolitan*, January 1892.

Edsall, Thomas B., "The People and the Press: Whose Views Shape the News," *Public Perspectives*, The Roper Center for Public Opinion Research, July/August 2001. Available online at http://www.ropercenter.uconn.edu/pubper/pdf/pp12_4d.pdf.

Gibson, E.J., "The Washington Correspondent," *Lippincott*, November 1894.

Peters, Charles, "Eternal Washington: To Get the Real Stories, Know the Real City," *Columbia Journalism Review*, September/October 2002, pp. 60-62.

Ritchie, Donald A., *Press Gallery: Congress and the Washington Correspondents*, Harvard University Press, Cambridge, Mass., 1991.

Rosten, Leo C., *The Washington Correspondents*, Harcourt, Brace, New York, N.Y., 1937.

Rozell, Mark, *In Contempt of Congress*, Praeger, Westport, Conn., 1996.

Tuchman, Gaye, *Making News, A Study in the Construction of Reality*, The Free Press, New York, N.Y., 1978.

2 KEYS TO SUCCESS

Washington is the goal for many political junkies, the pinnacle for journalists fascinated by the human hodgepodge we call government. The chance to cover Washington should be and often is the reward for distinguished reporting at city hall or the statehouse. But Washington is very different from those places, so different that if political minutiae and maudlinism do not hold you in thrall, you may be happier in Miami or Muskogee.

Satisfaction and frustration are constant companions in Washington. The glamour of walking the corridors of power is tempered daily by the demands of discovering behind which doors that power resides, and in what amount, and for how long. Many people here are ready to help reporters open those doors; some are not. For instance, many press officers at the Pentagon wouldn't tell you if your coat was on fire, but the staffs at the Federal Election Commission and the Congressional Budget Office often won't stop helping you.

People in Washington are busy. Even those who aren't pretend to be. (If you want to invite a withering glare, show up for an interview more than five minutes early.) Developing sources is thus a constant challenge. Even veteran reporters, with a few exceptions, have trouble getting people to return their phone calls. If you're not read in Washington—and most reporters who work here aren't—you face an extra hurdle in gaining the access to and the confidence of sources.

Getting through to the right person is not even half the battle. Separating fact from fiction, and rhetoric from reality, is a larger part of a reporter's job in Washington, where hidden agendas are more common than original thoughts.

Still, information is the coin of the realm. It's trite but true that information is power in Washington. In a city where purveyors of press releases, surveys, research reports, classified documents, polls, anonymous quotes, boilerplate analysis and "spin" are constantly competing for your attention, much of your energy is spent finding out the real story behind the story. The beauty of the place is that you usually can find out. Because it is almost always in someone's interest to answer your questions.

Washington is also a city of experts—many authentic, some self-appointed. At times, it seems, an expert in Washington is anyone with a title who returns a reporter's phone calls. In fact, the city is filled with people at think tanks, foundations, trade associations, libraries and universities and on congressional staffs who know a great deal about practically any subject you can name. Many of them remain obscure because reporters like to take the easy way out—and simultaneously impress their bosses—by patronizing the same experts called by The New York Times and The Washington Post. The point is that all sides of every issue are usually well represented in Washington; there is rarely a reason to write an unbalanced story.

Yet, even with a wealth of diverse sources and resources, much of Washington goes uncovered. On a typical day, you'll find dozens of reporters sitting in the White House press briefing room, scores more hanging out at the House and Senate press galleries, another 30 to 40 at the State Department briefing room—and a mere handful scattered across the rest of the entire federal bureaucracy.

"Congress, the White House and the Supreme Court are covered well," says St. Petersburg Times Washington Bureau Chief Sara Fritz, who has covered Washington for five different newspapers, magazines and wire services in a 30-year career. "The problem is, they (media) don't cover the Food and Drug Administration. They don't cover the Immigration and Naturalization Service. The things that really affect people don't get covered, and I'm just overwhelmed by the notion that the stuff here in Washington that's most interesting doesn't get much attention."

The trade press—specialty newsletters, magazines and so on—fills some of that void, but the trade press rarely is read except by bureaucrats and the industry it covers (and by alert reporters looking for tips).

It's not just that reporters often are poorly deployed in Washington. Reporters often develop a cynical attitude that hardens with tenure, a phenomenon that Charlie Peters, the crusading former editor of Washington Monthly, calls the wise-guy syndrome. He says that even some of the best journalists in Washington have an attitude that they've seen everything before, that there's nothing new about sleaze or bureaucratic ineptitude, that nothing can or will be done about it—and that therefore it's not worth covering. "The capacity for outrage is so long gone from these guys," laments Peters. "There is this wise-guy world-weariness that is just frightening."

Perhaps the most disturbing pattern of all, and one that reflects the other shortcomings, is what the late Jack DeVore, longtime press adviser to Texas Senator and Treasury Secretary Lloyd Bentsen, called goatherd journalism. Manifested most visibly in White House coverage, the goatherd school holds that there is safety in numbers, that if you write about what everybody else is writing about—if you "match the wires," in the parlance of the trade—you can't go wrong. If everybody's writing about it, it must be important.

What accounts for goatherd journalism? Many reporters and bureau chiefs, as well as government press agents, lay much of the blame on editors back home. Editors are a convenient target, for they labor under misconceptions about Washington. It's easy for them to take their cues from cable television or The New York Times.

To some editors, the federal government is city hall writ large. From afar, they do not appreciate the massive size and sprawl and complexity of the place. Even after years on the scene, it's hard to grasp the tangled layers of executive and legislative bureaucracy, which work more often than not, it seems, at cross-purposes. Editors often do not seem to understand that much of what is accomplished in Washington is a product of trade-offs, grudging concessions and subtle give-and-take. They have textbook notions that overestimate both the sanctity of the process and the importance of their representatives and senators.

Sometimes, too, editors contradict and overrule one another. Turf wars in the city room can play havoc in the Washington bureau. The lazy reporter in Washington, of course, will exploit every sign of ignorance and office politics that comes from back home and will voice all kinds of rationalizations: "That kind of story will take days" or "You can't just walk in the door and talk to the secretary of the Treasury" or "That's just another inside-the-Beltway story—who cares?"

Another tendency is to blame television for the lack of direction and diversity in Washington coverage. The power of the networks to set the agenda—and, ironically, to be manipulated—is awesome, especially at the White House. Television focuses on the White House because it's easy. There's a single personality—the president. There's a nice familiar backdrop for the cameras. Big shots come and go in big black limousines. Bands play. Pretenders to the throne wheedle their way in and babble on the way out. Members of the palace guard stab each other in the back.

By contrast, the networks largely ignore Capitol Hill. The place has no focus. It has hundreds of fiefdoms, but no king. Unless there's blood on the House or Senate floor, or a movie star is testifying at a committee hearing, Capitol Hill provides little appeal for television. And what about the Energy Department, the Bureau of Land Management, the Federal Trade Commission? Are you serious?

Esoteric debates about the philosophy of Washington coverage are not a prime concern of a reporter trying to navigate a new beat, nor are they a major concern of this book. What's most important is getting a sense of the place, and this book discusses some steps to accomplish that, though no list is finite or exclusive.

Becoming a respected reporter in Washington has little to do with lifestyle, and nothing to do with the imagery concocted over the years about what might appropriately be called cocktail journalism. Simply put, you don't have to host or attend Georgetown dinner parties, you don't have to take big-time lawyers to lunch at fancy restaurants, and you don't have to be a regular on the TV talking head shows. Most working reporters in Washington—as distinguished from columnists and commentators—aren't part of that world. The keys to success in Washington, as in the hinterlands, revolve around such basics as curiosity, preparation, energy and the right work habits.

TEN KEYS TO THE CITY

Define Your Beat

Washington has far too many moving parts, and far too many distractions, to permit covering a beat on an ad hoc basis. Whether you're responsible for covering the New York congressional delegation, the State Department or environmental issues, you and your editors need to decide the parameters and main focus of your coverage.

Covering any beat in Washington involves a lot of deciding what not to do and then putting that out of your mind. DeVore, the late Bentsen aide and a father confessor of sorts to a generation of Texas reporters in Washington, once said: "There's an infinite number of things to cover in this town. And to survive, one of the things you have to do in the first few months after you arrive is arbitrarily eliminate whole categories of things that at first impression would be interesting and in fact are interesting."

The tendency, if you find yourself alone reporting a story, is to wonder why you're there, and everyone else is somewhere else. What are you missing? It's not just the range of subject matter you must decide upon. You must also decide on your approach. Do you chase spot news every day, or do you try to anticipate major developments and trends? Do you write about the nuances of Washington infighting, or do you explain what programs and regulations and debates mean to citizens who care about the sausage but not how it's made? Getting the right formula is a constant subject of debate in Washington bureaus. Choosing your approach, in turn, leads to the next key to success.

Understand Your Audience

If you write for Congressional Quarterly or The Washington Post, your audience is markedly different from that of the Denver Post or the Rockford (Ill.) Register Star. You need to have some feel for your audience's interest in federal issues. Some local economies are heavily dependent on federal spending, and others hardly at all. Attitudes about federal regulations are as diverse as the nation's demography. It's easy in Washington to get carried away with inside baseball, to think that what interests you and the editors of The Washington Post must interest everyone. That's a mistake.

Get Organized

The rhythms and rituals of Washington life can frustrate a disorganized reporter. You can spend a lot of time spinning your wheels. For example: Most key decisions in the House of Representatives are made in leadership meetings between Tuesday morning and Thursday afternoon. More press conferences are held on Wednesday than on any other day. Bureaucrats are hard to find after 4:30 p.m. any day and almost anytime near a long holiday weekend. Lobbyists and congressional staffers often schedule vacations to coincide with congressional recesses, which are frequent. In August you usually can forget it all.

You can't just get up in the morning and say, "I think I'll start reporting today on a piece about trade legislation." You have to plan such projects with an eye on the calendar and some knowledge of local work habits. The smartest thing to do is what most of your potential sources will do: Keep weekly, monthly and yearly calendars. This not only will allow you to log in scheduled interviews, background briefings, press conferences, seminars, working social events and the like but also should encourage you to block out time to work on long-range projects and list the interviews and areas of research you need to pursue. In short, set an agenda. If you plan your day only after reading the wire service daybooks, you will forever be running in too many directions.

Develop Good Sources

Developing good sources is a slow, painstaking, hit-and-miss proposition. You have to work at it, and you have to be hard-nosed about it. The emphasis is on good. Thousands of people in Washington are ready and eager to talk to reporters, but their value as sources sometimes is inversely proportional to their willingness to talk. Remember, your time is important too. Good sources are to be treasured. But you may be tempted at times to call sources who are out of date in a subject area just because they are quotable, you know them, they are easy to reach or somehow connected to the audience you report for. Part of your job is to update your Rolodex on a continuing basis. Don't let laziness, friendship or parochial concerns interfere with a clear-eyed assessment of who's in the know and who isn't.

Know the Ground Rules

No matter who your sources are, you usually will have to deal with them under certain ground rules of attribution. It's a nettlesome issue. The purists, few of whom reside in Washington, argue that unattributed quotes should be used only in the most unusual circumstances. That is a worthy goal but rarely works in practice in Washington. In fact, it's questionable that it would ever work unless all major news organizations agreed in collusion to accept information only with full attribution.

Four types of interviews have commonly accepted ground rules in Washington, though press officers frequently get them confused:

On the record. No strings are attached to an interview of this type. Everything is attributable by name to the person speaking.

Background. The information is on the record, but the source is not to be quoted by name. The information may be attributed to "an administration official," an unidentified "department spokesperson," or some similar designation.

Deep background. You can use the information only on your own authority, with no quotes attributed to any person or any title. You may say, for example, "The president is known to be angry about thus and so," but it's you who is saying it, not anyone else.

Off the record. You can't use the information, period. This rule is frequently abused by some reporters, who accept information off the record and then try to smoke out the story somewhere else by using the information.

Nothing stays off the record for long in Washington, as a rule, but many officials and political operatives take the ground rules seriously. If you promise a source anonymity and then write a story in such a way that the source is obvious, don't be surprised if your next phone call is not returned.

Do Your Homework

Developing sources in Washington may be challenging, but discovering resources is not. Among people who deal regularly with the press in Washington, few things mark a reporter's reputation as quickly as sloth and ignorance. You shouldn't expect a congressional committee lawyer, an agency division head or a think-tank scholar to spend a half-hour or an hour to bring you up to date on an issue if you haven't taken the time to review the history and prepare questions. Until you are ready to ask intelligent questions, don't ask any.

Few places on earth are as rich with resources as Washington is. Libraries, archives, bookstores, press offices and databases are crammed with documents churned out by congressional committees, investigative bodies, think tanks, specialty publishers, trade associations and special interest groups. Even the laziest reporter can quickly get backgrounded on complex issues with a few clicks on the Internet, a few phone calls and a subway card.

If you want to be considered a serious reporter, act like one. Don't even pick up the phone in the morning until you've read The Washington Post. Remember, Washington is a company town and a town of big egos. To make a good impression quickly, study the background of the person you're interviewing and then make some casual reference to it early on.

Be Persistent

You can't spend a few minutes on the Internet and make one round of phone calls and expect to plug all the holes in a story. Officials who ignore the first e-mail or phone call may think twice if you message them or call again. Be polite but firm. Leave enough details in a message so the person you're trying to reach understands what your questions are likely to be. If someone else suggested the call, use that person's name (with permission, of course). Sometimes, reluctant sources will relent if they are convinced that (a) you're going to do the story with or without their input or (b) you honestly want their input. Few stories hinge on one or two sources. If you build your own network of contacts and use the many directories in Washington with skill, you can usually find someone who will give you the answer.

Learn to Sell Stories

In this era of television and fast-food journalism, it seems that fewer and fewer editors are interested in long explanations of government and politics. Competition for space is fierce at most news organizations. In that scramble, most editors place state and local news ahead of national news. Some editors have jaundiced views about the relevance of Washington stories. Thus, being an enterprising reporter is only part of the game. You've got to be prepared to make the case for a 3,000-word takeout on a legislative battle or bureaucratic snafu. If the story's importance to the casual reader isn't apparent in the first few paragraphs, you've got a hard sell.

Don't Be Distracted

The advent of 24/7 cable news has vastly increased the chances that you—or your editors—will be distracted by the hot story du jour. "It exacerbates the herd mentality," says Cox Newspapers correspondent Larry Lipman.

"Because when you see a story run twenty times a day on CNN or whatever, even if it's not much of a story, the constant barrage of images and emphasis, I think, makes everybody say, well, this must be a story; there must be something here. And that generates more of an interest and a frenzy to cover the story, and then move on to something else. The Chandra Levy (missing intern in 2001) story was a perfect example of that." If you have a firm understanding with your editor on your role and mission in Washington, you can rebuff those distractions.

Don't Be Co-opted

One of the biggest potential hazards for a Washington journalist is to get too cozy with sources. This is a particular threat to regional reporters, who can easily become too dependent on members of Congress and their staffs to help them cut through the rest of the bureaucracy. If you are a regional reporter, you may be tempted to do an occasional puff piece in return for an exclusive report or for being tipped off on a story that would otherwise have been missed. If anything about the relationship causes you to overlook or downplay an abuse of privilege or a questionable committee vote or fund-raising tactic by the legislator, you've been compromised.

The best advice is this: Don't become an insider. Washington can be an incestuous place. The lines between work and play are subtle and easily blurred. But you can be friendly and sociable in dealing with sources and still keep them at arm's length. With few exceptions, official Washington views its relations with the press as a part of doing business, whatever that takes. You should view it exactly the same way, but with a clear understanding of what won't be allowed.

3 CONGRESS

To many people in the United States and around the globe, the chief symbols of Washington and the American government are the president and the White House. But to most of those who live and work inside the Beltway, including journalists, the reality is different: It is Congress that sets the pace for daily life and is the focus of most everyone's attention. When Congress is in session, the city is busier, the streets are more clogged, the restaurants fuller. Few journalists or lobbyists or senior government officials dare schedule vacation when the lawmakers are in town. Many dinner plans, nights with the kids or evening strolls have been ruined for reporters because the Senate or the House decided to take up a major bill long after dark. To paraphrase Mark Twain, "No one's schedule is safe when the legislature is in session."

Rare is the Washington reporter who doesn't spend at least part of his or her time at congressional hearings or walking the halls of the Capitol and its adjoining campus in search of sources and stories. No matter what issue you tackle, whether you write for The New York Times, The Rock Island Argus or the Soybean News, sooner or later you'll end up on the Hill. In the view of former Washington Post correspondent Spencer Rich, "If you haven't covered Congress, you don't understand Washington. It's the heart of this town."

Fortunately, Capitol Hill also is unquestionably the most reporter-friendly terrain in Washington, considerably more accessible than the buttoned-down White House or the maze of bureaucratic offices that line Constitution and Independence avenues or the virtually impenetrable Supreme Court. More than 200 of the 275 Washington journalists who responded to a survey conducted as part of the research for this book said covering Congress was either "somewhat easy" or "very easy." Nearly 200 said covering the White House was either "somewhat difficult" or "very difficult."

Elaine Povich, a longtime congressional correspondent who now covers the Hill for Newsday, authored a study published by the Freedom Forum in 1996 on the relationship between Congress and the press. She says reporters are comfortable covering Congress. "It's the last place in Washington that you can actually reach out and touch the people you are covering." Shrewd journalists also quickly discover that having good congressional sources isn't just valuable to their coverage of legislative issues. Virtually every Washington story and issue could benefit from having a congressional perspective. Congress is a player in every game in Washington by virtue of its constitutional powers to make policy, create (and destroy) programs, allocate money to favored programs and places (and withhold it from those out of favor) and investigate virtually any activity its members choose. The result is that few things happen at the White House or in the most obscure federal agencies that aren't being tracked by someone on the Hill, often with a disapproving eye. This wide-ranging power and influence also means that wise federal officials find it in their best interest to give Congress the information it desires, even if they want to keep it secret, and even if they know that once it's on the Hill it soon will be public. Few members or staffers, it seems, can keep a secret, a fact that continually irritates upper-level bureaucrats and White House aides. Sometimes the leaks are fairly innocuous. Sometimes they appear to involve more serious matters. In the summer of 2002, the White House, so angry over reading details of its supposedly top secret communications intercepts, asked some members of Congress to take lie detector tests to see if they had talked with reporters. Not surprisingly, the idea was mostly met with cold stares from those in Congress. It is this gift of gab that attracts many reporters to sources on the Hill. "There are 535 people in this place and they all love to talk. What could be better?" Povich asks. How much you rely on a congressional member's office to obtain information held elsewhere can be a tricky question. You don't want to feel indebted, but on the other hand, many kinds of information you might seek would be made available to any constituent. But you should not expect simply to walk into a member's office, announce yourself as a journalist and expect the juicy leaks to start flowing. Getting to the point that the members and staff trust you with secrets—large or small—will take time, energy and cultivation. The process begins, of course, with knowing something about the place and how it works. And to get the most out of Capitol Hill you and your editors also will need to learn how to effectively pick and choose the stories in which you can have impact or bring an added dimension to the coverage.

The first step for any new Hill reporter is to apply for credentials to the congressional press galleries. You need them for access to buildings in the Capitol complex, to hearings and to the galleries themselves. When you apply for permanent credentials, you'll be given a temporary pass while the permanent pass is being processed. The galleries, which are run by committees of journalists, were established more than 100 years ago when Congress got fed up with reporters who doubled as political aides and lobbyists. There are separate galleries for daily print media, print periodicals, radio and television reporters and photographers. Today, there are more than 7,000 journalists with Hill credentials.

For many beginning Washington reporters one of the hardest tasks when it comes to covering the Hill is simply learning how to get around the Capitol complex. Perhaps the best advice for any Hill reporter is to wear comfortable shoes. To the uninitiated, the Capitol and the nearby office buildings can appear to be an endless succession of dead-end corridors and stairways that lead to nowhere (actually, some of the most important offices in Washington are squirreled away in the upper reaches of the Capitol). Lolita Baldor, who covers Washington for the New Haven, Conn., Register, recalls an early experience: "One of the first times I was in the Capitol, I couldn't get out. I actually wandered around the Capitol for what seemed like forever but I am sure it was only for a few minutes, looking for a door." Now she gives tours of the Capitol campus for fellow journalists—and says that even those who have been around town for a while ask for her help in navigating the hallways.

One of the easiest ways to think of Capitol Hill is as a city within a city: It has its own rules, culture and pecking order. At the top are the elected senators (100) and representatives (435). Actually, there are nearly 25,000 people in the "city on the Hill," when pages, interns and staffs of the various members, committees, caucuses and support offices are added in. And while many Washington journalists have fairly frequent contact with the representatives and senators they cover, the bulk of a reporter's work on the Hill will be with staff. Not only do staff members control access to the members, it's they who do the research, prepare witnesses for hearings, draft legislation, meet with lobbyists, work with constituents, and perform all the other tasks that are the daily fare for a representative's or senator's office. You will find the Hill staff a mostly young crowd, dominated by fresh faces from colleges and universities across the nation. It is an environment in which a relatively young woman or man can quickly accrue considerable influence and, even, power. While pay can range to more than $100,000 a year, most survive in expensive Washington on much more modest incomes, often below $30,000 a year. Many are merely using the Hill experience to make connections on their way to other professions, including the law, journalism, academia and lobbying. Others will stay to become fixtures—the congressional press gallery staffs, for example, are mostly made up of folks who have been working on the Hill for a quarter of a century or more. A few of today's staffers will show up as political figures in their own right—Republican Sen. Pat Roberts of Kansas, for example, served as a staff member to a Kansas congressman before being elected first to the House and then the Senate. Democratic Sen. Hillary Rodham Clinton of New York began her political life on the staff of a Watergate investigating committee.

While many people tend to think and speak of Congress as a unitary body, the reality is quite different. The House and the Senate are distinctly different institutions, some of which are connected to traditions that are two centuries old, others more directly tied to the political culture in which the members live. Perhaps the most important cultural issue to understand is that getting re-elected is at the top of the mind of virtually every member. The reason for this is simple, and is true for both the House and the Senate: Seniority rules. The more you get elected, the more power you get. Everything from office locations to committee assignments depends on seniority. If you want an office with a better view, get re-elected. If you want to be more influential on major policy decisions or if you want to be able to direct money from federal programs to your district or state, get re-elected. It also is true that you can have more power if you are a member of the majority party, which helps explain why the closely divided Congress of recent years seems to have helped heighten the partisan tension on Capitol Hill.

The stark fact of life for a House member is that the next election is never more than two years away. This alone makes the House a pretty good pulse taker of the nation. Probably the most dreaded charge in a House election is that the incumbent has "lost touch" with his or her constituents, so members go to extraordinary steps to avoid the allegation. House members soon learn at their peril that cutting bureaucratic red tape and remembering the birthdays and anniversaries of supporters are just as important, if not more so, than taking a position on Medicare drug benefits or the war on terror. When you have to run for office every two years, no issue is too mundane and no political antennae are too sensitive. In fact, many House and Senate members have relocated substantial parts of their staffs to offices in the home district to facilitate this so-called "casework." Many members who live in nearby states travel home every weekend. Others usually take advantage of frequent "district work weeks" to attend to political and other business back home. This frequent contact with folks outside the Beltway and the ombudsman role of members are key reasons why the House is such a valuable source of stories for reporters.

Because of its size, the House operates under a set of strict rules that controls such things as which proposed bills make it to the floor for debate and how long members may speak on an issue. This system permits the majority party, by its control of the House Rules Committee, to push its agenda through in most cases, even when the House is split down the middle, as it has been for much of the past decade. The Senate, by contrast, retains something of a House of Lords character. Operating under rules that make every member a king, the Senate still hosts an occasional great debate, it still has some colorful characters and it's still a launching pad (mostly unsuccessful) for presidential candidates. Unlike the House, where it appears efficiency is the order of the day, the Senate seems designed to build in delay and to act as a leveling influence when the more excitable House bolts out of control. Sen. Robert C. Byrd of West Virginia, the dean of Senate Democrats who has served as both majority and minority leader and chaired the Appropriations Committee, likes to recall the Senate's role, as envisioned by George Washington, would be "the saucer that cools the coffee." Just one senator can place a "hold" on a bill, effectively stalling progress for days or weeks or months or forever. In addition, unlike the House, the Senate has no limits on debate—a senator who grabs the floor can keep it as long as he or she can talk or stand. It has been years since a true filibuster has captured the Senate, but the mere threat of prolonged debate often moves members to reach compromises or to postpone contentious bills or nominations. Thus, the two most important words in the Senate are "unanimous consent," which means that no senator will object to the proposal. Without an agreement, Senate action often stalls, unless or until one side can assemble 60 votes to invoke cloture (which shuts off debate). But with the narrow political margins that have ruled Capitol Hill since 1994, getting 60 votes has proved impossible in many instances, such as the debate in 2002 over whether or how to add a prescription drug benefit to Medicare. Likewise, the Senate has no rules on "germaneness"—virtually any amendment can come to the floor for debate on almost any bill. Many reporters find the Senate's apparent random schedule irritating, and some senators agree. Sen. Thad Cochran, a senior Republican from Mississippi, told Povich in an interview for her 1996 study of the relationship between Congress and the press: "I don't know how in the world you can really cover things that are happening on the floor of the Senate on a regular basis without being frustrated by the procedure." He suggested that the Senate should try to make "things flow a little more predictably at least" (Povich, 127). So far, his advice has gone largely unheeded. Leaders in both the House and the Senate have tried in recent years to adopt and follow more "family friendly" schedules. But in the heat of a congressional session—especially near planned recess and adjournment dates—members, staff and reporters find themselves stuck on the Hill waiting for "the world's greatest deliberative body" to work its will.

GETTING STARTED

Define Your Beat

Before worrying about whether you'll be feared, admired, despised or just tolerated, you need to decide exactly what your beat entails. That may sound simple, but some reporters are wandering around Capitol Hill without a clear understanding of what they're supposed to be doing. People on Capitol Hill want to know two things about reporters: Do they know what they're doing up here, and do they know their audience?

You need to have an understanding with your editor or bureau chief on whether you should "match" the wire services on big stories or ignore spot developments in favor of more in-depth treatment. Do you provide day-to-day coverage of legislation at the hearing and markup stages, or do you write advance stories that explain what precipitated the legislation?

If you're a regional reporter, do you write about bill introductions, or do you leave it up to the ingenuity of a press secretary to figure out how to get such trivia into the newspaper? Do you cover hearings conducted by congressional members from your region even if the subject has little relevance to that region? Do you have the latitude to nationalize a regional story on your beat? Conversely, are you expected to localize national stories that may be in the headlines? Do you have the leeway to break away from the daily disorder on the Hill and devote three days or two weeks to a special project?

The truth is, you probably will be expected to do both spot coverage and longer pieces. Povich says: "My life is a balancing act between essentially covering whatever the big story of the day is and working on longer term stories and working on stories that are related to New York. It's sort of a three-legged stool. . . . My mandate is to know what's going on, to be aware of the big stories of the day and to cover them and report on them. To work on longer-term stories . . . and also to be sensitive to New York issues. How I juggle those on any given day depends on what kind of day it is. If it's a slow Monday, I will work on a long-term story." For journalists in small bureaus, getting the focus right is paramount. Brett Lieberman, who covers Washington for the Harrisburg, Pa., Patriot-News says: "You need to figure out first who your members are. Who do you care about? Then you have to figure out, what issues do we care about? Is there a big VA hospital in the area? Are there a lot of veterans? Or military issues?"

Some of these questions will be resolved in daily discussions with your boss, but you should have some firm guidelines and a general philosophy. Too many bureaus lurch from one formula to another, never quite sure which focus best serves their audience. Often, it seems to reporters and other observers inside the Beltway that much of the fault for this lack of focus comes from having editors who haven't covered the city themselves and who may not understand the legislative process well.

In the past, many Washington correspondents reveled in the fact that their editors, who usually are hundreds or thousands of miles removed from the capital, had a fairly hard time keeping abreast of issues and events in Washington. That gave the reporter considerable leeway when it came to defining how the job got done. But the advent of congressional coverage on C-SPAN, 24-hour cable news and instant communication through e-mail means editors back home can be more active in day-to-day coverage decisions. For that reason, among others, the Freedom Forum study of Congress and the media concluded that editors need training about the ins and outs of Congress. "Ironically, the best way to improve beyond-the-Beltway coverage may be to bring editors inside the Beltway for brief but intensive sessions (Povich, 5)."

Although it's important to understand how you'll cover Congress, it's just as important that you know your audience. One bureau chief for a newspaper in the Midwest used to boast that he hadn't been to the home city in nearly 20 years. Makes you wonder if he even read his own newspaper.

If you're going to do a credible job of representing a newspaper, radio or TV station in Washington, you've got to know something about its community. If you came to Washington from there, you are presumed to have that familiarity. If you didn't, you should visit when you take the job, and follow up with trips at least once a year, to meet with local officials, get a look at the economy and compare notes with other professionals from your own organization. Lieberman takes advantage of the fact that his paper is based just a couple of hours drive from Washington. He tries to get back to Pennsylvania to talk with his editors at least once a month. He tries to get on mailing lists of local organizations. Lieberman says: "If you know people in the community, it helps. You are finding out about issues and you are also building up a network." These contacts can prove invaluable in keeping tabs on members of Congress and the impact of federal programs. Reporters who came to Washington to work for one paper and have moved on to other papers face a different challenge. "I try to get back there at least four times a year," says New Haven's Baldor. "I didn't work for that paper while I was in Connecticut so I didn't know the editors and (visiting) really helps; people see your face, know who you are."

Take Advantage of the Press Galleries

The galleries are an indispensable part of Hill coverage. While Congress generally has left management of the galleries, including hiring and firing of staff, to the Standing Committee of Correspondents for each group, occasionally the lawmakers find excuses to get involved in matters that would affect Hill journalists. For example, a few years ago, stung by stories about their financial disclosure statements, a group of members led by Sen. Robert Byrd, D-W.Va., pushed for rules that would have forced reporters with Hill credentials to file disclosure statements, as well. Few journalists, or senators, supported the effort and eventually the drive ran out of steam. Shortly after he became Senate majority leader in 2001, Sen. Tom Daschle tried to kick the Senate Periodical and Press Photographers galleries out of their historic roosts on the third floor of the Capitol in order to make more room for the Senate Secretary's office. He lost the battle. And in 2002, members again tried to assert their authority by involving the Senate Sergeant of Arms in the process of hiring a new superintendent of the daily gallery to replace the long-serving and generally well-admired Robert Peterson.

From time to time the standing committees also get involved in fights with journalists. The committees have had a hard time figuring out how to deal with the new phenomenon of Web-based reporters. A perennial issue involves whether to credential representatives of organizations that say they are involved in news gathering and distribution but that also take stands on public policy issues.

Lots of Hill people are willing to help new reporters; for the folks at the House and Senate press galleries it's their job. The House and Senate sites on the World Wide Web provide access to a considerable amount of information about Congress and its operations, including extensive directories of members, sites for most individual members, floor schedules, calendars of committee hearings, the ability to track bills, votes on amendments and bills and other details needed for routine Hill coverage. But it would be wrong to think that you can do a thorough job of covering Congress without getting to know the gallery staff and without using the services the galleries provide. Using the Senate gallery as an example, the following is a rundown on the services available once you've introduced yourself to the superintendent of the gallery and the staff. (Separate periodical, radio and TV, and photographers' galleries provide services tailored to their members.)

Summary of floor action. Gallery staff members monitor floor action on a 45-minute rotating basis, write summaries of what happened and keep a logbook. "If you talk to reporters, they would say 'We save their lives a lot,'" one gallery staff member says. But don't expect the gallery staff to write your stories, get quotes and make up for your own shoe leather. It's obviously up to you to pursue the details, but this service provides some protection if you're elsewhere covering a hearing or conducting an interview.

Free answering service. The staff will take messages for you, an especially valuable service for one-person bureaus and for reporters working a story elsewhere on the Hill. The staff also will give you a quick status report on floor action over the phone.

Reserved seats. The staff will reserve a seat at a committee hearing if you call ahead and request it, a wise precaution in the case of controversial issues or high-profile witnesses. But if you don't make it, the staff will bring back to the gallery for you copies of testimony and reports entered into the hearing record. They also will save copies for you of bills, reports and amendments being considered on the floor.

Historical files. The gallery maintains extensive historical files that can help you broaden a spot story or develop a Sunday feature or perspective piece. Titles range from "Women in the Senate" to "Late-night Sessions" and "Cloture History of Development."

Major reference works. Included are daily newspapers, Who's Who, encyclopedias, Congressional Directory (since the 1870s), Congressional Staff Directory, the Editor and Publisher Yearbook and Bartlett's.

A place to work. Many major news organizations have permanent work space here, but transient work space also is available. The work areas include telephones and spots for computers.

In the main room of the Senate gallery, a TV monitor carries both floor debate and happenings in the TV-studio gallery. A computer monitor carries vote summaries, committee hearing lists and so forth. Racks hold press releases, and a bulletin board contains important advisories. On a typical day, the board includes a list of that day's committee hearings, a whip's notice on the week's schedule, a press secretaries' contact list, an index of clip files (some 150) available from the gallery staff, and assorted legislative bulletins, updates and notices from the Democratic and Republican policy committees. (Also see "Selected Resources" at end of this chapter.)

In addition, a five-person staff, headed by the gallery superintendent, provides a detailed knowledge of the Capitol and parliamentary procedure. Staff members also can help you—if you're on deadline—with some bare essentials on the phone, providing the bottom line on a vote, as well as how a state's two senators voted. If you want a full vote breakdown, however, you'll have to come to the gallery (or wait for the wires to move it).

With all this help you may get the idea—if you're lazy enough—that you can cover Congress by meeting a handful of press secretaries, sitting in the gallery, checking Web sites, watching C-SPAN, and using Congressional Quarterly as a crib sheet. You can, but your coverage won't be very good.

Establish Your Own Credentials

Covering Congress is no different from covering any other beat: To be effective, you've got to demonstrate that you're a serious player. You can't call a press secretary or a committee staff director once a month and expect to know what's going on or expect that person to be interested in talking to you. You have to make contact on a regular basis, and that means a lot of time on the Hill.

Steve Piacente, who covered Washington for papers in Florida and South Carolina before moving to a government agency in 2002, says it's important that Hill sources "know what your face looks like. . . . The personal contact will get you places you otherwise couldn't get." But with cutbacks in many Washington bureaus, Andy Fisher, press secretary to Indiana Sen. Richard Lugar, says it's increasingly rare to have a reporter just call to check in. "One of the frustrations I've had is the lack of reporters doing beat checks; it has become something of a dying art," Fisher says. "Many only call you when they need something, as opposed to checking in every week or so to see what is going on." He thinks reporters who make the effort at personal contact likely get better service from his office and others on the Hill.

Reporters agree that making regular rounds would be good. "In theory you would stop by congressional offices once a week just to pop in," Lieberman says. But that's not easy. "You don't have time to do all the checking you're supposed to or you won't have time to report or cover the things going on." And when reporters do show up in offices unannounced, "You get this look from press secretaries, 'what do you want?'" In the survey done for the book, only two of 110 Hill press secretaries who responded said that their most frequent interaction with reporters is in person. It's not just a matter of being there, of course. It's also a matter of doing your homework and asking the right questions.

Develop Contacts

Among the 25,000 or so staffers on the Hill are experts on every conceivable subject. The staff, especially senior aides on member and committee staffs, will have most of the answers. Some members of Congress are knowledgeable on issues and are worth talking to, but the more senior they are, the more difficult they are to reach. You can also go off the Hill to get informed opinions from Washington's many think tanks and legions of lobbyists. But for day-to-day coverage, the bulk of your contacts will be with Hill staffers.

House staffs are relatively small, with a limit of about 18 full-time staffers per member, regardless of the district. Members supplement this by using committee staff slots to handle tasks. Full committee and subcommittee chairs and ranking members (senior members of the minority party) control substantial blocks of staff time—another affirmation of the importance of seniority. Senate staffs tend to be much larger than House staffs, and the allocation of staff resources is related to the size of the state: California senators have more help than members from North Dakota.

The starting point for most reporters is with the press aide to the member or committee. In fact, many offices have made the rest of the staff off limits to reporters, except in rare instances. "Having different people talk on the record I think is confusing," says Wendy Belzer, press secretary to New York Democratic Rep. Nita Lowey. Belzer says few reporters ask to talk with legislative staff. If you're a regional reporter, you'll want to meet the representative or senator, and you should make it a point to seek the member out frequently in the first few weeks so that both your name and face will become familiar.

While the titles may vary from office to office, key people on the member's Washington staff usually include the administrative assistant, the press secretary, the legislative assistant or legislative director, the caseworker, and the personal or appointments secretary. Moreover, the relative power of staff members differs from office to office. Most often, the AA serves as a top political adviser and staff boss: You often can consider him or her the alter ego of the member. The press secretary may be a relatively low-level writer of press releases or may be a key adviser. LAs are important to know because they usually coordinate the member's legislative activity and often have the best contact with committee staffers, bureaucrats downtown and lobbyists. Case-workers spend most of their time working on district problems and thus can be good sources, as are staffers who handle the mail. Likewise, personal secre-taries can be a valuable source because they often know the most about the member's whereabouts and private life. One thing you will quickly discover is that a member's staffers are obsessed with one thing: getting their boss re-elected. This is especially noticeable on the House side, where the next election is never more than 24 months away.

Committee staffs also come in all sizes and flavors. The more-senior members (committee and subcommittee majority and minority staff directors and counsels) tend to know the most, but hundreds of others with legislative and political savvy rarely hear from reporters. Turf wars rage constantly among committee staffs, so your best bet is to find a reliable source high on the committee chair's staff to guide you through the battlefield. Typically, the chair controls about two-thirds of the committee staff; the ranking minority member, the other third. In addition, each committee member usually gets to name one committee staffer, although these aides are sometimes shunted aside by the professional staff.

In dealing with staff, you will have to assess the relative clout of each per-son before deciding which ones are worth trying to cultivate as sources. You may conclude, especially in House offices, that you're better off going straight to the member. You won't be able to do that as easily on the Senate side, where the demands on a senator's time are much greater. As a rule of thumb, the big-ger the state, the harder it will be to get one-on-one time with the senator.

If your beat has a wider scope, one that includes covering major Senate or House floor action or tracking the budget or a major issue, you'll want to aim for contacts that have a wider scope, like top aides to House and Senate leaders. "You want to get to know the leaders themselves as much as you can," says The Washington Post's Helen Dewar, who is one of the most respected reporters on the Hill. "But you've got to get to know their aides, and not just their press secretaries." Dewar says that while she needs to have sources among the staff, she also works hard to build contacts among senators— Democrat and Republican, junior and senior. She mostly relies on staff for details and members for policy and politics. "You've got to have the politics of it as well as the substance," Dewar says. "If you have one without the other you're in trouble."

St. Petersburg Times Washington bureau chief Sara Fritz says she has found that top aides to the minority leaders are "sometimes more helpful than the majority staffs, because they can tell you the dirt." Finding the right peo-ple, both in the leadership offices and on key committee staffs, takes work and time. Steve Bell, who has served Sen. Pete Domenici of New Mexico in a variety of senior staff positions including as press secretary and as chief of staff, advises building a network of sources. "If you're new on the Hill you've got to go find yourself five or six people who, over a long period of time, two to three years, you're going to be able to go back to on a steady basis to check not to quote them (but) to say, 'I am hearing this kind of thing is operating; what do you hear? Who do you think I ought to talk to about it?'"

FOLLOWING THE ACTION

Know How the Place Works

Knowing how many votes it takes in the Senate to invoke cloture is not what really matters. What matters is knowing how the place really works: the forces and alliances and personality clashes that drive and contort the place, the ground rules that govern most conversations between Hill staff and press, the political imperatives that permeate every nook and cranny.

For starters, you can read the writings of the National Journal's Richard Cohen. Among many Hill staffers, he is regarded as the reporter with the best fix on the place's nuances. Cohen, incidentally, says his best sources on the Hill are the members themselves. You don't have to be chasing a quote every time you ask a member of Congress for a few minutes.

Know the Issues

With thousands of bills introduced each year and hundreds given serious consideration, with thousands of committee hearings and hundreds of press conferences, you can't stay on top of all the issues bubbling on Capitol Hill. But you will need to get up to speed on several major issues and dozens of minor ones in any given year, often on short notice. Congressional aides should be able to help you.

If you're lucky, you might find a person willing to go to the lengths used by John Sherman, who worked for Rep. Dan Rostenskowsi when the Illinois Democrat chaired the House Ways and Means Committee:

> I would give (a new reporter) clips—we got them daily—and I'd say "read as much as you want. Here's a stack." Then I would say, "Here's all the written material we have. You read that and call me and I'll set you up with a staff person for two hours." Because it was to my advantage to get a reporter who knew what he was talking about, who had a running head start. It made our job easier because we could then sort of incrementally educate the reporter and the public.

That kind of procedure is followed routinely in the best-run Hill offices. At a minimum, the press secretary should put you in touch with the legislative aide most knowledgeable on the issue and should provide you with reading material. The better ones also will direct you to committee staff professionals on the subject, though you may be asked not to quote any staff member by name.

If the issue is complicated, such as the federal budget, you will need to develop some technical expertise. You can't even ask intelligent questions until you at least understand the definitions of terms thrown around on the budget.

Gain Access

You will find rather quickly that virtually every member of Congress and every staffer has a pecking order, however informal, in dealing with the press. Not surprisingly, most members and their staffs give priority to reporters representing news organizations in their district or state. Andy Fisher, who has been with Lugar for more than 15 years, says the secret to getting attention from the office is simple: "Be from Indiana. All Indiana calls get returned first. He [Lugar] needs the voters from Indiana to be re-elected. We work very hard at keeping all the Indiana contacts going." Fisher's perspective is not unique— nearly half the Hill press secretaries who replied to the survey said that "location of the media outlet" is the most important factor in determining the order of callbacks. This approach gives regional reporters an edge over other journalists, at least until the member latches on to a national issue that snowballs or achieves the seniority that makes the member a power broker. Even then, reporters from the larger papers and TV stations back home are rarely snubbed. But even if you have to wait a bit, you usually can expect a return phone call from a congressional press secretary: Of the 110 who responded to the survey, 98 said they "return nearly all the calls I get."

If you're covering a specialized beat on the Hill, the pecking order relates more directly to the size and location of your audience. It's a basic truth that if you're read in Washington, you're going to get more access. That gives reporters from The Washington Post, The New York Times, The Wall Street Journal and USA Today a decided advantage. The smart members of Congress, of course, try to accommodate both regional and national press.

It shouldn't be surprising, then, that if there's a pecking order for granting access to reporters on the Hill, there's usually a pecking order of sorts for leaks. One top aide to a Senate leader described the leak formula this way:

> The best place to leak something is to just walk through the press gallery and drop a few hints with some of the regulars. If it's a more sophisticated political story, you try to get it into The Wall Street Journal's Washington Wire on Friday. If you just want to get something out there, just to

start a story, you want to get it on the front page of USA Today in that column on the left side. Everybody reads it, even if they say they don't. If it's bad, if you just want to get some dirt out, you'd go for the Periscope column in Newsweek or Washington Whispers in U.S. News. And sometimes, you'd plant it in one of the weekend TV shows, like "Inside Washington."

Steve Bell, who describes himself as the "designated leaker" during his tenure as staff director of the Senate Budget Committee, says he viewed The Post as the "favorite leaker's ground" but also targeted specialty publications. "If you want to leak something to stir up opposition and you're on the Energy Committee," Bell says "you put it in the Oil Daily because it'll go to every lobbyist and it'll go to Houston and Denver and stir those folks up. You want to put it in the publication which gets to the grass roots the quickest, because grassroots lobbying is the big thing now."

Keep Up

On a typical day on the Hill, dozens of hearings are held, investigations are launched, bills are drafted, nominees are confirmed by the Senate for judgeships and executive branch posts, resolutions are debated, caucuses are held, reports are released, press conferences are staged and members of Congress react to the latest headlines with a range of emotions and rhetoric. Keeping up with all this is impossible; just keeping up with the major events that bear directly on your beat is a major challenge. Flipping through news releases or depending on a press aide to call you won't suffice.

At a minimum, you need to read The Washington Post closely and scan The New York Times and The Wall Street Journal for stories that relate to pending or past congressional action. You should read the wire service daybooks, inspect the committee hearings list for House and Senate and, if you have access to it, study the National Journal's Congress Daily or Congressional Quarterly's CQ Monitor. Both of these are newsletter-style publications that provide the highlights of expected action on the Hill, quick summaries of the previous day's action, and a detailed list of hearings, often including witnesses, for that day and several weeks hence. Both publications also offer Internet and other electronic updates throughout the course of the day, but it takes deep pockets and a lot of time to get the most from these resources. And if you really want to appreciate the institution, spend some time with the Congressional Record (see "Selected Resources" at the end of this chapter).

Required weekly reading includes National Journal and Congressional Quarterly, universally referred to as "the bible" on the Hill. If your beat includes an issue specialty or you're following a major piece of legislation, there almost certainly will be trade publications to monitor.

Daily and weekly reading is just a starting point. To really keep up, you've got to work your sources. Sara Fritz, who specialized for years in defense and foreign relations topics for the Los Angeles Times before joining the St. Petersburg Times as bureau chief, says she made selected calls each day to people she knew on various staffs and committees. She often talked to sources on the Senate and House committees that deal with military and foreign affairs issues, and other calls were targeted to "places where you think something might be going on."

Use Shoe Leather

You can't get by just working the phones, however. The reporter who complains that a member of Congress hasn't returned a phone call hasn't tried very hard. Finding members and senior staff can be relatively simple. Donna Smith, who covers Congress for Reuters from a desk in the Senate press gallery, finds "if you can't get somebody on the phone a lot of times you can just walk through the Capitol and find them or just pop into their office." Reporters who want to speak with a member who is on the floor or in the lobby can hand a note to a doorkeeper, who will pass the request along. Virtually every day that the House and Senate are in session, members of Congress make several trips from their offices to the floor. Most of them don't mind a reporter walking or riding the subway over or back with them. You also can often buttonhole members on their way in and out of hearing rooms. Nor do the good press secretaries mind if you do this. The better ones, if you tip them off, will alert their boss that you may be approaching them. If you're interested in getting a thoughtful answer, it helps if the member is tipped off. Smith says she makes a point of visiting the second floor members' lobbies every day. "Even though it might not produce an immediate story, you're building on your information so when you have to sit down and write the story, you have a knowledge base that you are working from," she says.

Most of the serious coverage of the Senate takes place on the second floor of the Capitol, outside the Senate chamber. That's where you can catch members leaving the floor and take them aside for a quick interview. It's also the area where the Tuesday lunches of the Democratic and Republican caucuses take place. Stake out those lunches if you want to stay on top of Senate business—not to mention gossip. In fact, the "scrums" outside the rooms where the senators have their policy lunches are some of the biggest gatherings of reporters on the Hill. You can also monitor the majority and minority leaders' offices, bird-dogging not only the leaders but also their visitors. Most days, the Senate majority and minority leaders meet with reporters to discuss pending business.

Monitor Subcommittees

Watching subcommittee hearings not only gets you in on the ground floor of the legislative process but also gives you a feel for future agendas in the House and Senate. Not all hearings result in legislation, but if hearings are held enough times on the same subject, legislation eventually emerges. And yet, day in and day out, two or three hearings with big-name guests draw the TV cameras and hordes of reporters while dozens of others go largely ignored. Competition to attract press coverage is intense. Frequently, a committee staff will billboard a hearing by leaking a report the day before to The Post or The Times. This is often true with oversight hearings, in which committee investigators are primed to grill an administration official and want to attract as much media as possible. The House Energy and Commerce Oversight Subcommittee and the subcommittees of the House Government Reform Committee are especially adept at this.

Some reporters insist on an exclusive before they'll trumpet hearings. How much success you have in getting such scoops depends on how much trust you build up with committee staffers, how important your audience is to the investigation and how hard you work to get the scoop. A quid pro quo of sorts is involved, naturally: You protect your sources while giving plenty of attention to the subcommittee or committee chair, who probably arranged for the leak in the first place.

THE BUDGET STORY

Of all the powers the Constitution confers on Congress, one is paramount: Not a dime of the $2 trillion-plus the federal government spends each year gets spent without congressional approval. Thus, sooner or later, every Hill reporter has to confront some aspect of the federal budget, sometimes in stories examining the process and politics, but more frequently by looking at individual bills that provide money for government projects and programs that affect a particular area or constituency. The world of the budget is one in which the meaning of "arcane" is raised to new heights. Some programs (such as Social Security) are "mandatory" and some (such as Head Start) are "discretionary." One person's "drastic cuts" are another person's "renewed commitments." Taxes become "tax revenue." Spending is "investment," when you're in favor of the item. Some things are "on budget," while others (which still cost money) are "off budget." The future is "out years." There is the "budget" and the "unified budget," along with the often-used, but poorly understood and somewhat obscure "Social Security lockbox." How much money is being spent depends on whether you are talking about "outlays," "appropriations" or "authorizations." Every program and project has to be "scored" to see if will fit inside the budget plan, which Congress is supposed to pass every spring, but frequently does not. (In late 2002, the Senate was in the process of passing, for the second consecutive year, appropriations bills setting spending even though no "budget resolution" was in place).

Here is a solution to the problem of budget jargon: Prepare a sidebar glossary when you're providing major coverage on the release of the president's budget or on the passage of the budget resolution. This device will not only help readers. You will be surprised how many times you refer to it and how many of your colleagues ask to see it when they're caught in the throes of a budget story.

There simply is no way a reporter can adequately convey how much $2 trillion really is and there is no nifty set of guidelines to make you a happy budget reporter, but here are some hints.

Understand the Big Picture

First, take all budget claims at something less than face value. At bottom, most arguments over how to divide up in excess of $2 trillion are not about money, but about policy and politics. Second, the major decisions on how the money will be raised and spent have been made long before any details are debated. Essentially, more than 50 years of political decisions have resulted in this reality: The federal government spends its money in four major ways— Transfer payments to individuals, chiefly through Social Security and Medicare (roughly 50 percent of the budget); national defense (roughly 17 percent of the budget); interest payments on bonds and other obligations of the federal government (9 percent); all other programs (25 percent). And it raises its money chiefly through taxes on individual incomes, including the Social Security and Medicare taxes (85 percent of all federal receipts). That does not mean the budget story is unimportant, especially as the federal government faces new security demands in the light of the Sept. 11, 2001, attacks on the World Trade Center and as the looming retirement of the huge baby boom generation further squeezes Social Security and Medicare resources. It does mean that after those two gargantuan appetites for money are satisfied (and they will be satisfied before any others absent a huge political upheaval), the amounts left over for other programs tend to be fairly small and the arguments tend to be at the margins. Still, a wise reporter will keep in mind the long-ago aphorism attributed (perhaps wrongly) to the late Republican Sen. Everett Dirksen of Illinois during a Senate debate more than 40 years ago: "A billion here, a billion there, and pretty soon you're talking about real money."

Read the Document

Sounds simple, but many reporters skip over the main budget document and head for the budget-in-brief. The main book is several hundred pages long, excluding all the tables of data, and it's as dry as dust. Before the Internet, you risked back injury just trying to lift the budget documents; today they all are available from the Office of Management and Budget. But they still are not any easier to read or understand, unfortunately. But if you want to understand what Congress is being asked to approve and why, you've got to read it. (That is not the same as saying you should take it seriously, or that Congress will.) Then familiarize yourself with the budget schedule, which involves certain deadlines for congressional action after the president submits a spending plan in late January or early February. Fortunately, OMB and most agencies deliver extensive briefings for reporters on the day the president's budget is released.

Seek Help Shamelessly

Some people on the Hill get their kicks explaining budgets and the budget process to reporters. Humor them. Ask for help. Both the House and Senate budget committees have staffers who will arrange extensive orientations for you.

Former Senate Budget Committee press secretary Dennis Beal, who now has his own public relations and lobbying firm in Washington, says he found reporters reluctant to seek help. "Reporters are intimidated by the budget process," Beal says. "They will fight like hell to keep from being assigned to cover it. Once they're assigned, they'll do the very superficial-type story. They'll cover the budget resolution debate a little, but they'll hardly ever come back in and ask for a second-level-type story. I don't find a lot of reporters getting below the politics of the budget to the second level."

A second key source of help on the budget story is the Congressional Budget Office, or CBO (see "Selected Resources" at the end of this chapter). The CBO is an especially valuable stop for reporters doing overview stories, because it has several experts who develop independent assessments of the economic assumptions underlying the president's budget, although the CBO's assumptions themselves often are the object of political bickering.

Another source is the Washington lobbyists for governors, mayors and state legislatures. Many of them routinely prepare analyses of how the budget will affect their clients.

In addition, Washington is brimming with think-tank scholars, academics and special interest groups who do their own budget analyses. Some of them have an ax to grind, of course, and you should allow for that. Their assessments can still be worth examining, however, because they may be familiar with obscure details that escaped your notice altogether. Besides, you can be sure that their analyses will find their way into the hands of key members of Congress.

Look for the Pork

For most regional reporters, as well as many beat reporters, the major interest in the budget is what the guardians of the pork barrel—the House and Senate appropriations committees—decide. (Just to put things into perspective, the chairs of the 13 House appropriations subcommittees are known collectively as the "College of Cardinals.") Legislative battles come and go in Congress, but the funding of government programs is the major business year in and year out. It's the subject of most interest to many in your audience. It's the preoccupation of hundreds of interest groups, especially in the late spring and summer, when the appropriations subcommittees are grinding out the 13 major spending bills. And it's the major preoccupation of most members of Congress, who fear, above all else, the charge that they are unable to deliver the bacon to their home districts or states.

Members of Congress and their staffs are not bashful about taking credit for every federal dollar that enters their district or state, so you'll get plenty of help on pork stories—as long as there's no hint of hanky-panky. Aides to Appropriations Committee members are usually the most help, and few are the equal of George Behan, press secretary to Rep. Norm Dicks, D-Wash.

Both Behan and Dicks cut their teeth working for the late Warren G. Magnuson, once acknowledged "king of pork" when he chaired the Senate Appropriations Committee (early in the 21st century, that distinction belongs to West Virginia's Robert Byrd). Dicks learned well from the king: Dicks' service on the Defense and Interior subcommittees of Appropriations gives him the clout to deliver to the Washington state economy. And Behan has developed the promotion into an art form. Every time an appropriations bill comes out of committee, he provides reporters with a precise breakdown of what is in the bill for Washington: how many billions for defense, how many millions for research at the state university, how many millions for national parks and forests and so on. Those state breakdowns go not only to reporters but also to other members of the Washington House delegation.

Behan may be more aggressive than most press secretaries, but all state delegations have someone on staff who knows where the pork is. A congressional member's staff is obviously the place to start when tracking spending, but sooner or later you'll need to develop sources on the staffs of the appropriations committees. It can be tough sledding. Appropriations staffers tend to look down their noses at others on the Hill, but you've got to charm enough of them.

No matter how many sources you develop around the Hill, however, you'll have to do some basic research of your own. You need to get a copy of any spending bill you're reporting on and—most important—the committee report that goes with it.

Spending bills deal in large chunks of money for a variety of activities under departments and agencies. But the committee report breaks down the spending as line items. These not only include the individual projects that may be of interest to a city or state or institution but also sometimes include items slipped in at the last minute with no publicity. In addition, some subcommittee chairs devise their own checklists for keeping track of the pork. Laying your hands on one of these lists can be a real coup.

EVALUATING CONGRESS AND ITS MEMBERS

With an army of press secretaries and other aides, members of Congress rarely miss a chance to get their story out, to put their spin on what a congressional action means for their constituents, to react to national and local headlines, to take credit for the most mundane piece of legislation. If reporters don't jump at the chance to rush any of this into print, the members are comforted in the knowledge that a satellite press release is apt to be run intact by the TV stations back home and that the member's next op-ed column will run verbatim in many weekly and daily newspapers in the district. And then there's always the newsletter that goes out next week by the tens of thousands at taxpayers' expense.

Much of what a member does is legitimate news, of course, and regional reporters especially are expected to give adequate coverage of those events and developments. Defining adequate, however, is a problem as old as the Washington press corps. It boils down to this: If you are responsible for covering members of Congress, you have to decide if you or they will define their image. Are you going to look only at what they say, or are you going to look even more closely at what they do?

Even with the close party split in Congress that has been the dominating feature of Washington politics for most of the past 10 years, more than 90 percent of House members are re-elected if they choose to run, which suggests something more than the advantages of incumbency and gerrymandered districts. It suggests that the press is not doing its job. Reporters who, at minimum, don't do an in-depth evaluation of members they cover at least every election year simply are not doing their job. All it takes are some orderly files (or a photographic memory) and some old-fashioned legwork. An election-year profile should include an assessment of performance versus promises, as well as the member's voting record on the floor and in committee, work in committee, use of congressional perks, reputation among colleagues, morale of staff and response to district or state needs.

How do you find these things out? You read the record, and you talk to people. For starters, review the campaign literature and speeches of the incumbent in the last election, including newspaper clips. This is especially important if the incumbent is a first-termer. If the member's staff won't make that information available to you, track down the opponent in the election or talk to the opposition party's House or Senate campaign committee. Compare that material with the member's voting and legislative sponsorship records. What bills did the member initiate? Which did the member cosponsor and why?

Assessing a voting record is subjective. Candidates promise to do things they can't always deliver in the real world of Congress. But if it's a clear-cut issue, take note. If the candidate promised to support higher defense spending and then voted to cut the Pentagon budget at every turn, you should point that out.

Examining the voting record should be done carefully. Votes on final passage might appear to contradict votes on amendments. If there's a logical explanation, point it out or give the member the chance to explain it. In this regard, you may have access to the dozens of report cards on Congress issued yearly by special interest groups. Use them cautiously. Some are downright misleading, many have an ideological bias, and even the authors of the more reputable ones, such as Americans for Democratic Action and the American Conservative Union, will advise you not to use the ratings alone without the context.

At the same time, Congressional Quarterly's annual voting studies are well regarded for positioning members on several spectrums. The four CQ studies rank members on their level of support for the president, their percentage of support for their own party's position, their alliance with or opposition to the conservative coalition in Congress and their voting attendance record. These studies make good spot stories each January but are especially helpful for election-year profiles.

To assess a member's work in committee or reputation among colleagues, you need to find committee staffers or ex-staffers who are willing to give you a candid opinion. If the member is prominently identified with any of the regional or issue caucuses, talk to his or her staff or other members. Eventually, almost every member of Congress settles into a niche, usually by the end of the first term. The member comes to realize that he or she can't be all things to all people, can't be on top of every issue and can't make a mark in Congress without focusing on two or three issues. Committee assignments have a lot to do with the issues chosen, and vice versa. But sooner or later, the member is going to become identified with certain issues or causes. And as soon as that happens, relevant interest groups in Washington will try to get a fix on him or her. If the member you're evaluating has left no impression on the committee staff and no impression on the lobbyists, you've got a very unusual legislator.

As for congressional perks such as foreign travel, records are kept with the House clerk and the secretary of the Senate. Travel records are scattered deliberately, to make it more difficult for reporters to construct junket stories. Congressional Quarterly makes a stab at compiling a list each year, with mixed results. In addition, the semiannual report of the secretary of the Senate and the House clerk's quarterly report provide figures on payroll costs, travel expenditures and other spending.

Office morale is another legitimate line of inquiry in preparing a congressional profile, but a delicate one. Many young staffers are so anxious to get Hill experience that they will put up with miserable working conditions without complaining. But if the member has a reputation for being a slave driver, for paying widely disparate salaries to men and women or for abusing the line between congressional duties and campaign work, that should be a part of the story.

You also need to make some judgment on how effective the member has been in representing the district or state's more parochial interests. Has the member made a difference in preventing a plant closing or getting federal aid for public works projects? Have you heard horror stories about the member's indifference to mail from constituents or requests for personal appearances? Talk to lobbyists in Washington who might have been involved in a funding crisis; to officials of the gubernatorial, mayoral and state legislative associations in Washington; to local officials back in the district and state; to interest groups that worked hardest for or against the member in the last campaign. If you can, go home with the member on a campaign swing during recess. This not only gives you a renewed perspective on what a crazy place Washington is but also gives you a chance to see how hectic and thankless a lawmaker's job can be.

After you've done all this, you're ready to sit down and write an evaluation that is detailed, authoritative and fair. A similar story, with much less detail, can be done about an entire state delegation. As committee assignments change and members gain seniority, an examination of how a delegation's power is growing or waning can be revealing.

Evaluating the Institution

Writing about the legislative process can become a rote exercise. Subcommittee holds hearings, marks up bill, moves it through full committee to the floor, and so forth and so on. Too often, when the bill leaves the Hill for the White House, that's the last word written about it by the Hill correspondent. What's missing in this process is context—too few reporters bother to go back to see whether programs that were desperately fought over at the outset are working as was claimed. One notable exception comes to mind: In the wake of the mid-1990s welfare reform program, many papers undertook the task of following up. Jason DeParle of The New York Times won a George Polk award in 2000 for his stories that put a human face on the impact of the program in Wisconsin.

Many of the best reporters on the Hill say there just isn't time for much work like DeParle's. Sara Fritz of the St. Petersburg Times says:

> By and large, Congress is the kind of institution that does not lend
> itself to just regular spot reporting. And yet it gets almost nothing but that.

You can do a better job of covering the place if you can stand back and look at it from a distance. You see things coming over the horizon, and some reporters will mention it in a daily story. But it sure helps readers understand what it's about if you can look ahead and write a piece that says "Here comes an issue—it's building," rather than say "The subcommittee voted today . . ."

For example, stories about defense budget battles on the Hill tend to focus on the next year's request. Few stories examine what those programs will cost five years down the road, when a combination of inflation and stretching out procurement could make them seem much less affordable. And many reporters and editors lament that the explosion of cable TV and the Internet have put even more of a premium on being there first, even if not with the most, and moving on quickly.

SELECTED RESOURCES

In covering Congress, you should never run short of reference material or people to help you interpret it. The Hill is awash in books, reports, directories, databases, research assistants, experts, newsletters, and daily and weekly publications. The following lists include some resources that have proved to be most helpful. (You also will want to check out the annotated lists in Chapter 13.)

Institutions and Organizations

• The General Accounting Office. At any one time, this congressional watchdog has about a thousand investigations under way. Its job, says a public affairs spokesman, is to "follow the dollar wherever it goes." The office is known as a career agency with high credibility; it might be the single most respected office in Washington, and one of the least political: only the two top officials are appointed. The GAO staff, headed by the comptroller general, includes auditors, lawyers, health experts, computer experts, economists and specialists on subjects from agriculture to defense. Although the official policy is not to talk to reporters while a report is in progress, experts are made available after reports are released. Diligent reporters manage to skirt the official policy by developing discreet agency sources. About 80 percent of GAO's work is in response to requests from Congress; the rest is generated internally. Reports requested by Congress are available for release by Congress for 30 days before GAO releases them. The GAO is another agency that has used the World Wide Web to speed up and enhance its information delivery. Its Web site offers daily updates of reports and testimony, plus the ability to search reports and testimony going back to 1975. You also can get on an e-mail list that will notify you of reports you might be interested in. Besides its reports, which tend to be excellent backgrounders and primers on whatever subject they tackle, the GAO does financial audits looking for (and often finding) that elusive "fraud, waste and abuse" in federal programs.

• The Congressional Budget Office. Created as part of the 1974 law overhauling the congressional budget process, CBO has become one of the most user-friendly agencies in town for reporters. CBO puts out three major works a year, along with about two dozen studies of fiscal policies and government programs. It also does a cost estimate of every bill reported out of a full committee—several hundred a year. Some include breakdowns by state. The major works are an economic and budget outlook for five years, released annually as the president's budget is sent to Congress; an analysis of the president's budget, which trails the release of the budget by three to four weeks; and a volume of options for reducing the federal deficit, released around the first of March. The economic outlook is updated each year in August. CBO officials routinely hold background briefings for reporters and are eager to get you on their mailing list. If you'll let them know your reporting specialty, they'll alert you to studies in your area. CBO's official policy is that no one other than the CBO director and the director of CBO's Office of Intergovernmental Relations is to be quoted by name. But they can be a good resource if you're looking for experts to balance the views and forecasts of the Office of Management and Budget.

• Congressional caucuses. A phenomenon of the past two decades on the Hill has been the explosive growth of issue-oriented coalitions of House and Senate members. A study done for the Woodrow Wilson Center, a nonprofit research organization, found that the number of caucuses grew from 59 in 1980 to 173 in 1998. Most of the caucuses are organized to help build support for a particular issue or industry, or they bring together members with shared geographic or regional interests. Some, such as the Lewis & Clark Bicentennial Caucus (made up mostly of members from the Northwest) and the Mushroom Caucus, consisting of representatives from areas that grow mushrooms for market, seem a bit bizarre. But the larger and more effective caucuses are the ones with the widest reach. The Congressional Black Caucus has considerable influence inside Democratic Party politics in the House. The Sunbelt Caucus, for example, was created in the House to counter the influence of the 200-member Northeast-Midwest Caucus. Several of the larger caucuses have formed affiliated "institutes" that are tax-free but are allowed to tap lobbyists for financial support. The important thing for reporters to know is that the caucuses produce studies for their members that often provide excellent material for regional economic stories. It also might be a good idea to check on how the caucuses operate and how they spend their money. When Republicans took over the House in 1994 they restricted the practice of letting House members use federal funds to pay dues to the caucuses, but that hasn't slowed the spread of these groups and their affiliated foundations and organizations.

• **The Senate Library.** Many reporters don't even know that this library exists or that many of its resources are available to the press. The library, open weekdays as well as nights and weekends when the Senate is in session, has an exhaustive collection of reference books. The staff also answers general reference questions and has access to numerous online databases.

• **The Library of Congress.** The Library of Congress has a special reference service for reporters accredited to the congressional galleries. The service responds to simple requests, such as verification of a quote or a biographical fact. The library also releases to reporters materials produced for congressional members by its Congressional Research Service if the requesting member approves the release. The CRS gets more than a thousand requests from Congress each day, and about 90 percent of its product is never published. The enterprising reporter will develop sources among CRS researchers to help cut through red tape. CRS has resisted calls from interest groups and some members of Congress to routinely make the files available on the Internet. A few organizations, including the State Department's Foreign Press Center, have put selected CRS reports on their Web sites. Rep. Christopher Shays, R-Conn., makes the text of reports available through his office Web site. And a Washington area publisher, Penny Hill Press, has been able to obtain CRS reports and offers abstracts on its Web site and full text on a subscription basis.

• **Congressional offices.** Many congressional offices keep extensive clip files from newspapers in their district and state. Some even do weekly summaries for staff and press who cover them. In addition, most offices have computer access to a range of databases and such wire services as the Associated Press.

• **Offices of the House Clerk and the Secretary of the Senate.** These offices hold treasures, especially the quarterly House reports and semiannual Senate reports that list disbursement of funds by members and committees, which Congress still refuses to make available electronically. Here you can find salaries of congressional staffers and calculate some of the costs of foreign travel. These offices also have available the registration of domestic lobbyists, as well as the financial disclosure reports by members of Congress, candidates and high-level congressional aides. The forms report income, financial holdings, transactions, liabilities, gifts and reimbursements, with much of the information in broad ranges. These offices are also the repository for reports on foreign travel.

• **House and Senate campaign committees.** Both parties maintain campaign offices for Senate and House candidates: the Democratic Senatorial Campaign Committee, the Democratic Congressional Campaign Committee, the National Republican Senatorial Committee and the National Republican Congressional Committee. Developing sources here is a must for campaign-year stories on candidate recruitment, financial assistance from Washington, the political climate in a district or state, the political dirt being dug up by the opposition, and primary and general election strategies. These committees frequently run seminars for candidates and their managers.

Reference Books, Periodicals and Services

AP, UPI and *Reuters Daybooks.* On a typical day, dozens of press conferences, seminars and hearings take place in Washington. The most complete calendars of the day's events are put out twice a day by the major wire services. They produce a first version in midafternoon that is updated early the following morning. A listing of congressional committee hearings runs separately.

Congressional Record. Some reporters on the Hill ignore the Record, and some read it cover to cover. Most just scan it occasionally. There is more to the Record than is actually said on the floor. Much of the material entered into the Record is never uttered on the floor. Instead these "revisions and extensions" appear in a separate portion of the Record. However imperfect, the Record gives you a sense of what is bugging members of Congress, what they're hearing from their constituents, and so forth. It includes a crazy quilt of tributes, editorials, bill introductions, reactions to events, notices of official actions (such as the appointment of conferees), and even some real debate. It also provides a helpful daily digest at the end that reviews the day's floor action, and on Fridays the Record includes a calendar for the following week, as well as a list of upcoming committee hearings.

Congressional Quarterly. Serious coverage of the Hill requires access to the Congressional Quarterly's Weekly Report. This is the record of Congress, not only an account of all action at the full committee level and above but a repository of good trend stories as well. The report also features a complete list of roll-call votes from the previous week, a box score on other legislative action, and handy charts that show the status of all major legislation, including the appropriations bills.

National Journal. National Journal has established itself in Washington as the premier explainer of government action. It probably also is the most plagiarized publication in Washington, because reporters find the coverage so compelling. Each weekly issue contains four or five full-length pieces, plus an assortment of special columns and features, including a "People" section on job changes in both the government and the private sector that is unequaled.

Congressional Directory. The official directory of Congress, the CD includes brief biographies of the members of Congress, their committee assignments, their committee staffs, key officials in the other branches of government, and a lot more, such as maps of the Capitol complex, maps of congressional districts and a directory of members of the press galleries.

Congressional Staff Directory. This directory, published by Congressional Quarterly, is used daily and sometimes several times a day by many Hill reporters. It lists job titles, assignments, addresses and phone numbers of members of Congress, committees, subcommittees and staffs. Of particular use are the biographies of top staff members. Before calling staff members you don't know, it's good to check out their background; it might suggest an opening line. CQ also offers a Web version that is updated frequently.

Almanac of American Politics. Since 1972 the Almanac has become a reliable companion of Washington journalists. This comprehensive guide to members of Congress and their districts and states is published by National Journal and updated every two years.

Politics in America. This publication, which competes with the Almanac of American Politics, duplicates much of the information in the Almanac but is especially strong in its analysis of each congressional district's economic, social and political makeup. Politics is published by Congressional Quarterly every two years.

Vital Statistics on Congress. If you like to spike your stories with facts and figures, this is the book for you. Published by the American Enterprise Institute, the book is a fascinating compendium of data on members of Congress, voting alignments, campaign finance, congressional workload, congressional staff, and so on.

Setting Course: A Congressional Management Guide. Published by the Congressional Management Foundation, this little handbook tells you everything you might want to know about setting up and running a congressional office. A how-to book for new members of Congress, it will help you understand the personal, logistical and political challenges of the office. A new version is published every two years.

Congressional Yellow Book. Published by the Monitor Publishing Company and updated quarterly, this directory of congressional members, committees and staff includes pictures of members as well as legislative responsibilities of aides.

"How Our Laws Are Made." This primer, compiled by the House parliamentarian, is for people who forgot the lessons they learned in high school civics class. If you don't understand the fine differences between the consent calendar and the private calendar in the House, for example, this little book will get you up to speed. You can buy the book through the Government Printing Office or browse it online at the Library of Congress.

<u>REFERENCES</u>

Povich, Elaine S., *Partners and Adversaries: The Contentious Connection Between Congress & the Media,* Freedom Forum, Arlington, Va., 1996.

4 FEDERAL DEPARTMENTS AND AGENCIES

The dust had not yet settled on the site of the World Trade Center in New York and the Pentagon before Washington had its response to the Sept. 11, 2001, terrorist attacks. First, there would be a worldwide war on terror. Second, there would be a new federal agency: The Department of Homeland Security, which eventually will consolidate the functions of dozens of other agencies and will have a work force of more than 170,000. In that regard, the American government was on familiar ground: Crises at home and abroad often have spawned new federal agencies. The Defense Department is an outgrowth of World War II, the Secret Service established to flush out counterfeiters in the mid-19th century, the Marines to deal with the pirates of Tripoli, NASA to coordinate the space race after Sputnik.

All told, there now are 15 cabinet-level departments and more than 125 independent agencies (the alphabet soup of the federal government—EPA, FCC, FEC, SEC, CIA, and so on). Additionally, nearly every agency has a set of "advisory" boards and commissions designed, ostensibly, to help provide the public with a way to channel information into the vast federal decision-making apparatus.

Two things are true about this far-flung bureaucracy.

First, an agency once created almost never dies, even if its purposes have been superseded by time, technology or other developments. That's because over time an agency acquires constituencies including its own employees (and former employees), the authorizing and appropriating committees of Congress, interest groups and industries affected by the agency's work and the public at large. Additionally, agencies adapt their missions to deal with new realities. Thus, the dwindling numbers of full-time farmers has had little impact on the Agriculture Department. (A joke: Why was the USDA employee crying? His farmer died.) County agricultural extension agents now spend more of their time helping urban gardeners figure out solutions for their lawns and less time helping farmers find the highest-yielding corn variety. When the end of the Cold War seemed to some to obviate the need for the Voice of America, the VOA reinvented itself and became a content provider for broadcast stations in the newly emerging democracies of Eastern Europe. Problem solved. Agency saved.

Second, journalists who venture into these agencies will be mostly alone, at least until some major event, like the Sept. 11 terror attack, sends reporters flocking to places like the Transportation Department, where the Washington pack usually wouldn't be seen. Although "faceless bureaucrats"—not members of Congress—shape most of the rules and regulations that touch almost every facet of American life, news organizations in Washington spend little time and effort examining what goes on behind the bureaucracy's doors. While it is true that nearly every major agency has a small, permanent press corps, most of these reporters represent small, specialized newsletters or trade press outlets. Few national or regional papers assign anyone full time to any agencies except the Pentagon and the State Department. American Journalism Review reported in 2002 that no Washington newspaper or wire service reporter was assigned to regularly cover the Interior Department, with a $13 billion budget, or the Veterans Affairs Department, which spends more than $50 billion a year, or even the Social Security Administration. No one would argue that these agencies should be covered just because they are large. But almost anyone would admit that good stories, important stories, are being missed. The Interior Department manages the national park system, administers millions of acres of federal lands in the West, and handles health and education programs for Native Americans, among other things. Veterans Affairs operates one of the world's largest health care systems.

No doubt there are countless reasons for this paucity of coverage. Certainly, one problem for bureaucrats is that, well, they are bureaucrats. Reporters find it more exciting to cover a White House briefing or a Senate press conference than a meeting of the Federal Energy Regulatory Commission, even though the latter may have much more real impact on their audience. Brookings Institution scholar Stephen Hess, who has spent much of the past two decades studying the Washington press corps, explains it this way:

> Washington is the political capital. Everything is looked at through a political lens rather than, say, a public administration lens. . . . Thus the typical reporter here, if you looked through his Rolodex, it would be political appointees or elected officials . . . relatively few members of the permanent bureaucracy. . . . The news is skewed in that direction also by the inclinations of reporters. They become reporters to cover senators and Cabinet officers—not to cover GS-14s. But there is a need to cover GS-14s as well.

Washington bureaus also try to shift federal regulatory issues to the home office, arguing that statehouse and local government reporters can track those stories more easily through regional and local federal offices. Federal agencies sometimes abet that notion by proposing that state governments enforce federal rules and regulations. The result is that stories fall through the cracks.

But the best explanation is much simpler: Getting stories out of the bureaucracy is hard work. As elsewhere in government, the bureaucracy has its turf battles and political feuds. But unlike, say, on Capitol Hill, there is usually no ready source of leaks, counterleaks and political potshots in a federal agency. The flow of official information to the press is often tightly controlled, sometimes requiring White House clearance. Despite the protections of the civil service system, most career bureaucrats are chary of saying quotable things or even talking to reporters unless they've built up trust over time.

Frank Aukofer, who covered Washington for more than 30 years as a reporter and then bureau chief for the Milwaukee Journal Sentinel, says he couldn't justify the time and energy required for systematic agency coverage: "My attitude toward covering agencies and departments was it wouldn't profit me very much to spend a lot of time developing sources at a huge agency because I didn't have the time. I'm a generalist. I'm covering the whole Wisconsin delegation. We had individual members—congressmen and senators—who were on very important committees. They were on judiciary, they were on agriculture, they were on government operations. So one day I could be covering dairy policy and the next day I could be covering patent and trademark law and the next day I could be covering defense issues. I was all over the map. For me as an individual reporter to try to cover a federal agency like HHS or HUD just didn't make any sense." Aukofer says he was able to use good contacts on Capitol Hill—remember, every agency reports to at least four committees—to get leads and information about agency happenings.

Regulatory agencies are especially tough to deal with because their actions are apt to be both controversial and viewed in a political context. The smart agencies, however, like to have press coverage so long as it's balanced, of course—because press coverage can have a tremendous impact on Capitol Hill.

THE ROLE OF GOVERNMENT PRESS OFFICERS

A reporter's first approach to any federal agency typically starts with the press office, so it's important to understand the role that press officers play. Whatever you call them—flacks, PR types, public affairs officers, press aides, public information officers—the one thing most veteran reporters in Washington agree on about government press agents is that they are a very mixed bag.

The Chicago Tribune's managing editor James O'Shea, who covered Washington for the Des Moines Register and the Chicago Tribune before moving into management, tends to rank press aides according to their political clout:

"As a general rule, unless they have a good relationship with the person who heads the agency, they really aren't very helpful." O'Shea describes the "real pros" he dealt with this way: "If you write something their boss doesn't like, and you call back, they don't sit there and gripe about it all the time . . . or they're not so insecure that every time you call over, you have to go through them."

Several points regarding press officers are important. First, there are two distinct kinds of press officers in most departments and agencies: political appointees and career employees. Political appointees usually fill the top two or three public affairs or press spokesperson slots, though some smaller agencies have only one such slot and some larger ones may have half a dozen. The top appointee sometimes has responsibility for both public affairs and congressional affairs. Top appointees are usually in tune with the thinking of the cabinet secretary or agency administrator, are conversant with agency policy generally, and are often authorized to enunciate that policy. They are especially important to know if you're assigned to cover the agency full time, because they usually know about coming policy pronouncements. They are also likely to be out of a job when a new administration takes over the White House.

Says Sue Hensley, head of public affairs for the Labor Department during the administration of President George W. Bush: "The public affairs shop is here to be the voice of the leadership of the administration and the department. . . . You're here not only to serve the department but (also) to serve the president (and) to advance the administration's goals."

Chet Lunner, the chief spokesman for the Transportation Department, adds: "We stay in constant contact with our counterparts in the White House and then down through our agencies, so we all know we're on the same page with whatever the developments are on the presidential agenda. Part of our job is to amplify the president's message as it pertains to our piece of the national message."

Career public information officers are more attuned to the nuts-and-bolts operation of the agency and the day-to-day needs of the press. They usually stop short of expressing political opinions. They often remain in place through several administrations. John Heine, deputy public affairs director at the Securities and Exchange Commission, says, "A career bureaucrat has more loyalty to the institution whereas the political people have more of a loyalty—understandably—to the person who appointed them."

Second, press officers, like reporters, are often very busy people. Though some agencies have gained a reputation for being generous havens for flacks biding their time until retirement, many others have lean staffs that work long hours.

The Labor Department's Sue Hensley recalls one day in her life as the chief spokesperson. "I knew I wouldn't have time for lunch so I made myself a peanut butter sandwich before I came in—I got in at 6:45 in the morning, and you know when I ate the peanut butter sandwich? At 7 o'clock at night. Some days are just like that—no time to breathe, to eat, to anything."

At the Transportation Department, which became a hot spot for reporters in the wake of the Sept. 11 terrorist attacks, Lunner finds similar issues. "People forget that we've got a hundred other people in the news media tracking 50 other things at the same time. It really becomes a monumental task some days just to keep up with it."

The Securities and Exchange Commission, which found itself buried by the corporate accountability scandals beginning in 2002, has only six public affairs officers for the whole country.

So, when you call a press officer, he or she may be simultaneously

• Seeking information within the agency for six other reporters who called ahead of you
• Trying to get the last of six or eight department officials to sign off on a press release
• Trying to figure out where a reporter's Freedom of Information Act request should be routed
• Preparing to background an assistant secretary or administrator about likely questions in an upcoming press interview
• Fending off a persistent citizen who wandered in off the street and should be in the public documents room.

Not surprisingly, press officers establish priorities and pecking orders. If you're a regular on the beat, you're probably going to get your phone calls returned more quickly than if you're doing a one-time story. If you work for a major news organization, your phone calls and interview requests will get attention sooner than if you work for a small paper or chain, barring special circumstances. Cindy Skrzycki, who covers federal agencies as a beat for The Washington Post's business desk, freely admits: "It helps amazingly to be a top-tiered newspaper."

And sometimes it's simply a question of who can get the story out quickest. Christi Harlan, who became director of public affairs at the Securities and Exchange Commission in early 2002 (just in time to handle a barrage of inquiries about Enron and other troubled companies), says, "If I had requests pending at the same time for the chairman to talk to Business Week, which wouldn't be out for a week and a half, or CNBC—CNBC gets the interview because I want him out there fast talking about these things."

John Heine, a career public servant who is Harlan's deputy, says not all phone calls or requests do get answered the same day. "There usually are 3 or 4 phone calls that I wish I could have returned but it just got too late," Heine says.

You can speed the process of getting access by first determining the structure of the press office you're dealing with. Many of the larger departments and agencies have beat systems under which some press officers concentrate on certain programs or divisions and other press officers serve as backups when they're away. The more specialized the press officer, the more apt he or she will be able to answer your questions firsthand.

Third, press officers have tough and sometimes thankless jobs. They are bureaucratic buffers, facilitators, greasers of skids. It's not unusual for them to feel they are stuck in a rut. The federal government has no system for moving its career public information people around when they get bored or stale. Press officers often find themselves caught in the middle between demanding reporters and insensitive bureaucrats. Some bureaucrats are almost as contemptuous of press officers as they are of reporters and are quick to blame the press office when something embarrassing leaks.

Fourth, good press officers can be invaluable. If you demonstrate that you're serious about your job, and you have made the effort to learn a little about the subject you're seeking help on, the good press officers will respond in kind.

Besides providing factual information, the good press officers offer guidance on background. That guidance might be as simple as suggesting which government watchdog group is best to approach for reaction, or it might be as intriguing as a tip on a long-forgotten government study contradicted by new findings you're about to report. As elsewhere around town, top press spokespersons in the bureaucracy spend much of their time offering key reporters background guidance on what some public utterance by the cabinet secretary or agency head really meant.

Finally, the best press officers are the ones who play devil's advocate for both sides. They promote agency positions to the press, but in the agency's inner councils they are willing to argue the media's point of view.

In short, press officers are a valuable link in covering the agencies. Even the best reporters rely on them as a starting point. But the best reporters are always trying to get beyond press officers into the bowels of the bureaucracy.

DEVELOPING BUREAUCRATS AS SOURCES

Now comes the tricky part: finding government officials in responsible positions whom you can cultivate to serve as your eyes and ears, sounding boards and unofficial "confirmers" within agencies. This is a slow process. Most bureaucrats are nervous about talking to the press unless they've developed a special relationship over time. Most assume they're not supposed to talk to reporters without clearance from above, when in fact policy varies from agency to agency.

So in all likelihood you're trying to develop sources whose names you don't even know yet and who, once you've identified them, are apt to be nervous about talking to you and skeptical of your intent. What to do? Suggestions, ranging from the patently obvious to perhaps the not-so-obvious, include the following:

• Have an open mind and don't assume that all you're going to find is "dirt." Christi Harlan, who spent nearly 20 years reporting for such organizations as The Dallas Morning News and The Wall Street Journal before getting into public affairs, first in Congress and then at the SEC, finds an attitude that troubles her. "What I was seeing in reporting before I left and what I'm seeing now is the assumption that the government is wrong or it's driven by some political ideology. It's easy to write the black and white protagonist/antagonist story. It's much more difficult to write a gray story about here's an idea, here's something that might work. This kind of reporting doesn't serve the reader or the people you're writing about."

• Neither should reporters assume that they are being shut out of information just because officials or press officers don't like or respect journalists. Lunner, who moved from newspaper reporting to Capitol Hill and then to the Transportation Department as chief spokesman, says the view from the inside is quite different from the view from the newsroom.

> We try to be timely, open and accurate to the extent that we can be. That's complicated by this new security regime, because again we don't want to say anything that's going to tip the bad guys to methods and procedures and technologies that we have now employed to stop them. And again while you will see with your seemingly innocent question about something—one strand of that formulation—if you put it all together as a terrorist could by running a Nexis search at his local library (see) that all these things mount up into a pattern that (he) could use to defeat the system. So what looks like stonewalling for bad purposes can often be stonewalling for the positive national goal.

• Get the department or agency's phone book. If the press office won't give you one, go to the Government Printing Office bookstore and buy one. In some agencies the directories are available online and can be searched by a variety of indexes. Study it. Figure out which people with which job titles are most likely to have the answers you're looking for. You're not ready to call them blind yet, but it's good to familiarize yourself with some names.

• Read closely the agency coverage in The Washington Post, especially in the "Federal Page." Not only will you see names being quoted that may be of use to you, but you'll also see unnamed sources quoted whose identity may become apparent to you as you learn more about an issue and the politics surrounding it. Study the top trade publications and newsletters that focus on the agency. Every government agency of any size is now covered intensively by at least one newsletter.

• Use the leverage of sources you already have. Perhaps you know a lobbyist or consultant or think-tank expert who used to be in a government office you're now trying to crack. Maybe that source is on good terms with his or her successor or the people around the successor. Ask your source to make a call for you or at least to vouch for your trustworthiness. Also pump your sources on the Hill. Congressional committee staffs work hand in glove with agency staffs, especially on spending decisions. Oversight committee staffs often know where the bureaucratic skeletons are buried.

• Aim for midlevel officials. George Anthan, the retired bureau chief of The Des Moines Register and for many years Washington's premier agriculture reporter, says he concentrated on Agriculture Department officials at the level of the division chief or assistant division chief (USDA has scores of them scattered throughout its many services). "At this level," says Anthan, "you'll get a professional bureaucrat or economist who'll give you good information. At the deputy- or assistant-secretary level, they get political. I wouldn't go to them except for quotes. To build a story, I'd start lower." The Agriculture Department remains a fairly open agency. You can get the names, phone numbers and e-mail addresses of agency officials and the midlevel economists and program specialists from the Web site. In other departments, the route to the people directly involved in program management often is more circuitous.

• Dazzle the bureaucrats with your knowledge. Even if you're a stranger, a government official is apt to be more receptive if it's obvious that you know a great deal about the relevant subject matters. The official may be willing to help you plug the last few holes in your story. You can get up to speed on any subject in Washington in a day or two by using the city's many libraries, databases, think tanks and congressional experts. You can get an elaborate briefing that will prompt intelligent questions.

• If all else fails, do a project. Doing a big project is an excellent way to break into a new beat and will work just as well when you're trying to learn your way around a government agency. Newsweek's Roy Gutman recalls that when he was first sent to the Pentagon in the early '80s for Newsday, he decided that the way to get to know people was to undertake a massive reporting project on the Reagan-era defense buildup. He chose to focus on how the United States would react to Soviet threats to international stability in the Third World. Gutman first spent a long time interviewing people outside the Pentagon to find out whom to interview inside the Pentagon. The resulting series was picked up in the Pentagon news clips and got a lot of attention throughout the building. That in turn produced new contacts, who led to other contacts. Thus, if government officials see that you're doing solid reporting, they'll be less hesitant about taking your calls. Once you've established personal trust, you'll be able to maintain the kind of back-channel communications that take the flack out of the picture.

• Cultivate your sources. Too often, it seems that reporting on an agency is like having a series of one-night stands. Judy Burns, who covers the SEC for the Dow Jones News Service, says: "I guess the thing I would stress is if you are going to be a beat reporter covering a beat you not only want to begin relationships but you have to maintain them. Basically the way to do that is to stay in touch with people regularly." Skrzycki of The Washington Post counsels arranging meetings or lunches with new public affairs officers and senior officials. But that's not enough, she says: "Check in daily on the phone. You can also check their Web site. You can look at other Internet-based publications, but nothing is going to take the place of picking up the phone and saying 'Hi, this is Cindy Skrzycki with The Post. How are you today . . . what's going on?'" Burns finds other ways to build goodwill, such as letting a source know a potentially troublesome story is on the way. For example, she says she would call Harlan's predecessor at the SEC and say: "'I'm working on a story and I'm going to report this — do you want to comment,' just so he would know—just so he wouldn't be surprised. And once or twice he'd say, 'The only comment I have is I wonder who the hell you're talking to'(or) 'How do you get this stuff.' If I hadn't called him up he would have been surprised when the story came in print. And so that way I felt like I wasn't totally irritating him and I gave the opportunity to comment. People don't want to be sand-bagged. If you got the story and don't need them—OK you don't have to call them—but unless you really want to tick them off you can just say 'FYI I'm going to run this.' That way they can tell their boss ahead of time and they look good. Because there will be a time when you—the reporter—will need to pull something from the favor bank." Finally, Burns says, "If you mess up, then fess up and make the correction."

THE RULE-MAKING PROCESS

The growth, care and feeding of federal regulations is a story that bores many reporters who get paid a lot less than the Washington lobbyists who earn six-figure salaries tracking the evolution of the most obscure rules and standards. Lobbyists appreciate that regulations are important to the economic health of their industry, whereas reporters believe that what matters is results, not the interminable processes that produce them. Granted, rule making is a time-consuming, tedious process. It's not so important that you write about the process. What's important is that you understand it well enough to be able to monitor it and spot stories before they've become hot enough to attract five different congressional investigating committees.

You can start with just one basic document, the Federal Register, in which all regulations must be published before they go into effect. It's a fairly simple document, but if it intimidates you, go to the National Archives site on the Web (www.archives.gov) and download a manual called "The Federal Register: What It Is and How to Use It." The manual explains both the Register and the Code of Federal Regulations, which codifies all regulations under one of 50 titles that are revised annually. To be sure, not many reporters sing the praises of the gray, dense Federal Register, but listen to The Washington Post's Skrzycki:

> One thing that many reporters who cover the federal agencies don't do is read the Federal Register. I view it as the most important thing to do. I've insisted that The Post actually get a paper copy of the Federal Register, because you can take it with you. You can read it on the Metro. You can tear pages out of it. You also get a sense from the Federal Register of the overall load of fed regulation by how thick the book is. You can find executive orders in there; you can find all sorts of things. . . . People petition the agencies—this is something that a lot of reporters don't even know—and some really big stories come out of this.

By monitoring the Register, you can learn when new or amended rules are proposed, how long the public has to comment on them and when final action was taken. You will also find notices of public agency meetings, presidential executive orders, and so forth, all listed in a table of contents that spares you from scanning every page. If you want more information on a proposed regulation than is contained in the Register, you can go to OMB and request to see all draft submissions from the sponsoring agency. This is a good way to explore the history of a proposed regulation.

The Register is particularly valuable twice a year, in April and October, when agencies are required to publish their agenda for the next six months, outlining the rules they expect to propose, the ones they have under review, the priority and timetable attached to them, and so on.

KEEPING TABS ON THE BUREAUCRACY

You don't want to have to depend on one source of information, of course. Experienced reporters quickly discover that Washington is crammed with people and institutions and resources that will help them keep tabs on the bureaucracy, most at no cost except perhaps publicity for a cause. Among those sources are the following:

Public interest groups. Led by the likes of Ralph Nader's Public Citizen, these groups almost always have an ax to grind, some to the point that they strain their credibility. But whatever their cause, they frequently have channels into the bureaucracy that can prove enormously helpful if you're pursuing a story they're interested in. They also do studies of their own that make headlines. Get to know them, monitor their publications and ask them about their future agendas.

Congressional research and watchdog agencies. The GAO and the CRS at the Library of Congress are gold mines of information about the internal workings of the bureaucracy. The GAO will gladly send you its reports free; to obtain CRS documents not previously made public, you're required to make a request through a congressional office. When you get these reports, don't just read the executive summary. Study the names of members of advisory groups who contributed to or reviewed the findings. Among them may lurk a great source just waiting to be cultivated.

Private research groups. In recent years, Washington has seen the creation and growth of many organizations and groups that have been able to parlay a seemingly narrow interest into broad-based political roles. Among those is OMB Watch, started by Gary Bass in the mid-1980s to "lift the veil of secrecy shrouding the White House Office of Management and Budget." Today, Bass and his OMB Watch publications churn out several newsletters each month and have become a force in such issues as access to federal information and the environment. The newsletters are free and available online (www.ombwatch.org). Bass also is generous with tips for reporters learning their way around the federal maze. The newsletters do tend to take a fairly liberal approach to issues, but they also can contain good leads for stories.

Consumer complaint files. Virtually every federal department and agency has an office that receives and files complaints from the public about programs and regulations under its jurisdiction. This is a natural place to start if you're looking for tips on what Uncle Sam is doing wrong now.

Inspectors general. All cabinet departments and most independent agencies now have internal watchdogs under legislation passed during the Carter presidency. The inspector general position is an awkward one: a presidential appointee whose job is to ferret out waste and corruption and report it to the head of the agency and to Congress. Some IGs have been accused by Congress of having ignored more fraud than they exposed. Their semiannual reports to Congress are worth getting nonetheless. Their summaries of investigations, prosecutions and audits provide a quick overview of acknowledged agency mismanagement. More information about the role of inspectors general is in Chapter 11.

Lobbyists. As noted above, lobbyists get paid big bucks to know what's going on in every nook and cranny of the bureaucracy that can influence their clients. Because many of them used to work in those nooks and crannies, they'll have less trouble uncovering information than you will. No significant regulatory proposal gets far without lobbyists' fingerprints all over it. Lobbyists may not reveal their lobbying strategy, but if they know you well, chances are that they'll share gossip about what others are up to.

The Freedom of Information Act. If you suspect that an agency has information you're after, don't be deterred by a bureaucratic runaround. File a request under the Freedom of Information Act, being as specific as possible about the information you're seeking. Talk to the press office and the Freedom of Information officer first. They may give you some guidance or even handle the request on the spot. Be polite but persistent. The Reporters Committee for Freedom of the Press can help you if you are new at the FOIA game or are involved in a nasty dispute. For more information about using the FOIA, see Chapter 11.

A WORD ABOUT WATCHDOGS AND WHISTLE-BLOWERS

Organizations like the GAO, the watchdog arm of Congress, have been a boon to generations of Washington reporters. They are a fertile source of unbiased, hard-nosed investigative evidence about government waste and mismanagement. A reporter tracking any segment of the bureaucracy is well advised to develop sources at GAO and to monitor its activities closely.

However, the watchdog fad has spread far beyond the official realm of the GAO. More and more public interest groups are conducting their own investigations of how government regulations are working or, as is more often the focus of their studies, not working, and the groups are following up their studies with lawsuits. Groups such as the Natural Resources Defense Council, which targets pollution and toxic substances, and Public Citizen, which focuses on health, highway safety and nuclear energy matters, have become major players in the constant Washington battle for influence and press coverage. Members of these groups are good people to know. Although the groups almost always are working for a cause, they sometimes produce newsworthy material.

But remember that without the cooperation of the press, few of these groups would last long. Without publicity to point to, contributions from foundations and assorted wealthy do-gooders would dry up. Don't permit yourself to be used as a soapbox by organizations that may give you an exclusive on a story in return for a promise of good play. Always assume that there is another side to the story, without which the story is incomplete. Indeed, you often need more than the other side; you also need the expertise of a neutral third party. Much the same goes for whistle-blowers. The best compromise is to take everything you can get from whistle-blowers, but be sure to scrutinize it with a skeptical eye.

SELECTED RESOURCES

Agency Publications

One thing all government agencies do with great success is turn out paper. Reporters may give much of it short shrift after they become familiar with it, but there's no better way to get a basic understanding of how a department or agency functions than to study its publications. You can begin with its annual report to Congress and whatever budget documents it puts out. Most agencies make your reading task easier by publishing an annual list or index of all their regular staff reports, studies, guides, and so forth. Press officers will usually provide copies of the documents at no cost; you can also review them at the agency public reference rooms (see below). Whether it's the Uniform Crime Reports from the FBI, a Health and Human Services study on the shortage of nurses, or a National Transportation Safety Board study of medical evacuation helicopters, such reports are authoritative, and they frequently make headlines.

Public Reference Rooms

All regulatory agencies have rooms for public display of documents involved in most of the cases before them. Nowadays, almost all this material also is available, with some digging, on the agency sites on the World Wide Web. Here, for example, is a partial list of what you'll find at the public reference room and on the Web site of the Federal Energy Regulatory Commission, the agency charged with handling such matters as rates for electric power, pipeline regulation, and related issues (www.ferc.gov):

• Applications, complaints, petitions and other pleadings requesting FERC action, along with responses, protests, motions, briefs, contracts, rate schedules, tariffs, and commission and staff correspondence relating to any proceeding
• Commission orders, notices, opinions, decisions and approved commission minutes
• Agendas for public commission meetings and lists of actions taken at the meetings
• Transcripts of hearings, hearing exhibits and prepared testimony
• Actions of administrative law judges
• All reports required to be filed by regulated companies (including, now, many reports that are filed electronically)
• Legislative proposals, correspondence and reports concerning FERC that have been released on Capitol Hill
• An index of commission actions by subject
• Filings and records in court proceedings to which the commission is a party

Agency Libraries

Most of the larger departments and agencies have libraries to which you can almost always gain access. These are ready sources for reference books and studies and are valuable repositories for newsletters and trade journals that cover the field.

Newsletters

No cause or institution in Washington is too small to have its own newsletter—and often several of them. High-profile departments and agencies like Energy, Defense, Health and Human Services and the Environmental Protection Agency, and the issues they deal with, are the subject of numerous well-circulated newsletters. Others, such as Sludge, Mobile Phone News and Peelings, the last put out by the Potato Museum, are more obscure. Newsletters are closely monitored by bureaucrats and lobbyists because the publications are narrowly targeted and often are a forum for leaks and scoops, which Washington's general press corps routinely steals without attribution.

Federal Register

As noted earlier, the Federal Register is essential for any reporter covering the activities of an agency in depth. It not only carries notices of public meetings but also provides advance details on proposed rules changes, as well as final notices when new government regulations are about to take effect.

Books

The following reference books are most helpful in tracking agency personnel and responsibilities.

Federal Regulatory Directory. Published biennially by Congressional Quarterly, this all-purpose book gives you a historical overview of federal regulatory activity, biographies of top commissioners and administrators, key contacts in the agencies, crisp summaries of the agencies' history and responsibilities, and valuable descriptions of libraries, public reference rooms, and Freedom of Information Act offices, as well as the federal titles under which agency regulations are codified.

Federal Staff Directory. Published annually by Congressional Staff Directory, Limited, this book lists top and midlevel staff by title in all departments and agencies. It includes some 2,400 biographies of top bureaucrats and political appointees.

United States Government Manual. Published annually as a special edition of the Federal Register, the manual is the official bible of the government.

It contains a brief history of departments, agencies and their major divisions; a list of key personnel; a description of each unit's legislative and regulatory authority; and sources of information within the agency.

Federal Executive Directory. This directory, published and updated six times a year by the Carroll Publishing Company, lists by name and by agency position the phone numbers of nearly 90,000 top and midlevel officials in the executive and legislative branches. The frequent updating allows you to keep up with job changes.

Washington Information Directory. Although this book, published annually by Congressional Quarterly, contains much of the same information about agencies you'll find in the Federal Regulatory Directory and the U.S. Government Manual, it has a valuable added attraction: It lists by subject matter the congressional committees that deal with each agency, as well as private-sector groups interested in the agency's jurisdiction. This is a great place to start if you're trying to identity watchdog and special interest groups that match up with a particular agency. As a bonus, this directory includes other reference lists, such as lists of diplomats, labor unions, and state and local government officials based in Washington.

Many of these books are a bit pricey, especially for small bureaus, but local libraries, including the Library of Congress and libraries at most of the major Washington-area universities keep them on their reference shelves.

5 SPECIALTY BEATS

Three main schemes dominate Washington coverage patterns: National reporting with a focus on Congress or the White House, regional reporting (see Chapter 6) with a concentration on issues and people from a particular part of the country, and specialty reporting, in which the journalist devotes most of his or her time to a particular issue, such as defense or health care. Few Washington reporters in the general press fall into the last category. The exceptions are at the Associated Press, the news magazines and a few major dailies like The New York Times, The Washington Post and The Wall Street Journal. Those newspapers have numerous specialists and sometimes assign more than one to major beats such as economics or national security.

Furthermore, specialization, such as the two medical doctors who cover health for The Washington Post, is a luxury that fewer and fewer news organizations can afford.

True, there are hundreds of reporters in Washington writing for specialty magazines and newsletters who are extremely specialized. Their numbers have been increasing in recent years. But most specialists in the general press corps are jacks-of-all-trades who have carved out some expertise by dint of hard work and demonstrated interest in a subject. In many cases, specialists cover a combination of beats that usually—but not always—have some relation to one another. The economics reporter, for example, may be expected to cover the federal budget, trade and labor (or workplace) issues. The defense reporter may also dip into foreign policy, which permits hobnobbing with the striped-pants set at the State Department.

The environmental reporter will usually cover natural resources issues at the Interior Department and may also be in charge of energy issues. The science reporter may be expected to cover health and medical topics, as well as the exploration of space.

Beats generally reflect the audience being served. Even a small bureau may have a defense specialist if a large military installation or defense contractor is located in the readership or viewership area. A small bureau serving a western state will probably have an expert on water, conservation and energy issues. A bureau serving a large Midwestern or Northeastern city would almost certainly have a beat focusing on labor, trade and perhaps transportation issues. Regional reporters in Washington routinely become experts on subjects and issues that affect their local audiences, including such topics as agriculture, offshore oil drilling or the insurance industry.

Whatever the modifications and mutations, few of these beats are unique to Washington. Institutional coverage of the White House, Congress and the Supreme Court requires a Washington presence, of course. And it would be hard to cover an issue such as arms control without being based in Washington. Most other issues could be—and are—covered from Omaha or Miami, but being in Washington has its advantages, especially if you can get out of the capital now and then.

DEVELOPING THE BEAT: A FORMULA THAT WORKS

Set Parameters and Priorities

Although they may not think about it much, or even realize it, most good beat reporters in Washington use similar techniques in their work. The basics of reporting here are no different from elsewhere, but the number of potential sources and available resources is mind boggling. So are the options and distractions and potential roadblocks.

In approaching a specialty beat, the first thing you need to do is to set your parameters and priorities. You and your boss need to agree on what the beat entails. If you have to fight a turf battle every week, you're never going to get much serious work done.

If you're covering trade, the environment or energy policy, do you follow the beat where it leads you, or do you have to stop at the edge of Capitol Hill in deference to the congressional correspondent? Do you cover the federal budget as it relates to your beat, or do you leave that to the wires or your bureau's budget reporter?

Do you develop enterprise and trend stories, or do you cover spot developments? Are you expected to do both? Do you go to press conferences to "gather string" or to compete with the wires? Can you travel outside Washington in pursuit of a story? Also, do you know what your readers or viewers are interested in? Are you planning to focus on things that interest you? Can you identify the most important business and political groups in your audience, and their interest in your beat?

One of the best models for true beat coverage was created by Sonja Hillgren, now the editor of Farm Journal, when she covered agriculture for UPI,

Knight-Ridder and Farm Journal in the 1980s and early 1990s. In her UPI days, Hillgren was based in an office deep in the Agriculture Department and she had incredible sources inside the sprawling agency's bureaucrats and officials. But Hillgren didn't confine her coverage to the building. She roamed the city, from Capitol Hill to the White House to the EPA.

Hillgren also made a point of giving heavy coverage to international trade issues that are of vital importance to the success or failure of the American farm economy. And she spiced up her Washington-based stories with information gleaned from frequent trips out of the capital to meet and talk with farmers, academics and other agricultural experts. Hillgren says: "The best way to develop a beat is to focus on the major, real problems and issues confronting a sector rather than to get sucked into covering only what the interest groups, administration or Congress are pushing publicly. You have to find out what is really keeping people up at night. It also is important to find out from people across the country how laws and regulations are affecting their lives. No coverage should stop with enactment of a law."

Get Up to Speed on the Subject

Once you know what is expected of you, it's time to do your homework. The late Edwin Dale, a longtime New York Times economics reporter who later worked in government posts on Capitol Hill, at the Office of Management and Budget, and at the Commerce Department, was once asked for his advice to a reporter new to the beat in Washington. Dale replied: "Number one: Read! Number two: Read! Number three: Read! Read your eyes out. Read all night. Read transcripts of committee hearings. Read Federal Reserve reports. Read the fine print of statistics. Become a genuine intellectual in your field."

Mark Thompson, who covers defense industry issues for Time magazine, backs up that advice. "On the defense beat, you need to have a lot of knowledge. It's not like the White House, it's not like Capitol Hill where you have to know a little about a lot of things. In defense, you have to know a lot about a relatively smaller number of things. And the way you get smart at that is by reading everything you get your hands on. If you're a general reporter for a regional newspaper, you need to read the trade press that covers whatever parts of the military you're interested in. When I worked for the Fort Worth Star-Telegram, I was very interested in the F-16 jet; I was very interested in helicopters because both of those were made in the Fort Worth area. So you read Aviation Week, so you read Helicopter News, [and other] trade publications on a weekly basis to give you a lot of knowledge and direct you to story ideas."

You can start with materials as basic as textbooks if you're totally cold on the subject, but the fastest way to get plenty of current material is to get on the mailing lists of key federal agencies, congressional committees and subcommittees with jurisdiction (and their chairs), trade associations, special interest groups, think tanks, and so forth. Author Philip Shabecoff, who was dean of environmental reporters in Washington when he worked for The New York Times, once estimated that his daily stack of mail was between 12 and 18 inches high. You'll learn how to sort through that much paper pretty quickly, but until you've thoroughly boned up on the subject, you'll want to study much of it. And, of course, these days the World Wide Web offers a welter of information, not only from official government agencies and companies but also from a spectrum of public interest groups, think tanks, and the like.

The Bureau of National Affairs' (BNA's) Elizabeth White counsels reporters to take advantage of the technology by visiting Web sites frequently for both routine and depth information. She also says: "You can subscribe to all these different listservs (electronic mailing lists) as a reporter. One of the first things you do is try to get on the key listservs. The Department of Health and Human Services has a service that you subscribe to as a health care reporter, that will, you know, spit out over e-mail . . . five or six things in one day."

For background, you especially want to get your hands on the following:

• Annual reports to Congress from the federal agencies with jurisdiction in the subject area.

• The budgets of those agencies, which provide a rough road map of future plans.

• Relevant investigative reports submitted to Congress and agency heads by the General Accounting Office, the Congressional Budget Office, the departments' and agencies' inspectors general, and advisory bodies to the departments and agencies. Be forewarned: Agency reports to Congress are sometimes more detailed than the versions made public by the agencies. But for a beat reporter who is looking for depth, and not just a quick-hit story, the details can be invaluable.

• Congressional hearing transcripts, which not only give you background on congressional concerns but also provide the names and testimony of policymakers and experts from around the country. The question-and-answer sections of transcripts can be particularly revealing.

• Agency news clips. Most departments and agencies circulate news clips early each morning to top officials internally and to jurisdictional committees on Capitol Hill. Reading these for a few weeks will give you a good overview.

Develop the Right Sources

To figure out whom to develop as sources on a new beat, answer this question: Who is trying to influence the process? You want to meet as many of those people as you can. So get on the phone. Attend press conferences. Introduce yourself. Write letters. Ask for interviews. Review campaign finance records. Look at the public comment files for recent agency proposals.

You can start by meeting the top press officers at the relevant federal agencies. As an issue-beat reporter, you're most interested in the department's spokesperson or political appointee in the press office, because he or she will be more conversant with the top dog's thinking. Then try to identify officials below the assistant secretary level who are involved in programs related to your beat.

Dale Eisman, who covers defense for The Norfolk Virginian-Pilot, says: "You deal with the media office, and over time you try to develop people outside the media office who you can call on, depending. If am working on a story about shipbuilding then there are certain people I know who are active in the decisions that are made about shipbuilding that I've tried to develop relationships with."

As in almost every Washington assignment, the Capitol Hill connection, meanwhile, is absolutely essential. You need to get to know the staffs of committees and subcommittees with legislative, spending and oversight jurisdiction in your area. Members of Congress themselves sometimes prove to be valuable sources, as do their administrative and legislative assistants. The ideal is to find a member who is truly knowledgeable on a subject, has some clout and is comfortable with reporters. Minority staffs can be fruitful sources if they disagree strongly with the direction that the committee majority is headed on an issue. Also, Congress is home to dozens of single-issue caucuses and ad hoc coalitions.

You can also finagle an introduction to members of an agency's congressional liaison staff. "Most reporters don't think to talk to them," says James Webster, a publisher of agriculture newsletters and a former top press aide at the Department of Agriculture. "They have access to the secretary. They know what policy is, even if they won't tell you. And sometimes over drinks, they will tell you . . . especially if they're mad at some member of Congress."

Next, look to the private sector. Start with special interest groups, some of which prefer to be called public interest groups, but all of which exist to promote one or a multitude of causes. Many of them—environmentalists and advocates for the elderly are two examples—have enormous influence on both Congress and the bureaucracy. You should not have much trouble developing sources here; they crave publicity.

Eisman of The Virginian-Pilot says: "I've had some success working through the retired military community for expertise. When people are telling you certain things about weapons systems, and there are a lot of recently retired military who are knowledgeable about these things and, who once they're out of uniform, aren't so constrained in what they say. So that's been a good network for me to develop. And you learn who the people are in the think tanks who are inclined toward certain views, and you use them on the defense beat like reporters use them on every beat, you balance the right with the left, the liberal with the conservative."

Also get acquainted with lobbyists for key industries and organizations concerned with your beat. Generally, they don't crave publicity, except that which is planned by public relations arms. Even public relations spokespersons for individual corporations will sometimes defer to their trade associations in Washington. Cultivating lobbyists is a time-consuming proposition that works because lobbyists are paid to know what's going on. Often, they will tell you more about what the opposition is doing than what they themselves are doing.

BNA's Elizabeth White, who covers health care issues on Capitol Hill, gives this advice: "It's very important to get to know the lobbying groups who are interested in the issues that you cover. They are very knowledgeable about what's going on. They're following the process intricately, they're going in and they're meeting with these (congressional) aides on a very regular basis to say this is what we want in the legislation. So they very much know the issues that are in play. So you want to get to know lobbyists on both sides of the issues that you cover and get them to trust you, and you want to develop a rapport with them where you get past the point where they're just spinning you all the time and where they trust you and want to talk to you and want to tell you what's actually going on so you can advance your stories rather than just get their spin."

Then get to know the watchdog groups. Government watchdogs such as the General Accounting Office have well-established reputations. Once upon a time, few agencies had full-time professionals in the private sector looking over their shoulders, and often the bureaucrats and politicians dismissed them as "gadflies" or "nuts." Today, virtually every major agency has folks who fall into this category (usually from across the political spectrum), and winning their backing often is key to winning support for an idea or cause.

Just who in the private sector qualifies as a watchdog group is subject to interpretation. Some of the "public interest" groups that try to do government exposés are as political as the Democratic or Republican national committee. You have to make your own judgment about the credibility of groups and their information. Generally, if they have broad bipartisan support in Congress and do not openly lobby for legislation, their information is more credible. Watchdogs can act as intermediaries that will connect you to government whistle-blowers. Remember to question everyone's motives.

Many ex-bureaucrats end up in think tanks, another wellspring of sources for Washington reporters. Some journalists dismiss think tanks as "quote factories." The careful reporter will discover that some sources at think tanks are more valuable than others. Among the most valuable are those who recently left government or are strong bets to return to government. If you develop a good relationship, chances are that they'll still take your phone calls when they return to government. Also, if they're from the party out of power in the White House, they may have informed criticism to offer. At the very least, they can help you formulate thoughtful questions that will impress the people you're trying to cultivate inside the government. The revolving door between the government and think tanks such as Brookings, American Enterprise Institute and the Heritage Foundation, to name the most prominent, never stops.

Academic sources also can be invaluable when you are trying to build a beat or filling in a story on deadline. In the colleges and universities in the Washington area and across the country you can find professors who are experts on any issue. And college public relations people are more than willing to put you in touch; most have their "experts" listed in a handy online directory. One good resource in this area is Profnet (www1.profnet.com), an online service that will route an inquiry to academic and other experts around the world. Think tanks such as Heritage will even steer you to professors who generally share their philosophy.

You should also develop sources outside Washington. People in the capital tend to talk to each other and read the same things. You need a non-Washington perspective. You may have sources from where you worked before or from where your audience is. If not, develop new ones. Study lists of congressional witnesses from around the country. Use state and local officials, business executives and community activists as occasional sounding boards. Fortunately, thanks to the World Wide Web and e-mail, it never has been easier or cheaper to find non-Washington sources for your stories.

Finally, use other reporters on your beat as sources. If they are not in direct competition with you, most veterans will share tips with newer reporters. They can give you guidance on how reliable a potential source may be or where to find information. A lot of reporters who cover foreign policy or international trade develop valuable friendships with foreign reporters based here. Some of those foreign reporters are major figures in their own countries. They can be tapped for names and an explication of their government's policies. One caveat: Some may be doing double duty as intelligence agents.

Most reporters on a new beat must do more than make a few phone calls to develop sources. They also have to hang out. Meeting someone in person is better than a phone introduction, but arranging for a sit-down interview may take weeks or months. Why wait?

The places to hang out include agency hearings, congressional hearings, press conferences, even government cafeterias. Some bars in Southwest Washington are known as hangouts for employees of nearby agencies such as the Environmental Protection Agency and the departments of Housing and Urban Development, Transportation and Energy. Press conferences in Washington don't draw just the press. They sometimes draw observers from other organizations, both friend and foe. When a Senate committee is grilling a nominee for confirmation to a high government post, or a House subcommittee is deciding how much money a government program should get for the next year, or an agency head has been called on the carpet by a grandstanding oversight committee chair, the hearing room will probably be filled with lobbyists, lawyers, consultants and all manner of aides. This is a good place to meet people who are trying to influence the process. Take along a good supply of business cards.

Discover the Resources

If you get on all the mailing lists, including the electronic lists from the agencies and groups on your beat, you'll receive plenty of reading material, some of which will prompt story ideas. But you can't rely on handouts for covering a beat. Also consider the following:

Reference books. Few major commercial works equal the guides to the Supreme Court and Congress published by Congressional Quarterly, but most departments and agencies produce overviews and major compilations of data that are helpful. At the Department of Education, for example, it's an annual report on education statistics. At the Defense Department, it's the secretary's annual report to Congress. Most agencies put out thick volumes that provide great detail. And any number of Washington directories, outlined in Chapter 13, are helpful.

Federal Register. This official bible on agency proceedings includes notices of proposed regulations and rules changes, public comment periods and public meetings of government bodies. You'll want to scan the index regularly.

Periodicals. The two most popular chroniclers of government and politics in Washington are the Congressional Quarterly and the National Journal. CQ is the most authoritative voice on the legislative process, and the National Journal provides in-depth treatment of current issues, lobbying, politics, regulatory activity and agency operations. Again, you can either get them in traditional paper format or, by paying a bit more, through the Internet.

Newsletters and trade press. Hundreds of newsletters and magazines focus on issues and the many parts of the bureaucracy. Beat reporters tend to favor two or three in their field and ignore the rest. Newsletters particularly are read closely by industry officials, their lobbyists and federal bureaucrats, and thus they are fertile sources for leaks and story ideas. Agency press officers can tell you which are considered the best.

Journals. Medical, science, environmental and foreign policy reporters are most apt to follow the scholarly journals, and they disagree on how much technical knowledge a Washington beat reporter needs to absorb.

Libraries. Starting with the Library of Congress, Washington is bulging with libraries that make research rewarding if not a pleasure. Most federal departments and large agencies have libraries. The Library of Medicine at the National Institutes of Health, for example, is a utopia for reporters in that field. It has all sorts of medical journals, and the staff will do computer searches for reporters.

Public document rooms. Most regulatory agencies have rooms where all public documents concerning the agency's activities, including correspondence between regulator and regulated, are kept on public file. At the Nuclear Regulatory Commission's public document room, you would find, among many other things, annual reports from nuclear power plants concerning the on-site storage of nuclear wastes, as well as semiannual environmental assessments of radioactive releases through venting at all power plants. Most materials in an agency's public reading room now also are available through the agency's Web site.

Conventions, conferences and seminars. The principals on virtually any beat have meetings that are designed with press coverage in mind. Medical and education writers are especially big at covering conventions and conferences in places like Las Vegas and Monterey, Calif., but many organizations also convene legislative conferences and seminars in Washington to get maximum exposure to both the press and members of Congress. Conventions are usually far more valuable for cultivating sources than for the news they produce. (The "news" is usually canned far in advance and spoon-fed to the press.) For cultivating sources, though, they are worth attending for a few years if you're new to the beat.

Demonstrate That You're a Contender

News sources in Washington tend to make judgments about reporters rather quickly. If they get the impression that you don't know what you're doing, they'll give you short shrift. After you've defined your beat, boned up on the subject, composed a list of potential sources, and figured out the key resources, it will help to do the following:

• Have a plan. Your plan should be an outgrowth of the discussions you had with your boss. If the sources you're developing get the idea that you have big plans for the beat, they'll be more interested.

• Do a project. One of the most effective ways to meet new sources and establish your reputation is to undertake a major reporting project. It helps, of course, if your potential sources have an interest in the subject being aired. Reporters sometimes do stories simply to ingratiate themselves with sources. You don't have to go that far, but neither is it smart to announce that you've come to unearth skeletons long ignored by your predecessors.

• Circulate your clips. Don't be modest about it. Don't assume your sources saw your story. Unless you work for one of the Big Four newspapers (New York Times, Washington Post, USA Today and Wall Street Journal), there's a pretty good chance they didn't. But don't despair. It is possible to build credibility even if your work doesn't have a Washington-based outlet. Smart agency officials and politicians always have paid attention to coverage in key places: For example, USDA policymakers follow The Des Moines Register for its agriculture reporting. And today more and more agencies are watching online news sites and using online archives such as Lexis-Nexis to track outside-the-Beltway coverage of inside-the-Beltway topics.

• Anticipate stories. "You can't ignore spot news stories," says James O'Shea, managing editor of the Chicago Tribune, who spent several years as a Washington reporter. "But you try to anticipate, try to see a story coming and get to it ahead of the pack." When he was reporting, O'Shea says he tried "to figure out what's going to be a story two or three months down the road" and get to it while he still had access to people. "It's a much more difficult environment to report in when the pack arrives," he says.

• Take the story out in the country. Says Frank Swoboda, who covered labor for The Washington Post: "You can't cover workplace issues unless you know what the workplace looks like."

• Be concerned about your reputation. That's not the same as having an outsized ego. It means playing straight with your sources and playing straight with the facts. When it comes to reputations, Washington is a small company town.

IN PROFILE: THE DEFENSE BEAT

Of all the specialty beats in Washington, the defense beat is one of the most demanding, and it can be one of the most rewarding. For that reason, we'll explore it as a case study of beat reporting before we look at overviews of selected other beats.

The defense beat centers on the Pentagon, although many sources and resources related to the beat are scattered across Washington, the nation and the globe. And something about that sprawling building, with its maze of hallways and military acronyms, intimidates new reporters. Whether it's press attitudes about the military left over from the Vietnam War (fueled unfortunately by too much reporting that seems to reflect a naïveté or downright hostility toward the armed services) or press perceptions about the military's attitudes toward the press (which often seem to range from paranoia to dismissiveness), young reporters aren't exactly beating down doors to cover the Pentagon. According to a report in October 2002 in American Journalism Review (AJR), only 20 newspaper and wire service bureaus assigned anyone to cover the Pentagon full time. And that was after the terrorist attacks of

Sept. 11, 2001, including a devastating attack on the Pentagon itself that killed more than 180 people, sent national security and homeland defense to the top of the issue list.

The Pentagon beat isn't necessarily considered prestigious. John Fialka, who covered the defense beat for The Wall Street Journal and who now covers the environment for The Journal, says that among reporters outside the Pentagon, the standard reaction was, "Why did you get sent to the Pentagon? What did you do wrong?" But it "ought to be exciting," Fialka maintains, to cover a building where most of the decisions about the government's money and actions outside social programs are made. "With that money," he says, "also goes a lot of decisions, non-decisions, scandals, ineptitude, brilliant decisions, heroic decisions. This is the only civil service where people actually get paid to put their lives on the line."

The Tribune's O'Shea, who covered defense for several years in the mid-1980s, calls the Pentagon a "fascinating place," but that's the most positive thing he has to say about it. He found his assignment there "really frustrating and very difficult because it's hostile, the most hostile environment I've ever been in as a reporter." He adds: "Basically, the people don't like you. There was still a residue of the Vietnam War that permeates the place." O'Shea explains why it's a tough beat, beyond the attitudes:

> It takes you about two to three years to really get to know the place, to get to the point where you really understand what's going on. . . . You really have to be a knowledgeable person about politics, about weapons systems, about science, about economics and the political and budget beats, and you have to know a little about military tactics and history. It takes an awful long time to get up to a point where you can really cover it and begin developing sources.

Making inroads into the military beat can be easier said than done. Not only is the military a somewhat closed society, but it also is mobile. Dale Eisman says: "You really have to, when you are covering the military, work largely through public information officers' people. The military trains people not to talk to us." And he adds: "The military culture is a lot different than what most reporters are used to dealing with. I used to cover city hall and then a statehouse beat, and you could walk into legislators' offices and you could do this on the Hill, and just sort of shoot the breeze with staffers. You don't do that very much in the Pentagon. You walk into offices and people say, 'What can I do for you, sir?' and they answer your question or tell you they can't and then they show you to the door—which makes it more difficult to build relationships that reporters like to build and get tips, etc." The military's mobility also creates difficulties in building source relationships, Eisman says. "About the time you think you've got a good source, they're liable to be gone somewhere."

Still, Time's Mark Thompson says there is no substitute for trying to establish one-on-one relationships with military sources both in and out of uniform. One way to do that, he says, is to try to break down the mystique that sometimes seems to enshroud the Pentagon and other complex organizations.

> It's important for reporters on this beat to realize that the Pentagon is not a monolith. It's not millions of people that all agree with one another. They have fights and disputes just like any big organization. If you're reporting an Army story, a lot of your best sources might be in the Navy or might be in the Marines or might be on Capitol Hill. So you can't think of it as this impenetrable block of granite. Rather, you need to think of it as limestone with lots of cracks, and water seeps into those cracks and freezes, and when it does the limestone breaks apart. And your job as a reporter is to find those cracks, get in there and wait for some cold weather so you freeze and break open the source. A lot of people are intimidated by the building, meaning the Pentagon, because it's so huge, but as I say, you've got a million and a half people in the military, you've got their families, you've got the Reserve, you've got the defense contractors, you've got the defense contractors' families. If you add all those people up, you got 8 million people. That's the size of New York. And like any big city, there are good neighborhoods and bad neighborhoods. There are gangs and places you want to go, and places you don't want to go, and so you just need to take advantage of all of those little individual groups, and you'll find that reporting is not so intimidating in that building.

Thompson says he even finds the transient nature of folks in the Pentagon to his advantage: "What's interesting is military people tend to get new assignments every two to three to four years, and so you'll talk to them in the Pentagon in 1980, and they'll be back in '84, and they'll be back in '88. And every time they come back, you have a leg up on your colleagues who didn't know that person before. And so once again, it's something that comes from an accretion of detail, and over a span of time, you know. It's nothing, you know, that can instantly happen. It just takes time."

Eisman agrees that by building sources with folks when they are on Pentagon assignments (and nearly every senior military official and nearly every up-and-comer in uniform gets rotated to the five-sided palace at several points during a career) can pay off down the road. "When the military is active around the world, and you need somebody in one of these other places, there's a reasonable chance you might have somebody who at least knows your name, which can be helpful."

Getting Started

The first thing you need to decide is the focus of your coverage. Unless you're working for a wire service or The Washington Post, you can't be expected to keep up with everything. After all, we're talking about more than 650,000 civilians and about three million active-duty and reserve personnel, multibillion-dollar weapons systems and a worldwide force that consumes about 20 percent of the federal budget. Additionally, the terrorist attacks of Sept. 11, 2001, have given the military a controversial, but more important, role at home. It would have been hard to imagine, before Sept. 11, the spectacle of having armed U.S. fighter jets flying patrols over the capital, with orders to shoot down offending aircraft, including airliners. Or to see uniformed National Guard troops with loaded M-16 rifles standing watch over airport security posts. So, do you want to concentrate on weapons procurement (and attendant scandals), or do you want to cover military strategy? Do you want to cover people, or do you want to become a budget expert? Should you concentrate on overseas military operations, or the military's role in homeland defense? If you're working for a regional paper or broadcast outlet, should you worry only about the weapons systems and military installations of concern to your audience, or should you look at the big picture?

Whatever your approach, you'll start with public affairs officers, the top ranks of which are located across the hall from the Pentagon press room. The Pentagon has hundreds of PAOs, and their orders—believe it or not—are to help you. The Defense Department has adopted a set of Principles of Information that say, in part: "It is Department of Defense policy to make available timely and accurate information so that the public, the Congress, and the news media may assess and understand the facts about national security and defense strategy. Requests for information from organizations and private citizens shall be answered quickly." But most reporters find that often these principles seem to be ignored.

The public affairs office is headed by an assistant secretary of defense. In addition, each of the services has its own public affairs officers located elsewhere in the Pentagon and the nearby Navy Annex. They are the people to see if you're inquiring about active-duty personnel or about visiting specific military installations. Also, many of the major defense programs have their own public information officers. The higher-ranking public affairs officers don't always advertise that fact, so it's in your interest to pursue inquiries as deep into the Pentagon as possible. Generally, the public affairs officer who is closest to the subject of your inquiry will be the most helpful. Your objective is to reach, through the officer, the project managers who really know what's going on. There also are public affairs officers at all major command headquarters and military posts.

Pentagon press officers, both civilian and military, have an extremely mixed image among veteran defense reporters. Surprisingly, perhaps, the military PAOs often get higher ratings. Whatever their image, working through PAOs is essential. They can set up briefings that will give you great detail on a service's mission or a command's deployment around the world. They can provide the material and arrange the interviews. If you pick a colonel out of the phone book and call with no introduction, the odds are heavy that you will be referred to the press office.

Another way to get your feet wet at the Pentagon is to attend the regular news briefings. For one thing, you'll need to be there if a major defense story is breaking somewhere around the globe. Second, being there is your signal that you want to be taken seriously. In normal times, these briefings were often perfunctory and highly forgettable. But with the war on terror and the prospect of U.S. military action in Iraq and elsewhere, Bush Defense Secretary Donald Rumsfeld managed to turn them into something of a show that made him a media star; cable news networks frequently carried the briefings live. Rumsfeld often used his sessions to chide and upbraid reporters for asking questions that he considered ignorant or worse. And he was able to invent new ways of deflecting questions and saying no comment that usually left reporters with little to write but the official line. The briefings also provide an opportunity to get acquainted with the spokesperson and his or her top aides, so that you can break through the pecking-order barrier. Pentagon press aides, like those anywhere else in government, grant and arrange access primarily on the basis of the size of the news organization and their familiarity with the reporter. "You have to make choices," says Robert Sims, who was spokesman for Secretary Caspar Weinberger during Ronald Reagan's presidency and author of a book about Pentagon reporting. "Often I'd go with the reporter with the widest reach." And it's likely things haven't changed much in the intervening years.

If you're having difficulty getting answers out of the Pentagon, defense reporters agree that you can almost always start somewhere else. In fact, there is broad agreement that you should start somewhere else, that the worst thing you can do is go to the Pentagon unprepared.

How to prepare? Washington has many defense experts who can explain what the problems are in a situation and help you figure out what questions to ask. Congressional staffers can sometimes persuade their bosses to request information from the Pentagon that you could never acquire. Other experts reside in think tanks, on college faculties and in the offices of defense contractors and government watchdog groups. They can help you piece together the framework of a story and the questions for defense officials.

Richard Whitmire, a former regional defense reporter for Gannett News Service, emphasizes the importance of researching a story thoroughly before going to Pentagon officials for interviews:

> Always approach them knowing as much as you can. Otherwise they'll slough it off. If you go in and you know something, they'll really warm up to you. They respect knowledge a lot. What they don't respect is the press coming in and asking open-ended questions. If you ask a question

imprecisely . . . they'll think you're going to be sloppy with the information. Then they'll think you're not worth talking to, and they'll worry about you. And that'll be the end of it.

Sources and Resources

There is no end to the people and material helpful to reporters on the defense beat. A few days on the phone can fill both your mailbox and your Rolodex. Here are suggestions from a cross section of defense reporters.

READING

You obviously want to bone up on the history of the modern military and study the organization charts enough to understand the many Pentagon hierarchies and command structures around the world. As for daily and weekly reading, in addition to following The New York Times and The Washington Post, many reporters mention Congressional Quarterly's Pat Towell, even though Towell does most of his reporting from the congressional perspective. National Journal gets somewhat less attention. The defense trade press has grown so fast in recent years that it's hard to keep up with. The favorite of many reporters remains Aviation Week and Space Technology, known for its authoritative coverage of military technology. Others are Defense Week, the Armed Forces Journal, the newsletter Aerospace Daily, the Army Times, Navy Times and Air Force Times and Proceedings of the Naval Institute, as well as magazines put out by the Air Force Association and the Navy League.

THE BUDGET

It's difficult to understand defense if you don't understand the defense budget, and that requires close scrutiny of long-range planning, taking into account the multiplier effect on costs when procurement of major weapons systems is stretched out over years and sometimes decades. "The budget is a good place to take off for a new reporter," says retired AP reporter and former Pentagon spokesman Fred Hoffman. As a press officer, Hoffman was happy to load up a new reporter with stacks of books that break down the budget by services and defense agencies, by weapons systems, by state expenditure, and so forth.

William Ringle, former chief correspondent for Gannett News Service, says he found the services to be particularly helpful after the major budget briefings conducted by the secretary of defense and his top aides. These smaller encounters allow you to ask any detailed questions you may have, and they also permit you to make contacts that may help you later.

GOVERNMENT REPORTS

In addition to budget books, the Pentagon spews out reports, starting with the defense secretary's annual report to Congress and a defense "posture statement" delivered orally to Congress. The written report is a valuable reference tool filled with charts, graphs, maps, acronyms and rationales.

The Defense Department's IG and the congressional GAO investigate and document waste and fraud in the military. The Defense Contract Audit Agency issues an annual report that inventories all audits under way or recently completed.

CONGRESSIONAL STAFFS AND HEARINGS

Tracking weapons systems and military spending is easier if you develop congressional sources and attend subcommittee hearings. The Hill has its experts on every phase of defense spending and strategy. Subcommittee hearings draw not only defense officials but also defense manufacturers and lobbyists, all of whom are people you want to get to know. The question-and-answer section of these hearings frequently proves to be more revealing than the prepared statements.

Transcripts of congressional hearings, even closed hearings, can be valuable resources, often containing a great deal of information that the military doesn't volunteer in public. Also, sources in other places can point you to such records. When Ringle was still reporting for Gannett a source at the Center for Defense Information tipped him to a Navy plan to build an expensive mock-up of the Trident submarine at a facility in upstate New York, where Gannett owns several newspapers. Although both the late Admiral Hyman Rickover, then the Navy's top officer, and the congressman from the region said the plan was top secret and refused to discuss it, the whole thing was laid out in a hearing record that had been sanitized by the Pentagon and made public.

GOVERNMENT CONTRACTORS

The drawdown of the military after the Cold War led to considerable consolidation among major players in the defense industry, especially those involved in large aircraft, missile and shipbuilding programs. But in other ways, the move to privatize many functions of government, which began most earnestly during the Reagan years, but which has proceeded apace in the two decades since, has had significant influence on the defense industry and the military community. Indeed, reporting by the Center for Public Integrity and others has shown that the military is relying increasingly on contractors, rather than troops, to perform every function from KP to base security. Even some of the military's most sophisticated weapons systems apparently couldn't function in combat without civilian technical support. And it seems quite likely that the war on terrorism is going to fuel another big jump in military spending, much of it directed into high-tech, high-dollar programs designed to limit battlefield casualties. At any rate, finding and building sources among contractors seems an important part of a military reporter's job.

Don't expect them to be always helpful. Through long experience, many Pentagon reporters have come to regard contractors as merely an extension of the military. Other reporters value contractors more as well-placed sources. However you regard them, it's important to get to know the manufacturer of a system when you're following a military program. All the major manufacturers have Washington offices staffed with engineers, lobbyists and publicists, many of whom move from company to company and know a lot about what others are doing. One of the best ways to check up on a weapon is to query the manufacturers who lost a bid to build it. They are often eager to point out the defects in the winner's product.

Contractors, not surprisingly, are usually gun-shy about talking to a reporter until they know they can trust him or her on a background basis. If you strike out entirely with a contractor, remember that most contractors belong to trade associations that speak for the industry. In the defense area, most contractors belong to either the Aerospace Industries Association or the Electronic Industries Association, or a newer group, the National Defense Industrial Association (www.ndia.org). These organizations probably won't help you much if you're pursuing a feud between contractors, but they can help you understand the industry's position vis-à-vis the military and Congress.

WATCHDOGS AND WHISTLE-BLOWERS

Among the best known of the watchdogs and whistle-blowers is the Project on Government Oversight founded by Dina Rasor (www.pogo.org). Rasor gained fame for exposing malfunctions in the Army's M-1 tank. Her work was inspired by Air Force cost analyst Ernest Fitzgerald, who became an icon in Washington during the Nixon administration for baring cost overruns in the C-5A aircraft. He was fired, but later reinstated; his saga was the genesis for a new federal law designed to protect whistle-blowers who tell Congress or the public about agency wrongdoing. The Military Reform Caucus in Congress also can be helpful. The caucus gained fame for its probes into the high price of military spare parts, but its agenda is much broader, covering many aspects of military preparedness. Rasor is an energetic former reporter who has developed a wide following in the Pentagon underground and the Washington press corps. Her modus operandi is to cultivate former military employees and disgruntled current or former employees of defense contractors, collect documents from them showing wrongdoing, summarize the material and release it to selected reporters with an embargo. She also advises reporters who want to pursue whistle-blowers on their own to seek out suits by ex-employees of defense contractors who think they've been unfairly dismissed. Such suits are usually filed in state courts.

THINK TANKS AND RESEARCH GROUPS

Think tanks are home to ex-bureaucrats, former defense officials, ex-military officers and ex-ambassadors, as well as all manner of garden-variety professors, researchers and consultants. Some of them have an ideological bent; some don't. Many of these institutions invested heavily in building expertise with the Soviet Union and now have been forced to retool their portfolios, first with the end of the Cold War and more recently with the advent of the focus on fighting terrorism.

- The Center for Defense Information, for example, has a peacenik image but also has a number of experts on military weaponry.
- The Brookings Institution has experts on military personnel, the defense budget and U.S. foreign relations.
- The Center for Strategic and International Studies has experts on all aspects of national security.
- The Heritage Foundation has conservative experts on almost any aspect of defense strategy.
- The Johns Hopkins School of Advanced International Studies has broad expertise on diplomacy but also has good sources on defense issues.
- The Arms Control Association publishes a newsletter, Arms Control Today, which offers helpful details about how nuclear weapons work and strategies on their deployment.
- Consultants to the Pentagon, like TRW and the Rand Corporation, will set you up with their experts.

FIELD TRIPS

You can't fully understand the military unless you get out and see it in action. The Pentagon is happy to arrange for you to visit virtually any nonsecret installation or unit anywhere in the world. Getting out of the Pentagon, says The Wall Street Journal's Fialka, "is critical for writing accurately, for assessing what the real problems are, for showing people in the building that you're credible, that you're concerned about what they're doing and that you know about what they're doing." For example, the Navy likes to set up trips to aircraft carriers sailing not far offshore of Norfolk, Va.

Defense Enterprise

Once you've established your credentials, what can you do to distinguish yourself in reporting? One thing you can try to do is to question the commonly accepted wisdoms. A contrasting story would explore the extent to which the Pentagon is forced to buy unnecessary equipment to placate congressional members indebted to manufacturers who are big campaign contributors.

The question of interservice rivalry, and how much it's costing the tax-payers (not to mention defense readiness), is an old story that could use some updating. Rivalries within the Joint Chiefs of Staff between the specified and unified commands are another part of that story.

Another good approach for a story is to go out into the field and gauge the reaction to proposed military programs. Talking to regional opponents and proponents of such programs can give you a human-interest dimension that you sometimes won't get in Washington. Finally, dismissing Hollywood's revisionist glorification of Vietnam in recent years, the Washington press corps pays scant attention to the workaday world of military men and women and their families.

The Foreign Policy Connection

Some reporters in Washington combine coverage of foreign policy and defense to create a sort of umbrella national security beat. If you have the lati-tude to cover both areas, there are enough overlaps to make them a natural com-bination. For example, is arms control a defense issue or a foreign policy issue?

Covering foreign policy will take you to the State Department, another confusing place where the dissection of nuance is the favorite pastime and where Washington's clearest form of journalistic elitism is on display. The State Department depends on the television networks for its mass communi-cation and on four newspapers—The New York Times, The Washington Post, the Los Angeles Times and The Christian Science Monitor—for communicat-ing to the foreign policy cognoscenti here and abroad. The news magazines run a close second, and everybody else is in third or fourth place, or off the boards. A further division exists between those dozen or so reporters who travel on the secretary of state's plane on foreign trips and get the access and exposure to the secretary that such travel affords, and those who don't make the cut. (According to the AJR study of Washington coverage, only 15 print bureaus staff the State Department's Foggy Bottom press room regularly.)

Thus, you have to work harder if you don't happen to work for one of the chosen organizations. "If you're not there full time, with a desk, it's difficult," says William Ringle, who covered defense and foreign policy issues simulta-neously for Gannett News Service. "These people (at the State Department) are very well educated, usually with some specialty and with a career at stake. They don't want to screw up their careers, and they have nothing to gain by talking to reporters."

But as at the Pentagon, there's no reason to be intimidated if you've pre-pared yourself. Foreign policy experts abound outside the State Department, as former insider Hodding Carter, press spokesman for Cyrus Vance and

Edmund Muskie, points out: "The best reporters on that beat always look outside the institutional framework. There are plenty of sources all over town willing to do fact and theory checks on what's being said at State, not the least of which is the embassies, but also competing power centers across the river (the Pentagon) and at the White House."

"What's being said at State" for the record is said daily at a briefing conducted by the chief department spokesperson. State briefings are variously known as the biggest circus in town (any reporter can ask any off-the-wall question and be tolerated) and as an occasion when the most careful press spokesmanship is conducted. "Exactitude is often required," says Carter. "Most of the time, the game there is not to do anything. You're there because you have to be there. And what you're trying not to do is create policy by saying something which is subject to mis- or re-interpretation." A favorite saying of State Department briefers seems to be, "I have nothing for you on that." The nonanswer answer could mean, that's a question that didn't occur to officials, or that they haven't figured out what to say, or that they have been given orders not to answer. Figuring out the code can be challenging, but more likely frustrating.

Consider this example of a daily State Department briefing from May 2002.

Question: Can you tell me whether the Inspector General is looking into the Ambassador of India? (The Washington Post had reported an investigation into morale at the New Delhi embassy that day.)

Ms. (Lynn) Cassel, State Department spokeswoman: I have nothing for you on that.

Question: Is the—wait a minute, wait a minute. You're not saying yes or no; you have nothing?

Ms. Cassel: Yes. I have nothing relating to that report.

Question: You mean you cannot speak to the report for some reason?

Ms. Cassel: I cannot speak to the report.

Question: Why? Is it classified?

Ms. Cassel: The—

Question: By the way, I didn't ask about a report; I asked if he is looking into it.

Ms. Cassel: I'm talking about the report in the newspaper. I can't speak to any allegation or anything regarding—Ambassador (Robert) Blackwill is our Ambassador, and—

Question: Yes, I know that. There have been more than one—there have been several reports that the Inspector General is conducting some sort of an inquiry into the way Mr. Blackwill has been running the Embassy.

Ms. Cassel: I have seen those reports, and I have nothing to give you on it.

Question: So you won't say they're untrue, right?

Ms. Cassel: No.

Question: Okay.

If that's not confusing enough for the uninitiated, the on-the-record briefing is often followed by group or one-on-one sessions of background guidance. "Some of the background guidances," says Carter, "were meant to provide both cover and a message at the same time to foreign governments."

This kind of message sending and tea-leaf reading is a staple of Washington, but it can get a little arcane for reporters who aren't required to cover the building at State on a daily basis. There are some advantages, in fact, in not having that responsibility, because it gives you more time to roam the city and cultivate outside sources. Gannett's Ringle, for example, developed vast sources among Middle Eastern diplomats because he had traveled and reported in that area extensively and because of the large population of Lebanese Americans in several Gannett cities.

One strategy that might work would be the one followed by Newsweek's Roy Gutman, when he was a new reporter on the beat in the 1980s. He went to the embassy of each country involved in an upcoming trip planned by the president and asked for briefings. Armed with those perspectives, he then asked to meet with several State Department officials at the deputy assistant secretary level to help him prepare for the trip. By the time State put on its official trip briefing for reporters, Gutman says, "I was as prepared as anybody."

Diplomatic reporters agree in general on what to read and where to find the best experts. The following are the most important resources and sources.

READING

The New York Times is nicknamed Pravda in the State Department, so you obviously need to read it every day. You should also monitor the World News Connection (wcn.fedworld.gov), produced by Foreign Broadcast Information Service. These files are put together by people who read newspapers and listen to radio in foreign lands and translate the information into English. They are published by region (China, Mideast, South Asia) and can give Washington reporters broader access to information than correspondents in those foreign countries sometimes get. One drawback is the price: The cheapest subscription would be about $900 a year.

Most diplomatic reporters read Foreign Policy magazine, published by the Carnegie Endowment, and Foreign Affairs, published by the Council on Foreign Relations. Many of the think tanks around town also put out foreign-policy-oriented publications. For reporters into arms control, an exceptionally useful, but costly, publication is called the Arms Control Reporter. Published by the Institute for Defense and Disarmament Studies in Brookline, Massachusetts, it costs more than $1,000 a year and provides monthly loose-leaf updates on every new development in arms control. The end of the Cold War and the demise of the Soviet Union have diminished interest in these topics, somewhat. But the second Bush administration has embraced another round of bilateral nuclear weapons reductions with Russia. In addition, Bush has been pushing hard for a renewed effort to develop a missile defense system.

THINK TANKS AND ADVOCACY GROUPS

Experts on arms control and most aspects of international relations abound at the Arms Control Association, the Brookings Institution, the Center for Strategic and International Studies, the Johns Hopkins School of Advanced International Studies and the Carnegie Endowment. The Middle East Institute is the home of several former Arab ambassadors, and the Washington Institute for Near East Policy has experts who'll tell you about the effects of U.S. policy in the region, with a special focus on the Israeli-Palestinian peace process. The Council on Hemispheric Affairs has liberal-oriented experts on human rights in Latin America. These are among the more visible groups; nearly every faction and cause in the world has at least one group studying it or promoting it in Washington. Since the Sept. 11 attacks, groups such as the Arab American Institute have gotten increased attention.

The National Security Archive, now housed at George Washington University, is a valuable resource for reporters researching the history of diplomatic relations and national security controversies. The archive is especially helpful in its efforts to resolve contradictions in the official record.

FOREIGN SOURCES

Developing sources in embassies is important to understanding and reporting on U.S. relations with foreign countries. The larger embassies have experts on military strategy, trade, intelligence, economics, and cultural and scientific affairs—as well as press officers—and most of those experts are eager to communicate with American reporters. Similarly, it's helpful to develop friendships with foreign reporters based in Washington.

CAPITOL HILL

Developing sources on the right congressional committees and subcommittees is helpful for reporting on future battles over treaties, foreign aid, confirmations and policies in general. Keys are the Senate Foreign Relations Committee and the House International Relations Committees and the relevant Appropriations subcommittees.

THE STATE DEPARTMENT AND OTHER AGENCIES

The point of entry at the State Department is the main press office, but once you've learned your way around, you may do better talking to press aides within the many regional bureaus at State. Over time, you also can develop contacts among the country desk officers; they are often exceptionally knowledgeable.

Technically separate from State but pivotal to stories about arms control and foreign aid are two other agencies, the Arms Control and Disarmament

Agency and the Agency for International Development. Both have press operations, but developing sources at either place is a hit-or-miss proposition.

OTHER BEATS IN BRIEF

The study of the defense beat illustrates that a basic formula exists for getting a handle on any beat. If you read enough at the outset, meet the agency press officers, attend press conferences and public hearings, get on the right mailing lists, find the experts in think tanks and on congressional staffs, work constantly to use new contacts to lead you to even more new contacts, and circulate your work shamelessly to those contacts, eventually you will have mastered the beat. You can then channel your energy and expertise toward anticipating and developing the kinds of enterprise stories that will set you apart from your colleagues.

Below is a quick summary of tips from veteran reporters on getting started on various specialty beats, some of which are grouped under umbrella headings.

The Environment, Natural Resources and Energy

The environment, natural resources and energy issues are frequently combined into one beat, though environmental reporting has become increasingly specialized in recent years. Institutionally, the major focuses on the beat include the Environmental Protection Agency, the Interior Department, the Forest Service (which, strangely, is a part of the Agriculture Department), the Council on Environmental Quality, the Energy Department, the Nuclear Regulatory Commission and various oversight committees in Congress.

Press offices have a mixed reputation. The EPA press operation is divided into beats, and your first objective is to get to the right press officer. In the sprawling Interior Department, most of the many bureaus and divisions have their own press aides, though the main press office has a solid reputation for backing them up. The Energy Department press operation is more bureaucratic, but it also has press specialists in areas such as fossil energy, nuclear weapons plants, civilian nuclear waste management, and so forth. The NRC press operation in suburban Maryland receives occasional criticism from reporters for being unresponsive. Best advice on the NRC: Be persistent and take advantage of the agency's public documents room.

SOURCES AND RESOURCES

Numerous newsletters track the inner workings of the key agencies, led by Inside EPA and the Environmental Reporter. Shabecoff suggests journalists need to read such publications as Science, Nature and Scientific American. Most of the relevant research and watchdog groups in town put out annual reports. Also, EPA and other agencies release reports on compliance with federal laws, such as Superfund. Make sure you get reports issued by the EPA IG for an update on audits of agency programs.

Official sources of information can be found far beyond the agencies themselves. Congressional panels, particularly oversight committees, are rich veins to tap on this beat: Environmental and antinuclear activism is strong on Capitol Hill. The National Academy of Sciences is a gold mine for reporters pursuing research, and the National Cancer Institute has a branch of radiation epidemiology that can be helpful on nuclear technology stories.

The city abounds in outside groups that can be helpful, with this caveat: They're all selling a cause or a point of view. Use them without being abused by them. Among the most popular advocacy groups are the Sierra Club (which has a network of regional offices that puts it close to grassroots sentiment), the Wilderness Society, the National Wildlife Federation, Worldwatch Institute, the Environmental Policy Institute and the Center for Health, Environment and Justice. On nuclear issues, the Union of Concerned Scientists, the Natural Resources Defense Council and Public Citizen's Critical Mass Energy and Environment Program will supply all the antinuclear material you want, whereas the American Nuclear Energy Council will give you industry's point of view. Getting industry's point of view is critical to balanced reporting, and Washington has plenty of industry sources, whether the subject is chemical wastes, acid rain, coal mining, offshore oil, timber cutting or hydroelectric power.

BEST TIPS

• Get to know people in the regional offices on this beat.
• Make sure you understand the federal-state division of jurisdiction on enforcement of environmental laws. There's a wide disparity in enforcement among the states.
• Look for lawsuits across the beat. They're being filed virtually every day from state and federal district courts all the way up to the U.S. Court of Appeals for the District of Columbia Circuit.

Economics, the Budget, Trade and the Workplace

For much of the 1990s and the early years of the 21st century, when the U.S. economy was roaring along, business and economic coverage seemed to retreat into its more traditional position as an afterthought for journalists. But the stock market crash of 2000–2002, an incipient recession and the discovery of corruption and wrongdoing in some of the biggest corporations in the nation have helped spark some renewed interest in this arena. Although some larger bureaus have specialists in the areas of economics, the budget, trade and the workplace, many bureaus lump two or more of them into what might be called a business or pocketbook issues beat. Being based in Washington has advantages for any of those beats, if you also have the opportunity to get out in the country and assess the impact. Because budget battles are fought here, legislation is written here and trade policies are shaped here, thousands of outside interests are perched here also. Developing sources should not be difficult. More difficult will be learning all the jargon.

SOURCES AND RESOURCES

At the institutions, many of the press officers in this field tend to be veteran publicists. If your specialty is business, economics and finance, you'll want to meet press officers and other officials at the Fed, the Treasury and Commerce departments, and the Securities and Exchange Commission. If you want to become a budget expert, meet lots of people at the Office of Management and Budget, tax specialists at the Treasury and analysts at the Congressional Budget Office. If the banking industry figures prominently in your beat, head first for the Fed, the Office of Thrift Supervision and the Federal Deposit Insurance Corporation.

If you're into trade, focus on the International Trade Administration at Commerce, the office of the U.S. Trade Representative, the International Trade Commission and the Export-Import Bank. If your beat is labor, which more and more newspapers now call workplace, you'll need to make contacts at the Labor Department, its Occupational Safety and Health Administration and its Bureau of Labor Statistics, for starters.

Congressional jurisdiction is more logical in this field than on some other beats: Finance and Ways and Means for taxes and trade; the Senate Commerce and House Energy and Commerce committees on business and financial issues. The Joint Economic Committee and the Joint Committee on Taxation are good sources for studies and analysis. The Labor committees in both houses are venues for many of the family issues, such as parental leave and child care. Oversight committees monitor government programs in all these areas.

Outside resources in this field are among the most powerful in Washington, starting with the AFL-CIO and the larger independent unions (some of whom have hired their own public relations firms), the banking and the savings and loan industries, and representatives of corporate America at the Chamber of Commerce and the National Association of Manufacturers. Trade lawyers abound. The Brookings Institution and the American Enterprise Institute lead the think-tank field with experts on budgets, taxes, trade and finance. Embassies for countries like Japan, Canada, Germany, Australia, the European

Union and Korea offer superb contacts for trade stories. Feminist groups are good sources for workplace and family issue stories.

As for reading, The Washington Post, The New York Times and The Wall Street Journal are obvious musts. Other favorites include the Financial Times, Business Week, Fortune, the Economist and the Japan Economic Journal. Newsletters are monitored for tips because lobbyists usually are less wary of talking to reporters. Among the top ones are Tax Notes, Inside Trade and Labor Relations Week. Financial consultants churn out dozens of newsletters that offer tips on things like interest rates.

BEST TIPS

• Keep the reader in mind at all times. Avoid clichés and meaningless jargon.

• Be skeptical of budget numbers. The late Ed Dale, a longtime economics reporter for The New York Times who later became a spokesman for the Office of Management and Budget, put it best: "Budget stories are horribly misleading, but it's nobody's fault. I don't know the solution to it, except to put in the second paragraph: 'All these figures are meaningless.' And how many editors are going to let that go? But it would be the truth."

• As with other beats, there is little substitute for regular reading. Nearly every economics journalist points to John Berry's work covering the Fed for The Washington Post as being among the most influential.

Health, Medicine and Science

The health beat has drawn increased coverage in recent years, and the beat has become increasingly complex. Issues range from such scientifically challenging subjects as the practice and ethics of stem cell research to seemingly imponderable questions of how to pay for the health care needs of the aging baby boom generation. And besides the science or math of these stories, they all are tinged by political views that range across the spectrum.

Abigail Trafford, who writes about health issues for The Washington Post, has seen the beat evolve:

> My first big story was covering the Apollo space program, the landing on the moon program down in Houston. And this was a terribly exciting program that combined science, politics, the human story, economics, page one, it was a thrilling kind of story. After the space program kind of wound down, a lot of us who were covering that turned to health and medicine. . . . And there was a huge infusion of health reporters, and it coincided at a time in the country where people got much more interested in their health, and health also politically was starting to cost a lot of money. And it was kind of a coming together of a lot of excitement of health and medicine so that I

think this brought a huge amount of energy. I think before then . . . newspapers had one person who would cover medicine, and they would just follow the medical journals and write stories about headaches. What has changed is that health has become a, I call it a multibeat, just the way the space program was. It's science, it's medicine, but it's also politics and economics and human story, it's page one and has an urgency and an energy that I think it didn't have 30 years ago. All of that has made it, I think, a terrific beat and sort of one of the essential beats in Washington. All of your newspapers now really concentrate on health stories, and if you look at a lot of the stories that win Pulitzers and get a lot of attention, often it's in health. They're about health. I think it's changed from, in a sense, a specialty that was nice into a beat that's essential.

Trafford says she enjoys the health beat because it is "very open and very accessible, unlike a lot of political beats which are very structured, where you have a lot of spin control and press offices." Besides the regular government agency stops, she says health reporters have to get out of the office. "I'm a great believer that you just got to get out there and hang out at hospitals and doctors' offices and in people's lives."

For pure medical coverage, the advantages to being based in Washington for the heath, medicine and science beat can be summarized by the acronym NIH. The National Institutes of Health, with 13 separate major components, including the National Library of Medicine, is perfect for reporters who want face-to-face contact with sources.

Trafford says: "I think the NIH is excellent. They have a very good press office." She also gives generally high marks to press operations at the Health and Human Services Department and the Centers for Disease Control, though she says CDC stumbled a bit on its handling of the anthrax scare in the capital in late 2001. But the NIH is hardly the only government agency with a stake in the story. The Food and Drug Administration, now an independent agency, the Labor Department, the Agriculture Department, the EPA and others have major roles in health policy matters.

SOURCES AND RESOURCES

The official list begins with the NIH, with special attention to the Library of Medicine, home to practically every arcane medical journal in the world. The library has several online databases, such as MEDLINE and TOXLINE, and will do computer searches for reporters.

Other key resources include the Institution of Medicine at the National Academy of Sciences; the National Science Foundation, which funds medical research; the Food and Drug Administration and the Health Care Financing Administration within the Department of Health and Human Services; the Uniformed Services University of the Health Sciences, where the armed forces train doctors; the Walter Reed Army Medical Center and the Bethesda Naval

Medical Center; the Smithsonian Institution, which does top-notch and little-noticed scientific research; the National Aeronautics and Space Administration; and the National Oceanic and Atmospheric Administration, within the Commerce Department. Most of these federal agencies have libraries of their own. In recent years, C. Everett Koop and others have raised the profile of the surgeon general's office.

The president's science adviser at the White House occasionally makes news and usually reflects the president's interest in science issues. On Capitol Hill, the panel that makes the most news is the House Energy and Commerce Committee's Health Subcommittee. The authorizing and appropriations subcommittees on health bear monitoring, as do the House and Senate panels that oversee science and technology.

Outside resources begin with the American Association for the Advancement of Science, the American Medical Association, which has a legislative office in Washington; the American Pharmaceutical Association; and the Pharmaceutical Research and Manufacturers of America. On the list of think tanks and private research organizations, the Kennedy Institute for Ethics at Georgetown University ranks high, as does Worldwatch Institute.

Recommended reading includes the New England Journal of Medicine, the Journal of the American Medical Association; Science; Nature; Lancet; the journals of the National Cancer Institute, the American Psychological Association and the American Public Health Association; Science News newsletter; the newsletter of the Mayo Clinic; another newsletter called The Blue Sheet, which focuses on the NIH; and NIH Week.

As was noted, Washington is a popular site for medical conventions and hosts the annual convention of the AAAS. But conventions, with their growing emphasis on prepackaged public relations, tend to lose their value the longer you're on the beat.

Agriculture, Food Policy and Rural Issues

Few, if any, other sectors of the American economy are influenced more greatly by government policy than food and agriculture. The federal government has spent trillions simultaneously trying to stem the tide of consolidation that has characterized American farming for more than a century and trying to mitigate the effects of that consolidation on the vast rural areas of the nation. Much of that money has been paid out directly in checks to farmers, either to cushion the impact of overproduction or low prices or to encourage them to grow less of crops the world doesn't seem to need. It was overproduction of grain and other foodstuffs that led to the creation of the school lunch and the Food Stamp programs. Trade policy is vital to agriculture, because more than half of some commodities are raised for shipment overseas. In the West, many farmers use cut-rate government pastures for grazing. Farming is affected by environmental policy, labor rules, land use and a host of other government actions.

The advantages to covering agriculture and related issues from a Washington base are highlighted in two observations by Gannett News Service reporter Chuck Raasch, who covered the beat for several years: The U.S. Department of Agriculture does an incredible amount of economic and social policy research, much of which goes ignored by the general press, and Washington is the center of the national and international food policy debate and is also the home of hundreds of lobbyists who are trying to influence that debate. Despite those advantages and the enormous impact that agriculture policy has on American lives, the beat is largely ignored here except by the trade press and by regional reporters who occasionally make forays into local farm issues.

This is a complex beat, one in which strong geographical interests tied to commodities hold sway on Capitol Hill; for example, Midwestern reporters focus on corn and soybeans, Southern reporters on cotton. Also, urban lawmakers tend to defer to the expertise of those with a constituent interest in agriculture. These two factors encourage a lot of legislative logrolling.

The passage of a new farm bill every five years or so is one of the most politically complex acts in Washington. Just understanding something as esoteric as dairy price supports won't suffice. To cover the beat broadly, reporters have to understand not only the intricacies of deficiency payments and farm credit practices but also trade policy, scientific advances and environmental law. George Anthan, a Pulitzer Prize winner who covered agriculture here for two decades for The Des Moines Register before he retired, says he attended seminars occasionally to keep up on trends.

You can start with press officers at the sprawling USDA, of course, and you may have mixed results. Anthan calls the USDA information people "some of the best in government." He says, "A lot are very dedicated and in most cases very straight."

USDA is a sprawling bureaucracy. Aim for press aides within the individual agencies and services. There is no doubt that the Agriculture Department also makes it easier than almost any other agency to get to folks beyond the press office. USDA's online telephone and e-mail directories list contact points for economists, commodity specialists, trade officials and hundreds of other lower-level bureaucrats.

SOURCES AND RESOURCES

The best advice is to use press officers who are helpful, but you should move quickly to meet and develop other contacts within the agency, on Capitol Hill and in the private sector. A good way to start at USDA, says newsletter publisher James Webster, who has worked as a USDA official, is to find someone who is working on the next farm bill. That person will know what the post-mortems were on the last bill and what alternatives are being considered. Then find someone on Capitol Hill who has been involved in previous farm bill fights and will share that knowledge with you. Congressional liaison people from USDA are another favorite source of Webster's because they are wired into policy making and understand the Hill environment. Hill staff members on the Agriculture and relevant appropriations subcommittees are good to know, and staff aides to committee members are often even better. Subcommittee hearings are a good forum for following current issues and personalities.

On the outside, Washington is teeming with trade organizations, consultants and research groups that can provide you with expertise and an occasional leak. Webster says he makes cocktail receptions and parties a part of his beat because they invariably bring together the heads of trade associations and USDA officials at the assistant secretary and deputy assistant secretary levels. Lobbyists, as always, are a source to be coveted and cultivated.

Major broad-based farm and rural associations include the American Farm Bureau Federation, the National Farmers Union, the National Rural Electric Cooperative Association and Rural America, but each commodity and aspect of farming has its own association—and sometimes several—in Washington.

As for reading, most of the best inside stuff in Washington can be found in newsletters and magazines. Anthan's favorites included Food Chemical News, Feedstuffs, and Milling and Baking News. In addition to various newsletters, Gannett's Raasch suggests reading Farm Journal and Successful Farming magazines. James Webster publishes agricultural newsletters that are read closely by lobbyists and federal and state officials.

BEST TIPS

• Talk regularly with people outside the government. "They always know what's going on in the bureaucracy," says Anthan.

• Get on good terms with people around the USDA secretary. "That's most important," says Raasch.

• Get out of Washington. Explaining policy debates or legislative strategy won't convey the importance of a drought or a genetically altered supercow.

Education

Education is traditionally a local beat, but in recent years it has taken on an increasingly federal flavor. Both political parties—although coming from distinctly different approaches—have made education a priority. One debate that continues to rage is over whether the federal government should take steps to enable parents to choose the schools their children attend.

There are advantages for the handful of reporters who cover it out of Washington. Most notably, all the top players for the major educational organizations are based here. School administrators, school superintendents, state boards of education, the principals, the state school officers, and so on—all have offices here because one of their functions is to exert whatever leverage they can on the federal government. Part of that effort involves holding press conferences, which draw not only reporters but also curious representatives of other education organizations.

Jay Matthews of The Washington Post, who moved to the schools beat after being a foreign correspondent, says: "The best way to cover education is to get inside schools and talk to lots of principals, teachers, students and parents. I try to find a long-range project each year that requires me to go back to a few schools repeatedly."

SOURCES AND RESOURCES

The government connection to education is centered largely on the Education Department, where you'll want to cultivate both the department spokesperson, a political appointee who should be conversant on policy, and the career press officers, who will be able to help answer nuts-and-bolts questions.

The department puts out an annual summary of education statistics that serves as a good resource. Because the federal dollar constitutes a small fraction of education funding, the congressional role is more limited than in many other fields. Major interest revolves around student aid programs and aid to the disadvantaged, as well as the occasional debate over tuition tax credits and vouchers. The two Education committees and appropriations subcommittees are the key panels for following Hill action.

On the outside, dozens of organizations have research staffers and lobbyists who can give you guidance. Most important are the National Education Association, whose staff rates high for its expertise on issues as well as its political clout; the other major teachers' union, the American Federation of Teachers; the American Association of School Administrators, representing superintendents; the National Association of Secondary School Principals; and the National School Boards Association. Among the think tanks, the Heritage Foundation is most aggressive in pursuing a conservative agenda on education issues. The Education Commission of the States, headquartered in Denver but with a Washington office, coordinates educational initiatives by the 50 governors and can be a good resource for statistical information on state educational regulations.

For reading, the essentials are Education Week for tracking elementary and secondary education and the Chronicle of Higher Education for tracking higher education.

Matthews says education reporters need to dig more deeply into the subject matter. "We don't go deep enough. We tend to accept whatever buzz words or programs are considered good by the government agency heads." One way to avoid that problem would be to get out and build sources, he says. "We don't develop enough relationships with classroom teachers and students because they are hard to reach during normal working hours."

BEST TIP

Being active in the Education Writers' Association brings you a lot of literature on education trends. Attending its annual writers' seminar will expose you to many of the big names in education.

Law Enforcement and Justice

Although the law enforcement and justice beat is sometimes merged with the Supreme Court beat, the larger bureaus cover justice-related issues separately. In many cases, the focus is broad enough to include everything from the war on drugs to customs and immigration matters, civil rights disputes, prison reform and the fight against organized crime. With the worldwide effort to hunt down and eliminate terrorists and their networks, the Justice Department has taken on a new prominence. In addition, the push in late 2002 for creation of a new Department of Homeland Security held the prospect for a sprawling new bureaucracy that combined and realigned several existing agencies.

SOURCES AND RESOURCES

On the inside, you want to make contact with press aides at Justice, the FBI, the Drug Enforcement Administration, the Immigration and Naturalization Service, the Bureau of Justice Statistics and the U.S. Marshals Service. At Treasury, you want to get acquainted with the Customs Service and the Bureau of Alcohol, Tobacco and Firearms. The Secret Service, which protects the president and other top officials, also belongs to the Treasury Department.

Two of the most prolific sources of data on the beat are the crime statistics put out by the BJS and the FBI. They are two very different indexes: The FBI's Uniform Crime Reports is based on information on crimes reported by some 16,000 local and state units of government. The BJS reports are based on 100,000 interviews conducted each year in which Americans are asked about exposure to crimes, reported or not reported. Not surprisingly, the BJS reports peg the number of crimes at more than twice that recorded by the FBI reports, and there is some debate about which survey is a more valid indicator. But both provide resources and starting points for good stories. Most of these databases are available online.

The Justice Department Library is another good resource available to beat regulars. And developing sources among U.S. attorneys and regional FBI officials around the country is a prerequisite to getting a good handle on things.

Working Capitol Hill is another key component of the beat. Outside government are numerous organizations and research groups that provide expertise and churn out studies and reports. David Burnham, a former New York Times reporter and the author of a book about the Internal Revenue Service, runs a Web site through Syracuse University (trac.syr.edu/) that provides online access to a storehouse of information about U.S. attorneys and other Justice-related activities. Among those favored by many Justice reporters are the Police Foundation, the Police Executive Research Forum and the National Organization of Black Law Enforcement Executives.

BEST TIP

Work on developing sources outside Washington. "You should always have some kind of relationship with somebody in the Southern District of New York," says Ronald Ostrow, who formerly covered the Justice beat for the Los Angeles Times, "not just the U.S. attorney but also the (FBI's) special-agent-in-charge. That office has always made news and always will."

Transportation

Transportation is such a broad field that few reporters cover all of it. Some focus on auto-related issues, others on air safety, others on mass transit or highway issues. The Department of Transportation is a sprawling bureaucracy that encourages that lack of focus. Under its umbrella are nine major agencies, including the newly created Transportation Security Administration, which took over responsibility for airport security in the wake of the Sept. 11, 2001, terror attacks; the Federal Aviation Administration; the Coast Guard; the Federal Highway Administration; the National Highway Traffic Safety Administration; and the Urban Mass Transportation Administration. The main press office at DOT has a beat system and clears all press releases from all "modes," yet it encourages reporters to target their inquiries to the press offices within those agencies. The National Transportation Safety Board, a tiny agency with a high profile, is not part of the DOT and reports directly to Congress.

The first task for a transportation reporter is to understand the jurisdictions involved. For example, the FAA inspects commercial aircraft for safety violations but does not investigate crashes; that's done by the NTSB. The FAA is in charge of air traffic control tapes, which can be crucial in an accident investigation; the NTSB is in charge of cockpit voice recorders. The FAA administers grants for airports and sets security regulations, but it doesn't run airports.

The DOT press operation has a mediocre reputation among reporters, and the FAA is considered downright difficult. The NTSB, by contrast, is one of the friendliest and most helpful. Because it has no regulatory powers, the NTSB relies heavily on press coverage to advance its agenda for reforms in the safety of aircraft, school buses, and the like.

SOURCES AND RESOURCES

Both the NTSB and DOT generate a wealth of reports that will suggest both spot and enterprise stories. NTSB, for example, does frequent safety studies that supplement its investigations of crashes and disasters. Typical would be a study of alcohol and drug abuse among railroad employees, or a study of the safety records of medical evacuation helicopters. The NTSB also has a data bank that will permit you to research your own questions on the performance of a particular kind of aircraft, say, or the involvement of a certain factor as a probable cause in aircraft accidents.

The DOT issues monthly on-time performance reports covering all the major airlines and all major airports; it also receives and files publicly all kinds of consumer complaints related to travel. The Federal Highway Administration tracks and reports on the compliance with speed limits in the 50 states as well as the inspection of bridges in every state. The FAA issues semiannual reports on security violations at airports, and its aeronautical center at Oklahoma City has the history of every aircraft registered (by tail number) in the country, a database that is available electronically through a variety of sources.

On Capitol Hill, the Appropriations subcommittees and the Aviation subcommittees of the Senate Commerce and the House Transportation and Infrastructure committees are prime sources.

On the outside, every aspect of the aviation industry has trade representatives and watchdogs in Washington. Key ones in the aircraft and air travel area include the Air Line Pilots Association, the Air Traffic Control Association, the Air Transport Association (major airlines) and the Aircraft Owners and Pilots Association (general aircraft). The Airport Operators Council International speaks for airport operators. In the watchdog and consumer category are the Aviation Safety Institute, the National Transportation Safety Association and Airline Passengers of America. Auto safety is addressed by the Motor Vehicle Manufacturers Association, the American International Automobile Dealers Association (imported cars), the National Automobile Dealers Association, the Center for Auto Safety and the Insurance Institute for Highway Safety.

Recommended reading includes The Wall Street Journal, which does a good job covering all aspects of the field. Beyond that, Aviation Week and Space Technology stays on top of airline safety issues, as does the magazine

Frequent Flyer. You also should check out Automotive News and Ward's Automotive Reports to help you keep up with the auto industry and auto safety issues.

BEST TIP

Aviation is a highly technical world. Beware of experts who have an ax to grind.

Social Services and Social Policy

This beat is loosely structured at most Washington news organizations. It took on new importance in the mid-1990s when Congress and the Clinton administration agreed to a major overhaul of the nation's welfare system. The toughest part of the beat is dealing with the huge bureaucracies in the 120,000-employee Department of Health and Human Services, which has a reputation of being one of the densest and least reporter-friendly among the large government agencies.

SOURCES AND RESOURCES

Once you've given up on penetrating the HHS bureaucracy, think of looking elsewhere for help. On almost any story you tackle, you'll find studies at the Congressional Research Service, the General Accounting Office and the Congressional Budget Office. You can also find legislative history and perspective on the staffs of the Ways and Means and Finance subcommittees and the Aging committees. Think tanks to monitor include the Urban Institute, Brookings, the American Enterprise Institute and the Heritage Foundation. The Children's Defense Fund and the American Federation of State, County and Municipal Employees do a lot of work on family issues, and Washington is the home of many organizations representing the disabled, the disadvantaged, the elderly and the professionals who care for them. Trade groups like the American Hospital Association and the Health Insurance Association of America are essential contacts.

If you scan the major reports that flow into your mailbox, you'll have plenty to read. You can supplement those with periodicals such as AHA News and newsletters such as Child Protection Report.

6 REGIONAL REPORTING IN WASHINGTON

Regional reporters in Washington are the ultimate generalists. They have to know a little bit about practically everything and a great deal about a range of issues, institutions and personalities of interest to the city, state or region that comprises their audience.

Despite periodic cutbacks in Washington bureaus during economic downturns, regional reporting is still a distinctive beat, and the reporting by the hundreds of regionals in Washington is the backbone of the coverage read and viewed by most Americans.

Regional reporters in larger bureaus often are pulled between big-time national stories and humdrum parochial stories—a schizophrenic existence that is nonetheless rewarding. For example, when CIA Director George Tenet was called on the carpet before Congress following the Sept. 11 terrorist attacks in 2001, Larry Lipman, correspondent for The Palm Beach Post, covered the hearings for the Cox Newspapers because the Senate Intelligence Committee was chaired by Bob Graham, D-Fla., part of the delegation that he routinely covers. Because of his Florida readership, Lipman has also developed an expertise on elderly issues that serves Cox readers not just in Florida but across the country.

Lipman, who's been in Washington since 1985, says "a lot of regional reporters, if they've been here long enough, develop that sort of thing. They become fairly well known in the circle which they cover, whether it's defense or agriculture or elderly health care kinds of issues. So I think a good regional reporter will figure out that there are areas of interest that his paper has, and become known in that area, so that when something happens in that area, he is on the call list."

Despite having wide and far-flung audiences, however, regional reporters share a disadvantage that attaches to any journalist whose work is not usually available to Washington's power brokers and bureaucrats. It is journalism's version of the tree falling in the forest, beyond the range of human ears. Some reporters use this as an excuse to explain any and all shortcomings; others battle it year in and year out with mixed results. They tend to gravitate to Capitol Hill for answers because the White House and big bureaucracies like the Pentagon traditionally give them short shrift—although the George W. Bush White House earned some plaudits for assigning a press-office aide to deal with regional questions. But while some of the best reporters in Washington are regionals, there's no denying that regionals face special problems, among them:

Poor preparation for the beat. Typically, a new regional reporter in Washington gets a two-hour Cook's tour of Capitol Hill, introduced to a handful of congressional press secretaries, run through the Capitol press galleries in five minutes flat, handed a pile of disorganized files from a predecessor (maybe, with luck) and left alone. "It's a very big, very complex government and I think anyone dropped into the middle of this for the first time, you are completely at sea," says Lolita C. Baldor, correspondent for the New Haven Register.

Editors who expect too much. Too often, the editor back home is someone who assumes that Washington is just a large city hall or county courthouse; that the reporter should do everything the wires do, except better; and that the reporter's range of sources should rather quickly include the deputy secretary of state, the White House chief of staff and three high-ranking spooks at the CIA.

Over-reliance on the local congressional delegation. Because regional reporters quickly discover that their local congressional offices are places that really will return their phone calls, they frequently make those members and legislative staffs the primary focus of their coverage. Although it's legitimate to cover a member like a blanket, and even ask for his or her assistance in penetrating the bureaucracy, it's all too easy to be lulled into quid pro quo arrangements in which the member expects favorable coverage in exchange for a scoop or a carefully targeted official letter.

No time for enterprise. If regional reporters have a universal complaint, it's that they never have time to stop chasing trivial spot news long enough to develop stories in depth. The advent of all-news cable television networks has exacerbated this. Much of the blame rests on editors who believe that daily bylines are more important than reflective stories that anticipate and explain. Many editors, of course, want both; they want a story on the local entry in the national spelling bee and an analysis of why the new farm bill is in trouble.

Unreturned phone calls. Access in Washington is almost always proportionate to the visibility and reach of the news organization you represent, which puts regional reporters at a disadvantage. Says Dale Eisman of the Norfolk Virginian-Pilot: "The big thing is getting people outside your area to return your phone calls and deal with you. The reality is, if I'm working on something and I have to deal with a congressional office from say, Pennsylvania or New Mexico, they have no incentive, really, to return my call. You spend a lot of time trying to deal with that."

Regional reporters have learned to live with these handicaps, but in recent years they've also taken advantage of programs designed to help them raise their visibility and exchange ideas on how to get an edge. Since 1987 some 15 regional reporters each year have been named Paul Miller Fellows, under a program established by the Gannett Foundation (now called the Freedom Forum) to honor Miller, the former Gannett and Associated Press chairman and one-time Washington bureau chief for AP. The program was recently taken over by the National Press Foundation with an endowment grant from the Freedom Forum. Although reduced in scope from the original curriculum, the program offers one day of seminars a month spread over a year. It exposes the fellows to federal officials, congressional aides, lobbyists, consultants, scholars and veteran reporters discussing Washington life and how to do a better job of covering it from a regional perspective.

"There aren't a lot of people reaching out to you in Washington," says Oakland Tribune correspondent Lisa Friedman, "so you need to reach out to what is there. The Paul Miller program is still a good resource."

Friedman moved from a Miller fellowship to take on the presidency of The Regional Reporters Association, another resource for reporters who see clout in numbers. Some 200 regional correspondents belong to the RRA (www.rra.org), which arranges periodic briefings with newsmakers and professional development seminars, including an annual session in January or February on covering the federal budget. The RRA also publishes a newsletter periodically.

"When I landed in Washington," says Friedman, "it was like landing on Mars . . . it was a whole new language. It was very daunting, and one of the reasons I got involved with the RRA was because this was a group of people who said, 'we can help you . . . it's not that bad; don't worry about it.' This is the group that represents none of the hotshots."

The frustrations are ever with you, however. For example, Eisman of The Virginian-Pilot says he feels like he's "treated as an equal" with national reporters by the Pentagon's Navy brass because of the heavy Navy presence among his readers. But in the Pentagon at large, there is a definite "pecking order" that sometimes leaves regionals in the lurch. "It's not uncommon," he says, "to find yourself having worked on something for days, or even longer, only to find that as you're about to write it, the same story turns up in The Washington Post or The New York Times or the Los Angeles Times. And you can tell from reading it that it's been spoon-fed to someone. That was very hard for me to swallow the first couple of years I was up here, and I guess I've mellowed to it, but you do encounter that when you're dealing with big bureaucracies like Defense."

GETTING STARTED

There is no sure-fire formula that will make you the model regional reporter, but you can take some steps that will at least put you in control of things—sort of.

1. Start by asking yourself who in Washington, besides you, cares what's going on in the region where your audience is. These are the people you want to get to know.

2. Next, be sure you understand your audience. Knowing your market is critical for covering Washington on a regional basis. Do you know and understand what the local interests are—economic, political, cultural, educational, religious? The best way to learn that, if you've never lived there, is to read local and regional publications regularly. If you're a print reporter, start with the publication you work for.

3. Learn the jargon, the language of bureaucrats. "If you don't know it, you're immediately pegged as someone who hasn't done their homework," says Eisman. In the Pentagon, for example, he says, "You're dealing with very disciplined career people, college trained or beyond, and it's helpful to you if they know that you cared enough to learn a little something about it before you go see them."

4. Identify local problems, and remember that everybody looks to Washington for solutions. Maybe there's a toxic waste dump or a problem-plagued nuclear power plant that is becoming a major headache. Maybe foreign imports are devastating local industries, or the mass transit system is bankrupt. Maybe the savings and loans have gone belly up, or maybe clean-air deadlines have long been violated. Maybe there's a veterans' hospital scheduled for closing or a military installation tapped for sharp cutbacks.

5. Identify people in Washington from your market (beyond members of Congress) who have clout—lobbyists, congressional aides, high-ranking bureaucrats. Make a list of these "hometowners." Meet as many of them as you can, and play on their hometown memories. Write stories about them if they're interesting.

6. List the groups and institutions with a constituency in your market. If you're from Florida, it might be the congressional Sunbelt Caucus or the AARP. If you're from New Mexico or Arizona, it might be the Bureau of Indian Affairs or the Hispanic Caucus. If you're from Detroit, it might be the offices of Ford or Chrysler or the United Auto Workers. Almost every governor's office and many larger cities now have their own lobbyists in Washington.

7. Figure out which people are the most influential among your constituents back home. Get to know them. One way is to search the Federal Election Commission's records of individual donors to members of your congressional delegation and to congressional leaders. Most influential people in the business world make political contributions.

8. Identify and cultivate officials and political leaders back home who can help you keep tabs on stories moving from the local scene to Washington. Knowing someone in the attorney general's office will make tracking Supreme Court cases from your state a lot easier. Knowing state and local political party chairs will help you in assessing the outlook for new members of Congress.

9. Leverage the assets you have. If you or your publication has particular expertise, trade on it. For example, The Des Moines Register's Washington bureau is an authority on farm coverage in Washington, and the bureaucracy responds to that. If someone in your congressional delegation is an expert on an issue or has a large amount of clout, take care to cultivate that person's staff.

10. Circulate your work. It's a lot easier in the Internet era. Washington officials are unlikely to see that you accurately quoted them or made good use of their background guidance unless you show them your work. E-mail them a copy of your story or the Web address of your newspaper.

TARGETING RESOURCES

As a regional reporter, the trick is to discover and anticipate local angles throughout the government that aren't packaged for you. The most obvious source is state and local breakdowns of government statistics, grants, awards, programs, and so forth. A few examples:

• The Census Bureau and the Office of Management and Budget both do state-by-state breakdowns of federal spending.

• The Defense Department does state-by-state summaries of military spending, a breakdown of prime contract awards by state and region, and an annual survey of the 100 largest prime contractors doing business with the Pentagon.

• The Department of Transportation issues biennial reports on the status of every bridge in America.

• The Department of Education annually issues educational statistics broken down by state, as well as a state-by-state "report card" that includes a ranking of Scholastic Aptitude Test scores.

• The Environmental Protection Agency issues annual air-quality and biennial water-quality reports with regional and local breakdowns.

• The Small Business Administration issues state-by-state reports on its programs.

• The Health Care Financing Administration within the Department of Health and Human Services issues voluminous annual reports on hospital mortality rates and nursing home performance, with each report broken down by individual institution.

• The FBI's Uniform Crime Reports breaks down statistics by city, and the Bureau of Justice Statistics releases frequent reports on crime surveys that occasionally include state breakdowns.

Perhaps the biggest overall source of local stories is the federal budget that the president sends to Congress early each year, and the appropriations bills that eventually emerge from the House and Senate. Different bureaus handle the budget story in different ways, but release of the president's spending plan almost always prompts a flurry of regional stories about Army Corps of Engineers projects, military construction projects, water and dam projects in the West, Veterans Administration hospital projects, and so on.

Another prospective target is state or local actions that have risen to the federal level. The U.S. Tax Court, for example, is a treasure of good stories, virtually all of them local, about feuds between taxpayers and the Internal Revenue Service. (See Chapter 8 for more details.)

The U.S. Patent Office's Official Gazette, updated weekly, provides state-by-state lists of new inventions that have been approved. Some of them make great local stories.

Most federal departments and agencies have consumer complaint files that are open to reporters and can yield good feature stories. Regulatory bodies like the Nuclear Regulatory Commission are crammed with documents outlining local-federal disputes.

Federal "pork" is another rich vein for regional reporters. Little of that slips by the congressional public relations mill, of course, but the alert reporter will independently track lobbying for federal largess, including defense contracts, block grants for local development, academic grants, and so on.

The computer and Internet era has made targeting local names and angles easier for the regional reporter. Organizations like the Center for Responsive Politics let you search campaign contributions or expenditures by state, city, ZIP code, family name, corporation, interest group, and so forth.

BEING ENTERPRISING

Regional reporters often complain that their editors never give them time for enterprise, but even the most spot-news-oriented editors should realize the value of in-depth projects from their Washington correspondent. The only thing that limits regional reporters in Washington is their imagination. Here are a few suggestions.

Evaluation of Congressional Members

Examining a region's legislators should be a requirement of any regional reporter based in Washington. At least once every election cycle, and more often in the case of U.S. senators, you should take a hard, fair and comprehensive look at the job the lawmaker is doing in Washington. To do this right will require several days of aggressive reporting. The object is to draw a 1,500 to 3,000-word portrait that will assess the strengths and weaknesses of the

member. If you talk to enough congressional staffers, lobbyists, political consultants, state and local party leaders, bureaucrats, local officials and other
members of Congress, you'll be able to evaluate the member's effectiveness
on issues, on legislative strategy, on serving constituent needs and on his or her
prospects for moving up the leadership ladder. (See Chapter 3 for detailed tips
on covering Congress.)

State and Regional Clout

When Ronald Reagan was elected president in 1980, California's profile in
Washington shot up. The same thing happened for Texas when George Bush
succeeded him eight years later, and again when his son won the White House
12 years after that. You don't have to have a president from your state to construct a profile of its clout in Washington. Take a look at the state's congressional
delegation and how it ranks collectively on committees and in the House or Senate leadership. Identify state figures in the president's cabinet and in other
high-ranking executive branch positions. For example, when former Pennsylvania Gov. Tom Ridge was named director of homeland security following the
September 2001 terrorists attacks, both he and homeland security became a big
story for Harrisburg Patriot-News correspondent Brett Lieberman.

Chart the Fortune 500 companies headquartered in your state and assess their
Washington operations. Figure out how many superlobbyists and superlawyers in
town have strong ties to your state. Explore the networks that exist among all these
figures, put all the information together and then draw your own conclusions.

Regional and Local Impact

Next to evaluating members of Congress, the most important job a regional
reporter can do is to explain the local and regional impact of federal actions. It's
easy to report on adoption of a new federal law or regulation, but it's not so easy to
explain how much regional or local impact either had after six months or six years.
That requires following the oversight function in Congress and among government
and private watchdog groups. It usually requires traveling outside Washington or
working closely with reporters on staff back home. Too often Washington-based
reporters resist the latter and assume they can't justify the former.

Profiles of the Locals in Washington

Doing feature profiles of the local-girl-or-boy-makes-good variety not
only results in good stories but also acquaints you with people who may

become valuable sources. The key to any kind of reporting in Washington, including regional reporting, is knowing a lot of people. This is one way to build sources and do interesting stories at the same time. Many states have societies in Washington that sponsor social events with members of Congress and come to life quadrennially during presidential inaugural festivities.

Federal Red-Tape Stories

Stories about small businesses or large corporations battling Washington are interesting, and you don't have to wait for someone to hold a press conference to explore local employers' problems with the federal government. If the company in question is regulated by the Securities and Exchange Commission, check at the commission for any financial problems. If you suspect that the company may be the target of discrimination suits, check public documents at the Equal Employment Opportunity Commission. If the company has pension problems, check at the Labor Department. For health and safety violations, check the Labor Department's Occupational Safety and Health Administration. If there's a history of union problems, check the National Labor Relations Board. If you suspect tax problems, check the U.S. Tax Court. For possible violations of pollution regulations, check the Environmental Protection Agency. For possible complaints about the company's advertising, check the Federal Trade Commission; for complaints about its products, check the Consumer Product Safety Commission.

7 THE WHITE HOUSE

The White House is still considered a glamour beat, though few ex-White House reporters remember it that way. Glamour, in this case, is in the eye of the beholder.

Life on the beat approximates being one of the four-legged members of the support cast in an old western movie about cattle drives. On the road, you are constantly being herded from photo opportunity to press plane to motorcade bus to background briefing to hotel press room. All this movement is broken up by long waits and infrequent—very infrequent—sightings of the president, provided you brought along your binoculars.

In Washington, you mostly just wait: Wait for the press secretary to brief, wait for the president to make an impromptu appearance in the White House press room, wait for a pool report on the latest photo opportunity, wait for a presidential adviser to keep an appointment already an hour overdue, wait for a second-level presidential aide to return your phone call.

Karen Hosler, a congressional correspondent for The Baltimore Sun who covered the White House from 1988 to 1993, sums up the experience:

> Covering the White House offers great overseas adventures, lots of prestige and great cocktail party stories, but it's not nearly as fun or rewarding as covering Congress. White House correspondents put up with tedium and indignities that don't come with any other Washington beat. There's so much standing around on the North Driveway waiting for someone who met with the president to come out and tell you what they told the president. They never tell us what the president said in return. And there's waiting in the briefing room for the spoon-fed news. There's waiting for buses, trains and planes. There's waiting for phone calls that never get returned. There's just plain waiting. I used to feel like I was hurling myself daily at the ramparts, hoping some little chunk of information would fall off. It was very difficult. And the beat is 24/7.

USA Today's Judy Keen, who covered the first Bush presidency and part of the Clinton presidency, then returned to cover the second Bush presidency, says it's "kind of like combat everyday. It's a struggle to coax information out of people . . . it's maddening sometimes."

Nonetheless, when asked what she still likes about the job, Keen has a ready response. "Boy, it matters, you know. It's the feeling of awe I get when I walk through those gates in the morning that will never leave me."

The added attractions, of course, are the opportunities to be called by your first name by the president of the United States, to accumulate presidentially autographed photos to show your children and grandchildren and—in recent years—to use the beat as a launch pad for getting on television talk shows, which in turn gives you a shot at making after-dinner speeches for big fees.

Whatever the lure, the size of the White House press corps keeps growing. Some 2,000 reporters are accredited to the White House, and about 60 to 75 of them are counted as regulars. Those from the largest organizations have small carrels in which to work on the main or basement level of the press room. It's not unusual for small bureaus to establish a White House beat just as soon as the congressional delegation and other pressing parochial concerns are covered. A White House beat provides an instant prestige that appeals to both bureau chiefs and editors back home, even though there may be a dozen other beats in Washington that would better serve the readership.

Although the war on terrorism following the attack on the United States in 2001 focused the spotlight on the White House, the truth is that a president can go days at a time without doing anything particularly newsworthy. Yet anything he does is apt to be magnified because of the size of the White House press corps.

The emphasis on the White House strikes some as excessive. Stephen Hess, a Brookings Institution senior fellow and former presidential aide, characterizes the White House focus as "too many bodies chasing too few stories." The end result, Hess says, is that "they have probably blown the president out of proportion." The contrast with congressional coverage is drawn critically by Mark Helmke, a former press secretary to Senator Richard Lugar, R-Ind.: "On the Hill, you've got 535 members of Congress, hundreds more staffers, each with their own agendas. Each of them is trying to convince reporters that he's got the story. At the White House, it's like everything uttered by whomever is news because it's coming out of the White House."

Veteran White House reporters over the years have complained that younger reporters coming on the beat don't seem to have much historical perspective about the place. "The best White House reporters," says Richard Moe, former chief of staff to Vice President Walter Mondale, "were the ones who'd thought about the institution, had immersed themselves in the presidency and that particular administration, and could take a story and put it in context and tell what it meant." The ability to "tell what it meant" is part of the continuing debate in newsrooms and Washington bureaus over how the White House should be covered: Should spot news be left to the wires in favor of analysis? Should the White House report be a blend of spot news with a twist? Should it be that and more: spot news, exclusives and analytical pieces?

The typical daily schedule of an informal and a formal press briefing lends itself to the herd instinct that characterizes so much of Washington journalism. Avoiding the herd instinct is a challenge to any White House reporter, but it's not the first one he or she will encounter.

GETTING STARTED

Gaining Access

The first thing you have to learn to live with while covering the White House is the security and restriction on movement. Most of the time, you'll be confined to the White House press room or roped-off areas on the North or South Lawn. (On the road, you'll be confined to a roped-off area or a press bus.) You can't go beyond the press office complex without an escort and an appointment. The Executive Office Building next door is similarly restrictive. Time was, you could wander there among the warren of offices occupied by middle- and top-level presidential aides. No more. You can enter only by appointment and clearance to a specific office, and you have to leave the building when that appointment is over.

The next thing you discover is that at the White House, unlike at Capitol Hill or even city hall, information is usually tightly held. Leaks are carefully targeted. Presidential aides are busy people who don't have time for strangers. They get caught up in rivalries that make it dangerous to be caught talking to reporters. They all owe their jobs to a politician; no career work force of any stature exists in the White House.

Moreover, the history of recent decades has shown that openness among presidential aides can be self-defeating. Aides to both Jimmy Carter and Bill Clinton used the press to send their boss a message. The top staffs of Ronald Reagan and the first President Bush were much more disciplined both in the campaign for the White House and once they arrived. But they were neophytes compared to the top circle around George W. Bush.

Reporters covering the younger Bush agree, almost with a note of admiration, that the senior staff around "W" have no equal when it comes to controlling access and "staying on message."

"In terms of controlling the flow of information from within the White House, they're very good at that," says Newsday correspondent Ken Fireman. "They do it as well as anyone I've ever seen do it."

Anne Kornblut of The Boston Globe compares the Clinton and second Bush White Houses: "The Clinton people operated under the impression that if you drown the press in paper and facts and detail that you will win out. The Bush people figure that the argument stands for itself. They work from the perception that less is better."

Part of the problem, says Cox Newspapers correspondent Bob Deans, is the profusion of outlets. The White House has to make a lot of tough decisions about access while being besieged by cable and broadcast television, the Internet, the wires and newspapers. "We've all got locked into a sort of undifferentiated mass here," says Deans, a former foreign and State Department correspondent. "The answer from the White House has been increasingly to restrict the access. . . . I no longer have the feeling that I'm actually covering the White House. I'm writing about it and I'm writing about that aspect of the White House that they choose to make public."

Developing Inside Sources

Developing sources in the White House is both difficult and frustrating. Most administrations have no more than a dozen or so top White House aides—and often fewer—who are wired into all major planning and decision making. A second layer of several dozen aides knows some things about some issues but lacks an overview. Establishing a working relationship with some of the few in the know is a first and lasting challenge for any White House reporter.

The best way to get a leg up, of course, is to cover the campaign first.

Beyond that, there is broad consensus among veterans of the White House beat that the best way to cultivate sources is to work long hours, be persistent but fair, and demonstrate a high degree of knowledge and interest. Leo Rennert, the former longtime bureau chief of McClatchy Newspapers, says:

> You do it by dint of staffing and patrolling the beat, by going to the briefings and lingering after and talking with aides, and building up a record of coverage that inspires respect. If you do your job well, it's like any other beat. If you're a good reporter, if your reporting is fair, accurate, however critical it may be, people are going to say, "Wait a minute. This guy is really serious." And I think it opens some doors. Not many. Penetrating the White House to get a really good background slant on a story is very difficult.

The importance of projecting a serious image and, ironically, its limitations is described by Jody Powell, press secretary in the Jimmy Carter White House:

> Believe it or not, having a reputation as a serious person and someone who is interested in knowing what's going on as opposed to somebody who's interested in trying to get a few quotes and will sit there and ask questions as long as it takes—does help. It is something you can say as a press secretary to the national security adviser or the domestic policy adviser or whoever: "Look, this is a serious person, worth spending some time with." That helps, but clearly it's the old limited-time-and-resources game. People have got to devote time and resources to things that have the most impact.

Powell adds:

> Clearly, if you're working in the White House and you're making time
> to give reasonable access or a lot of access to a reporter, what drives you up
> the wall the most is not the serious negative story but the gratuitous zingers
> that get thrown, and the use of a quote—not that it's inaccurate—the sort of
> cheap shot which nobody can exactly define, but we all have a sense of what
> we're talking about. . . . If somebody commits real news in an unguarded
> moment, that's different.

St. Petersburg Times bureau chief Sara Fritz, who has covered Washington for five different major news organizations, says preparation is the key to developing White House sources and extracting information from them. "If you know the right questions to ask, you're better off," says Fritz, who adds that if you've got information to trade, you'll learn a lot more. "Probably the greatest wedge to getting information out of the White House is your own information," says Fritz. "They're always testing to find out how much you know. Part of the reason people see you is to get a feel for what's out there: What do people know about the subject? . . . If you have an independent source of information and present that, you'll do better than if you go in and say, 'What can you tell me?'"

Other strategies can also help you develop a network of White House sources. As previously noted, one is to make every effort to cover the presidential campaign preceding your assignment to the White House. Assigning future White House correspondents to the campaign allows them to get to know and become known to the presidential nominees and to develop sources among campaign aides who almost certainly will end up in the White House.

Keen of USA Today is an example. Because she covered the first Bush presidency and his unsuccessful campaign for re-election in 1992, she knew the younger Bush even before he won the governorship of Texas and began plotting his campaign for the White House, which she also covered.

"There's an advantage of having known the guy for 10 years—and his family—but also having covered his campaign," she says. "There's also an advantage in terms of relationships with his top staffers. If people know you, know they can trust you, know you're not going to screw them on stuff, I think it pays off."

If you're assigned to the White House without that kind of warm-up, at least get a complete directory of staffers and look for familiar names. You may find some mid-level officials there whom you knew on a previous beat and lost track of—lobbyists, state legislators, consultants, business people, congressional staffers. You can also put yourself on the list for daily pool assignments. It permits you to see the president at close quarters, and it marks you among press office staffers as one of the regulars.

Getting to know the press office staffers well is another little step that can prove beneficial. They can provide logistical details to make your life easier, and with a relationship built up over time, the more-senior staffers can provide background guidance that goes beyond the line of the day.

The value of presidential press secretaries depends on your approach to White House coverage and on their relationship with the president. Wire service and television correspondents depend on the press secretary to keep them apprised of logistics and breaking news. Reporters for all major news organizations like to stay on the secretary's good side in case he or she has the clout to have them blacklisted with top presidential advisers. But the press secretary's value as a source on substantive matters depends on whether he or she is a part of the inner loop around the president and has ready access to the president. In modern times, Jody Powell was an exceptionally valuable source because he knew Jimmy Carter's thinking—some would say he knew it better than Carter. In the Reagan administration, by contrast, Larry Speakes was regarded by many reporters to be out of the loop.

Marlin Fitzwater, who succeeded Speakes and stayed on during the elder Bush's term, was highly regarded by the press corps because he was a veteran government press officer and had such seniority that he was trusted by the presidents he served. Mike McCurry in the Clinton White House was well versed on foreign policy because he'd been press spokesman at State, and was regarded as "in the loop" when he wanted to be, although he deliberately avoided a lot of meetings after the Monica Lewinsky scandal broke.

Ari Fleischer in the younger Bush's presidency held some measure of respect because he rarely played favorites in the press—he didn't leak to anybody. Judy Keen's description of Fleischer is typical: "Ari is maddening in terms of his reluctance to talk on background or help you when you're working on something sensitive. He's on message all the time. . . . On the other hand, he's a terrific briefer—he's pretty smooth and unflappable. He's good at what he does."

Getting to Know Support Offices and Staff

The hundreds of staffers within the White House and Executive Office Building complex are fertile ground for an aggressive reporter determined to build a network of sources. Depending on how the senior staff is structured—and it varies with every administration—the key offices to start with usually are those of the chief of staff, the domestic policy council, the counsel to the president and legislative affairs. If you can develop good sources in most of these offices, you'll have a shot at getting inside information on how the White House is being run, what its policy agenda will be and what kind of working relations are being maintained with Congress.

If you're interested in foreign policy, you'll want to develop contacts in the National Security Council—always a challenge. If you're a political junkie, you'll want to know people in the office of political affairs, though its importance depends on the clout of the director and the administration's relationship with the national party apparatus. If you're into economic policy, you'll want to cultivate professionals working for the Council of Economic Advisers. Presidential speech writers and members of the White House advance and presidential scheduling staffs can provide good logistical tips. Tracking the presidential assistants for public liaison and media relations can give you a sense of how well the administration is doing at lobbying interest groups, the media and grassroots voters outside Washington.

You'll want sources in the vice president's office, and you'll be smart to treat the Office of Management and Budget as part of your beat. Although many White House reporters give OMB short shrift, it's one of the most powerful agencies. Under policies instituted during the Reagan administration, OMB is the president's enforcer on regulatory matters, a function that has more impact ultimately than annual battles over budget levels.

Developing Outside Sources

You don't want to live or die by the quality of your sources within the White House. Washington, indeed the country, is flush with people who make it their business to watch the president closely and who are prepared to comment. Consider the following outside sources:

Political operatives. Ranging from state party chairs and national and congressional campaign committee staffers to political consultants, these folks, depending on the party in power, either have contacts in the White House or are in a position to speak critically and knowledgeably.

Congressional sources. The Hill connection is important both for critiquing the performance of the president and the administration's top staff and for ferreting out information the White House may be trying to keep secret. The Watergate and Iran-Contra investigations, as well as the impeachment proceedings against Clinton in the Lewinsky affair, are the most dramatic examples, but routine correspondence and meetings between the president and members of Congress can almost always be tracked more easily through congressional sources.

Private-sector advisers. Every president relies on friends, former aides and associates in the private sector for advice. Developing them as sources after their patron gets in the White House is difficult. If you knew them well "back when," however, you'll be well-served to lavish attention on them.

Lobbyists. It's the business of lobbyists to know what's going on in the White House on legislative, regulatory and budget initiatives. Some may have worked in the White House or may have close ties to presidential aides through a variety of networks. Whatever connections you have with them from the past, play on them.

Bureaucrats. Career officials are usually fairly circumspect about speaking for the record, but appointed officials sometimes are willing to provide background information on some subjects. The annual budget fandango is a good example. The White House likes to put out the good news and leave it up to the departments and agencies to announce the bad.

Special interests groups. Contact with special interest groups is more in the nature of simply getting the "other side of the story." Advocacy groups such as trade associations, Ralph Nader's Public Citizen and lobbyists for state and local governments in Washington are places to look for other perspectives in assessing White House pronouncements and policy proposals.

Think tanks. Washington's many research organizations are more valuable for providing background on White House policy initiatives than for outright criticism, though some also provide that. The relatively nonpartisan Urban Institute, for example, has long been a good source for detailed—and sometimes critical—critiques of presidential domestic policy proposals. The conservative Heritage Foundation usually greets new Republican presidents with massive public policy prescriptions.

Presidential scholars. Reliance on presidential scholars is a matter of personal preference, but some White House reporters find them to be immensely helpful in analyzing presidential performance and character.

THE DAILY GRIND

A certain sameness creeps into life at the White House, just as at city hall or any beat shaped by the cycles of political and governmental calendars. So many unusual things can happen, however, when you're covering the president. A major objective of any administration is to control the flow of information while trying to convince the many competing and demanding factions of the press corps that it has their collective interest at heart.

Although Lyndon Johnson tried to use personal persuasion to control reporters, Richard Nixon and every president since has tried to manipulate the press by orchestrating events and messages. Ronald Reagan's aides perfected the technique with a theme-of-the-day approach and such gambits as shouted exchanges over the roar of helicopters that permitted Reagan to get away with three-word answers or no answers at all. The first Bush administration brought an abrupt switch to civility and frequent informal access that some reporters soon branded as a new form of manipulation.

The Clinton administration presented reporters with a cacophony of voices, all spinning at the same time. Because Clinton and his top aides considered government to be a force for good, notes Bob Deans of Cox Newspapers, they were always willing to talk and talk at length about what they were trying to do. "His (Clinton's) instinct was to give you an expansive response. That set the tone for his administration. His folks felt they, too, had a green light to expand on subjects, and they did so."

Because the younger Bush favored a "minimalist" approach to government, and was himself a man of few words, says Deans, his aides were careful to let his few words speak for themselves and not go beyond them.

Whatever the frustrations or concessions, life for most White House reporters revolves around the daily briefing by the press secretary, which may be supplemented by one or more shorter, informal sessions in the secretary's office. (The second Bush administration instituted a 9:45 a.m. "gaggle" that became so popular it was moved from the press secretary's office to the briefing room. The ground rules were no cameras—on the record.) The environment at the daily briefing tends to reflect the state of press relations at the White House and the attitude of the press corps toward the press secretary. In the Nixon years, the briefing room was like a snake pit; in the Reagan years, it deteriorated steadily during the tenure of press secretary Larry Speakes. Jody Powell fared better during most of his tenure despite Jimmy Carter's poor image, because reporters respected Powell's knowledge and clout. Marlin Fitzwater fared well under Reagan and Bush because he was a professional press officer and reporters liked him to boot. Mike McCurry in the Clinton administration was generally liked, as previously described, while Ari Fleischer in the second Bush administration was the subject of regular griping because he was so stingy with information, but got grudging approval for his stewardship.

Most reporters who work for the daily media attend the briefings, though their reasons for doing so vary. Reporters for weeklies can get by reading the transcript if they miss an occasional briefing. For reporters who have few or no White House sources, of course, the briefings form the basis of their coverage. For those who have other sources of information, the briefings serve more as a source of intelligence.

"It's good to go to the briefing just to get a feel for what the attitude is," says USA Today's Keen. "And, frankly, to get some idea what the competition is working on, which you can sometimes glean from the questions they ask."

The advent of the Internet and all-news cable television has made this aspect of the job a lot easier, of course. Many briefings are televised now, and White House regulars are routinely e-mailed transcripts of briefings, presidential remarks, fact sheets, pool reports and schedules.

Another reality for White House reporters is that White House leaks go only to a favored few. With some exceptions, foreign policy leaks go to The New York Times, domestic policy and political leaks go to The Washington Post and leaks about economic policy go to The Wall Street Journal. In recent years, USA Today has gained attention as a favorite at the White House because of its wide reach. Most reporters grudgingly accept this situation.

They dismiss The Post and The Times as "bulletin boards," but they understand that there's no point in launching a trial balloon for a Washington audience in a paper that no one in Washington reads.

A presidential aide floating an idea in one of the major papers may have any of several purposes in mind: (1) to see if it gets knocked down, (2) to knock down someone else's ideas, (3) to cause trouble for another presidential aide, or (4) to send a message to the president.

Tom Griscom, known as a consummate leaker when he worked for Senator and later White House Chief of Staff Howard Baker, said he would leak information to television reporters if they were already working the story. If it was something more subtle, but he wanted national impact, he would go with The Post or The Times. Once in a while, he would deliberately leak something outside Washington.

To be a good leaker, Griscom says "you've got to have the confidence that you can put it out there and your footprints are never anywhere around . . . and be very selective." He adds: "I can tell you a leaker from buzzwords and phraseology. A good leaker knows how to say it and how to cover his tracks in the process."

PRESIDENTIAL PRESS CONFERENCES

Among the most debated topics in Washington over the years has been the presidential press conference. Is the president having enough of them or too many of them? Should the president be committed to holding them on a regular basis? Should press conferences be prime-time television extravaganzas or midday, low-key affairs? Do press conferences serve the public or just the press? Should the president experiment with small gatherings of reporters, no cameras allowed?

One thing's for certain: This is a debate confined to journalists and a few academics. There's little evidence that the public cares one way or the other. Another thing for certain is that any savvy administration considers press conferences to be part and parcel of its overall political strategy and knows, furthermore, that totally pleasing the press corps is impossible. In any event, it's generally agreed that the day and age of the big East Room press conference production is over. Clinton cut way back on such events after the Monica Lewinsky affair, and George W. Bush favors more spur-of-the-moment sessions with reporters, not in prime time.

In the ideal world, the White House reporter will be able to treat presidential press conferences with considerable equanimity. They seldom make big news; more often they leave the press corps trying to figure out the lead. In the ideal world, the White House correspondent will let the wires write the hard news summary and will pick out one set of answers and extract from them some kind of theme to analyze. Later, the correspondent will go back and carefully read the transcript to see if it contains signals, however faint, of a change in direction or policy.

SPECIAL EVENTS

Covering press conferences is among the least demanding tasks for the serious White House reporter. More challenging are the big events that get advance billing and often turn into media extravaganzas. Breaking out of the pack requires planning.

Start with the presidential inauguration. This essentially is a three-day feature story about parades and balls and ceremony and new lifestyles in the White House. It is also a time for little history lessons that put the new first family and the president's inaugural address into context. It's a time for a serious treatment of a presidential speech, not only analyzing its uplifting themes but also identifying the echoes of inaugural speeches past.

The same with the presidential State of the Union address to Congress. Few contain lines as memorable as Richard Nixon's "One year of Watergate is enough" or Gerald Ford's admission that "the state of the union is not good." But it is worth careful analysis for what it says about the president's vision for the country and grasp of reality.

Presidential summitry is another opportunity for White House reporters to shine, provided they go beyond the televised images so carefully scripted. The first trip abroad with the White House can be a humbling experience for a reporter new to the beat. The presence of so many journalists from other lands, all of whom purport to be foreign policy experts, can leave you feeling like you just walked out of the swamp. Don't be intimidated. If you talk to enough experts in Washington—in the think tanks, in the embassies of host countries, and in the White House—you can hold your own with the diplomatic types. And don't forget whom you're writing for in Kentucky or Nebraska or Oregon.

The annual release of the president's budget to Congress is an opportunity to break from the pack, which tends to cover the story as if it were the Second Coming. The truth about any president's budget is this: It may reveal a packaged glimpse of the administration's spending priorities, and those are worth comparing with campaign promises. Beyond that, the budget proposal is hardly worth the paper it's printed on. The government runs on continuing resolutions and spending bills fashioned entirely on Capitol Hill.

Another big event that occurs infrequently but should test the imagination of any resident or incoming White House reporter is the transition of power from one administration to the next. Presidential transitions are a great marriage of history, tradition and old-fashioned politics in the nation's most visible institution.

Planning for the transition begins in both nominees' camps soon after the political conventions, but action reaches a fever pitch in the 10-week span between Election Day and the inauguration. Thousands of the president-elect's supporters jockey for hundreds of choice government jobs: ambassadorships, cabinet posts, deputy directorships, advisory commissions. The hundreds already in those jobs wait nervously for the ax to drop, hoping against astronomical odds that they will be deemed irreplaceable. Work at the upper levels of the bureaucracy creaks to a halt.

Lobbyists, presidential friends, special interest groups and members of Congress work frantically to generate support for their favorite job seekers. For every appointment, there is a constituency. For every happy appointee, there will be a dozen or a hundred unhappy candidates who didn't make it. The president-elect sits in the midst of all this, trying to assemble a cabinet and develop an agenda. The outgoing president, often the symbol of a rejected political party, tries to be accommodating without losing dignity.

For reporters, the story possibilities are endless:

• Who are these cabinet nominees, and does it matter who they are? This story calls for a little perspective on cabinet government and wayward cabinet officers.

• Who's up and who's down in the new White House staff? How are they viewed by the power brokers in Congress, not to mention state and national political operatives in the president's party? What are their qualifications for their new jobs?

• What about all those campaign promises the president-elect made? Catalog them and then establish their new priorities in the harsh light of political reality.

• What kind of job is the new team doing in rewarding its loyal followers? Is one state or region getting more goodies than any other? Are women and minorities getting a fair share of the plums?

• What does the performance of the president-elect and the transition team foretell about their grasp of power and the ways of Washington?

• What is the legacy of the outgoing administration? In style and substance, what will the outgoing president be remembered for?

The list goes on. The enterprising reporter will triple it with good ideas.

WHITE HOUSE ENTERPRISE

Enterprise reporting in the White House, as opposed to spot news and analysis, has been in decline since the 1980s. In the White House context, enterprise reporting is essentially explanatory and assessment journalism. One of the best at it in earlier years was Congressional Quarterly publisher Bob Merry, then reporting for The Wall Street Journal. Merry had a knack for anticipating events, reflecting on history and placing the White House perspective in the context of both. He did it, he says, by spending a lot of time just listening to presidential speeches and trying to fit them into a strategy. He also paid close attention to the debates within the White House, as people grappled over power and disagreed on the direction the nation should take. "If you take both those steps," he says, "you can get help from inside (the White House) when you try to do an analytical assessment on where they're headed and what kind of pitfalls they've failed to recognize."

Several approaches work well in covering the White House in depth. Among them are the following.

Profiles

A well-written profile is an excellent way to tell a story because it gives it a human dimension. You should try to profile the president's top aides individually and the cabinet members as a group. Some of the best stuff out of the Carter and Reagan White Houses was the profiles of their colorful and otherwise interesting senior advisers. Because George W. Bush kept a small inner circle of top aides, profiles in 2001 of such senior advisers as Karen Hughes and Karl Rove were studied carefully for clues on how the younger Bush managed to gain stature during his first year in office.

Assessments

Just as a congressional correspondent has an obligation to evaluate the performance of members of Congress, a White House correspondent has an obligation to assess the job of key figures on the beat, starting with the president. Assessments don't have to be tied to the calendar; they can be done just as easily at 200 days into an administration as at 100. But they should be done regularly; those that are tied to one aspect of presidential performance—say economic or environmental policy—can be just as effective as those that are all encompassing.

Assessing a president's record on appointments to the judiciary, relations with Congress or use of the symbols of the office provides important information that contributes to the big picture. To do an overview assessment, talk to political leaders in both parties, political consultants, lobbyists, pollsters, special interest crusaders, members of Congress and well-placed congressional staffers. Seek more than inside-the-Beltway opinions. Get out of Washington, preferably to a mainstream political state, and talk to voters. Finally, draw on your own observations and judgment: Watch the president carefully in a variety of settings and gauge the public's reaction.

Assess the vice president periodically, as well as the collective perform-ance of the president's top staff. And keep your eye peeled for presidential actions that set a tone in style or substance or leave lasting impressions with voters. An example of the latter was Gerald Ford's decision a month into his presidency to pardon Richard Nixon.

The Political Context

Although turf battles often ensue, White House reporters should have the option of getting intensely involved in covering the purely political side of the presidency. This includes the incumbent's gearing up for a re-election cam-paign and, if you are staying on the beat into the next administration, the oppor-tunity to occasionally cover all major candidates to succeed the incumbent. Being able to get out in the country and talk to politicians and voters is vital for keeping perspective. Halfway through a term, you should be charting the elec-tion or re-election prospects of the president or the reigning party's leading can-didates, as well as the president's political relationship with party leaders. As part of that coverage, you should monitor the Federal Election Commission for reports of exploratory or full-fledged presidential campaign committees.

Question-and-Answer Format

Many of the issues that pass through the Oval Office are complex. The easy out for any White House reporter is to present an issue in a political context (for exam-ple, does the White House have the votes to sustain a presidential veto?) and then move on to something else. The conscientious reporter will carefully study the issue, consult the experts and go beyond the White House fact sheets. Then the reporter will try to explain not just the politics but also the substance of the issue, with some historical context. One reader-friendly way to do this is to treat the subject with a question-and-answer format that proceeds from the broadest and most general ques-tions to the nitty-gritty details that a more sophisticated reader will appreciate. The advantage of this format is that it permits you to synthesize and interpret.

WHITE HOUSE RESOURCES

The basic resources most useful for covering the White House are sur-prisingly few and most of them are provided by the press office on the White House Web site, including these:

Fact sheets and briefing papers. Every significant announcement by the president is accompanied by a fact sheet giving basic and sometimes extensive details—from the White House point of view, of course. On foreign trips and economic summits, the fact sheet blossoms into a thick briefing book with voluminous background on the host countries, their top leaders, the issues being discussed, and so forth.

Transcripts. Verbatim accounts of presidential speeches, press conferences, official toasts, impromptu presidential remarks, press briefings and the like are provided to reporters within minutes of their occurrence. Texts of major speeches, or excerpts thereof, are often provided in advance, followed by the as-delivered versions.

Pool reports. Regular White House reporters are assigned to writing pools on a rotating basis, whether the president is at home or on the road. Pool reports are expected at the end of the pool cycle or after any significant event and are quickly reproduced for other reporters by the press office. There are no guidelines on how to write a pool report. Some reporters like to quickly summarize the news and observations worth passing on; others like to be poetic and include lots of color. One rule: As a pooler, you can't keep things to yourself, nor can you file a story from your own pool report before it's distributed to your colleagues. The best advice: Never go on a pool assignment without a tape recorder.

Schedules. The president's daily schedules and schedules of upcoming trips, dubbed the "bible," not only govern the lives of White House reporters but also serve as boilerplate for many advance stories. They are usually distributed at least once a day by the press office, but frequently they are updated, especially when the president is traveling. Concerns about security following the terrorist attack on the United States in 2001 resulted in some restrictions on how much schedule information would be provided in advance.

OTHER RESOURCES

Any number of reference works can be helpful to the White House correspondent, including the Congressional Record, Congressional Quarterly, National Journal and the Federal Register. Of most help, however, is the Weekly Compilation of Presidential Documents, published and sold by the Government Printing Office. The Weekly Compilation carries bill signings, presidential speeches, veto messages, nominations—every official action by the president is there. Two other presidential documents, the budget and the annual economic report to Congress, are released within days of each other around the end of January and are useful as a checkpoint for later pronouncements on spending and economic policy.

8 THE COURTS

THE SUPREME COURT

Covering the Supreme Court (www.supremecourtus.gov) retains an aura of mystery that seems almost as imposing as the building itself. No other institution of government is so bound by custom, tradition and secrecy, and no other press corps in Washington seems to reflect so precisely the institution it covers. After a fewyears on the beat, Court reporters seem to take on the demeanor of lawyers and judges. They impart a sense of propriety and sobriety that would be entirely out of place in the White House press room or on a presidential campaign plane. It thus seems only natural that when the Court press corps has its biennial off-the-record lunch with the chief justice, reporters are seated by seniority.

Except for the handful of reporters assigned full time to the Court, it is a tough beat. Reporters who must divide their time between the legal beat and other agencies or specialties worry about falling behind in tracking the thousands of cases filed with the Court each year. Regional reporters who go to the Court infrequently to pursue a local case are at an even greater disadvantage. There are no press conferences, no claque of leakers and no public relations machinery—just a few basic documents. "It's the weirdest place you'll ever cover, because you can't talk to the people you cover," says the Associated Press's Anne Gearan. "They're off limits, and you really don't see them anyway."

Echoes Robert Greenberger of The Wall Street Journal, who moved to the Court in 1999 after covering the State Department: "What's different about it is that it is extraordinarily secretive. There's absolutely no effort to communicate with the press corps that covers it. You don't overcome the problem, you just write about the opinions and decisions that they make. And you never really get any insight of how they make them."

Covering the high court is one of the most specialized beats in Washington, which, despite its drawbacks, makes it one of the most professionally appealing. "It requires a tremendous investment of time, just to understand how the institution works," says the Chicago Tribune's Jan Crawford Greenburg. But Greenburg says the biggest appeal of the beat is that the Court press

corps is collegial and congenial, and that because information is so tightly controlled by the justices, there's none of the scramble for scoops that characterizes
many of the beats in Washington. "You don't have to waste your time trying to
get a story four hours before it's going to be released to the world, which to me
is just preposterous; that's one of the worst things about journalism."

The highly specialized nature of reporting and analyzing the Court's
actions involves one of the oldest debates in the Court press corps: Does formal legal training make for a better Court reporter? Most lawyer-reporters,
such as Greenburg, argue that legal training helps any reporter cut through
legalese and understand the import of a Court decision. "Certainly it's not necessary, and there are obviously terrific court reporters who don't (have formal
legal training)," says Greenburg. "But it helps immediately with the learning
curve when you're walking up to this imposing institution with all those
arcane rules and traditions. Just to understand some of the law behind the rulings is tremendously helpful." Reporters who are not lawyers, led by Tony
Mauro of Legal Times and American Lawyer Media, argue that because
reporters should always try to think like the audiences they're writing for, they
don't need any formal education in the law.

Getting Started

The basic requirement for covering the Court, either full time or sporad-
ically, is understanding how the place works, and you can start at the press
office. Kathleen Arberg runs one of the leanest press offices in Washington,
and gets generous praise from press corps regulars. She and her staff do not
grind out press releases or spend their days offering interpretation of Court
actions, though they can be helpful in explaining the technical meaning of the
Court's procedural action.

"We're facilitators here," says Arberg. "We don't do spin. We very rarely
speak on the record. But we do a lot of guiding, a lot of let me tell you what
the process is, let me tell you who you might want to contact, and here's the
counsel names and numbers, here's the brief you want to look at, here's the
great guidebook for the kind of questions you're asking. . . ."

From a small suite of offices in the northwest corner of the ground floor
of the Court building, Arberg and her staff supervise the flow of paper to
reporters. If you go to their offices cold, they'll give you a quick tour of the
facilities, show you where Court documents are filed and show you the press
room facilities, reference books, copy machine and a terminal that allows
reporters to check the Court docket. Only news organizations with full-time
Court reporters have work space assigned in the press room. Fewer than 30
reporters have Court press credentials, but anyone who needs to cover a case

can be admitted with a commonly recognized credential such as a White House or Congressional Gallery press pass.

Arberg will also put you on a call list for contact when there are fast-breaking events, such as emergency applications and stays of execution, on a case in which you might be interested. She'll go through the drill on paper flow. She'll promise to provide copies of the justices' schedules and speeches when they're made available to her, which varies widely among the justices. If you feel self-important enough to want to be introduced to the justices, she'll advise you to write them individually and introduce yourself. (If they think you're important enough, they'll invite you to their chambers for a handshake and an off-the-record chat.)

The next thing you need to understand is the paper flow. You are primarily interested in five things: the docket of cases filed with the Court, applications for emergency action (usually of most interest to regional reporters), the conference list of cases awaiting preliminary consideration by the justices, the orders list of cases granted review or denied review by the Court, and the opinions issued after oral argument and a vote by the justices. Despite some concessions to modern technology, such as posting docket information and opinions on the Internet when they are released, the Court still does not put cert petitions or briefs online. This means that you'll usually have to go to the Court to read the documents in paper form, although briefs are sometimes posted online by interest groups or parties to a case.

Although the Court is in session only about nine months a year, its work goes on almost year-round. When a Court session ends in early summer, the work of the next session, which begins the first Monday in October, is presaged by a carried-over orders list of cases that the Court already has agreed to hear. In addition, new cases continue to arrive at the rate of about a hundred a week. Each is given a docket number and filed in the public documents room, just down the hall from the press room.

By mid-September, and often much sooner, the press office will issue the first arguments list for the fall, running through October; others follow at roughly monthly intervals through April. It will also release a consolidated conference list of the petitions awaiting the justices' decision on whether to grant review. Reporters look at the conference list, which is not for publication, as a kind of tip sheet. If a case is listed on a particular conference list, chances are good that the Court will act on it soon thereafter.

When the Court begins sitting in October, new orders lists are released and oral argument begins. A press office tape recording will tell you which arguments are upcoming and on which days opinions will be released. Orders continue to issue three Mondays each month, with oral argument Monday through Wednesday two weeks of the month. Usually there are two arguments a day.

By mid- to late November, the Court begins issuing opinions on Tuesday and Wednesday, promptly at 10 a.m. There is no advance word on which decisions will come down, and the curse of Court reporters is having editors ask them which decisions are expected on a given day. For some reporters, this is the biggest frustration of covering the court. "It's absolutely ridiculous," says the Tribune's Greenburg. "They do nothing to make it easier for reporters . . . they could make things much easier and serve the public interest by, among many other things, letting us know when opinions are coming down and what they're going to be, so the press is prepared, so we've got our ducks in a row."

Meanwhile, new conference lists are released preceding the three Fridays a month in which the justices meet privately to consider petitions. Most of the decisions reached in those private meetings—whether to hear a case or not (grant certiorari or deny certiorari)—will be announced the following Monday as part of the latest orders list.

Oral argument continues until the last week of April, after which the justices take a one-week recess and then return for the end-of-session onslaught. With one-third to one-half of expected opinions still pending, the pace quickens: Justices begin sitting every Monday to issue orders and opinions, and they begin conferencing on Thursdays, instead of Fridays. By mid-June, they often sit more than one day a week, and as often as five days near the end. The press office tape recording during this period advertises the next week's opinion days as regular (four or fewer opinions) or heavy (more than four opinions).

Although the Court's schedule is dependable and predictable, knowing when a certain opinion will be rendered is neither. Consequently, Court reporters spend much of their time preparing for news that will break on deadline. The most concentrated preparation comes in late summer and early fall, when reporters must not only wade through a backlog of new filings but also background themselves on cases already set for argument in the new term. Reporters who cover national legal affairs full time, such as Greenburg, monitor the Federal Appeals Courts regularly and are often familiar with major cases before they're filed at the high court. But all serious reporters devise some system to keep files on high-profile cases.

If you're new to the beat, you can take steps to prepare yourself adequately. Most of them involve developing sources you'll need later. First you need to identify the cases that interest you. You can scan each of the petitions as they are filed at the Court, but that is time-consuming. Several publications, including the Bureau of National Affairs' U.S. Law Week, briefly summarize filed cases. In August or September, National Law Journal publishes an extensive summary of cases granted review for the fall term.

If you're a regional reporter, you'll want to watch for cases being filed from the appeals court circuit you represent. You'll also want to talk to the offices of the attorney general and the chief state prosecutor in the states you represent to see what cases they may be bringing to the high court or otherwise participating in. Similarly, you'll want to check with the state offices of the American Civil Liberties Union. The ACLU gets involved as a party or amicus curiae (friend of the court) in about one-fourth of all cases heard by the Supreme Court. You can also check with law schools in the states you cover.

There are many places in Washington to check also. At the State and Local Legal Center, organizations such as the National Association of Counties are frequently preparing amicus briefs for upcoming cases. The National Association of Attorneys General sponsors moot court sessions to help state lawyers prepare for argument before the high court. The association may let you sit in on these sessions if you'll agree not to write about them until after the real argument.

Trade associations and other lobbying and legal groups monitor and frequently participate in pending cases. Some, such as the U.S. Chamber of Commerce, the ACLU and the Washington Legal Foundation, hold press briefings or seminars to preview cases of interest in the new term. You should also maintain contact with the office of the solicitor general at the Justice Department. Not only does the SG argue the government's position in major cases before the high court, but the SG's office often has a part in deciding which lower-court rulings involving government agencies should be appealed. And it frequently files briefs in cases in which the government is not a party. The office will put you on its distribution list if you ask.

Once you've decided which cases interest you, the next step is to read all briefs associated with those cases. The growth of the Internet has made this task much easier than it used to be—most organizations filing amicus briefs now post them on their Web sites, and legal sites like Findlaw.com also carry them. Only then should you call participants; few lawyers have the time to explain from scratch what a case is about. If you've studied the briefs, you'll be able to ask reasonably intelligent questions.

Most national-beat Court reporters who plow through these hundreds of cases have some latitude in deciding which ones to focus on and at what point they will write in depth about them. Tony Mauro describes these options as "four bites at the apple," to wit:

- When the case is first filed with the high court
- When the Court agrees or refuses to hear the case
- When the oral argument is held
- When the decision comes down.

Major cases often warrant more than one "bite," and if you're a regional reporter, you may be asked to bird-dog a case at every step because of parochial interests. Mauro says he is least likely to write about a case when it's filed. A little background: About 7,000 cases are filed with the high court each year. Nearly a third come from state cases in which constitutional questions are raised; nearly two-thirds on appeal from federal courts. The Court usually refuses to hear all but fewer than 100 cases. Of those accepted for review, most are granted a writ of certiorari for full review, including oral argument and a written opinion. In a few instances, the Court may dispense with argument and issue a brief unsigned opinion called a per curiam. Most cases accepted by the Court arrive by way of petitions for certiorari.

Many cases, nonetheless, are written about when they are accepted—or rejected—by the Court. It takes four votes to accept a case, and as Mauro points out, "very often the very fact that the Court even agreed to step into a certain controversy is news." Granting review is also important because it means that interested parties may get involved as friends of the Court.

Conversely, denial of review can be newsworthy for the simple reason noted by lawyer Alan Morrison of the Public Citizen Litigation Group: "It means that this is the end of the line." The Court can affirm a lower court opinion without giving its reasons and without holding argument, and less experienced reporters sometimes overplay a denial of "cert" by suggesting that the Supreme Court is thereby endorsing a lower court's decision. The most accurate interpretation of a denial of cert is simply that the Court chose not to get involved in the dispute. There are many reasons why the Court denies cert that have nothing to do with the merits of the case.

The oral argument is often much less interesting than the publicity surrounding the case. The one hour of argument, divided equally between the lawyers for each side, often involves technical legal points that are boring to write about and even more boring to read. The wire services traditionally cover only about a third of the arguments, and most regular reporters at the Court focus on one argument a day, at most.

The courtroom press gallery accommodates only about 30 persons routinely; extra chairs are added for major cases, but most of those seats have a poor view. Temporary passes are available for nonregulars on a first-come, first-served basis, but the press office often uses a sign-up list for major arguments, which is announced in advance on the wire service daybooks.

It's sometimes worthwhile to cover an argument even if you're not going to write about that phase of the appeal. It's an opportunity to meet interested parties in the case—people whose time, expertise and quotes you may be seeking later when the decision is rendered. Also, Court regulars like to monitor arguments to see if the justices' questions give some hint of how the Court may be leaning in the case. Trying to project an outcome based on the give-and-take of an argument is risky business, of course. Justices enjoy playing the role of devil's advocate in their questioning.

Reporters often use an upcoming argument as the peg to explore a case in some depth. "Advancing" an argument is a convenient point at which to go to the place where the case originated and interview the litigants and their lawyers as well as other interested parties, some of whom may have filed amicus briefs. Television reporters, whose cameras are barred from most of the Supreme Court building, often use this occasion to shoot film for use on argument day or when the decision is announced.

The one risk in advancing an argument at great length is that the case may be decided on some minor point or technicality that will make your carefully crafted prose superfluous. It's a risk worth taking, however, in the view of most reporters.

Opinions by the high court get extensive coverage, both in the national and regional press. Because they are always issued just after 10 a.m., reporters for the wire services and online news outlets routinely write stories ahead of time with alternate leads to reflect that an appeal has been upheld or reversed. On busy Court days, even reporters working on morning newspaper deadlines experience a time crunch that dictates quick work.

Getting Help

The first help for the scrambling reporter comes in the form of a headnote, or syllabus, attached to each opinion. This brief summary tells how the Court ruled, who wrote the opinion for the majority, who dissented, who wrote concurring opinions on either side and who did not take part in the decision (though not why).

After you have read the headnote, the next obvious step is to talk to the lawyers on both sides in the case. If the case is significant, you'll want to talk to other sources, ranging from the original litigants, amici and other affected interest groups to legal scholars. Quoting "experts" impresses editors (if not readers), and the more quotable they are, the better.

It is in getting reaction to a court decision that the Internet has come to play a revolutionary role in the reporting process. "The word on what the court has said and people's reaction to it has really sped up," says David Savage, who has covered the Court for the Los Angeles Times since 1986. Savage, who recalls the days when bicycle messengers were used to deliver reaction statements around Washington, says the advent of the Internet and e-mail means that interest groups are able to see court opinions and e-mail their reactions to reporters by midafternoon. In the old days, reporters often had to call or fax summaries of decisions to such groups and wait for them to craft a response.

It is precisely the ease with which reaction is registered, however, that puts a premium on reporters being knowledgeable about the subject matter. Says the Tribune's Greenburg:

> One of the things you should be most wary of when doing legal reporting in general—it is so susceptible to spin. And if you don't have any outside expertise, or if you haven't done your homework, or if you haven't read

the briefs, you're just too susceptible to spin, because the minute now that an opinion is released the e-mails are flying fast and furious, the fax machines are cranking out reaction about what the opinion means, what it doesn't mean, who it's a disaster for, who it is a huge victory for. If you haven't followed that case, and you don't understand the legal issues, you really can do your readers and viewers a disservice.

It's kind of remarkable the whole machinery that's come into its own in the last several years to respond to Supreme Court rulings, and you really have to be able to shake all that off and do a steely eyed independent look at what the court is saying, and if you've read the lower court opinions and you've read the briefs, you've gone to the argument, you can do that.

There are plenty of people who can help, of course. Greenburg is partial to professors at the University of Chicago Law School, which she attended. Mauro frequently talks to Richard Lazarus, who heads the Supreme Court Institute at Georgetown University, and Washington lawyer Tom Goldstein, whom Mauro describes as a Supreme Court "junkie." The AP's Gearan sometimes trolls the Internet to find law professors who have expertise in certain subjects.

Keeping It Simple

Once you've gathered a full measure of quotes and interpretations, the challenge is to write the story in language that laypeople can understand and that conveys the import and essence of the opinion. In his book "The Reporter and the Law," Lyle Denniston, the longtime Court reporter for the Baltimore Sun, observes that "to be able to write simply, any journalist, on the court beat or elsewhere, must understand penetratingly."

Bruce Fein, a conservative Washington lawyer and constitutional scholar, contends that some Court reporters don't understand penetratingly. Says Fein:

> Often, the Court reporter in covering a constitutional case will fail to recognize that to deny a claim of a constitutional right is not to say your local council or state legislature couldn't enact the right as a matter of statutory law. Reporting typically proceeds along the line that if something is denied a constitutional status by the Supreme Court, then there isn't any way you can ever receive that right, which is a grossly misleading understanding of what are the powers of the Court and what it is doing.

Noting that the Court is bound by custom to precedent, Fein adds:

> Too often, newspapers assign reporters to cover the Court who don't have any background in what's occurring at all, and therefore they're totally inept at conveying to the reader how this case fits in with the others so the

reader can get a general idea of what the state of the law is. You can't have on-the-job training for everyone covering the Court. . . . It's simply not true that one can understand the high court's decisions by reading thirty cert petitions two weeks before the new term begins.

If you've studied law, on the other hand, the temptation may be to slip into legalese or to interpret the law yourself. One way to avoid that is to shun legal terms as much as possible. Denniston, who has written for several trade journals as well as a general newspaper audience, "long ago adopted a rigid practice of not using legal terms in copy, no matter the audience." He says, "If I have to use one in a quote, I'll immediately follow the quote with a definition." Defining legal terms—and getting the definition right—is a requisite of good Court reporting. Providing facts, definitions and examples can make the difference between a dull, impenetrable story and an interesting, understandable one.

Good basic reporting also includes the breakdown of the vote in a Court opinion, as well as the authors of majority and dissenting opinions. Lawyers obviously want to know these things, but nonlawyers who follow the Court are also interested in voting factions. "It's more important when justices do something out of character," says Public Citizen's Morrison. "For people who follow courts, it's the 'who' that matters."

Court Customs

No matter how many legal sources you develop, no matter how much law you study or court lore you absorb, no matter how many briefs you read—you'll still face a major frustration on the Supreme Court beat: The subjects you are covering are almost totally inaccessible. The Court's attitude toward the press hardened during the reign of Chief Justice Warren Burger, and it wasn't helped any by the publication of Bob Woodward and Scott Armstrong's "The Brethren" in 1979. Some members of the press corps think Burger's successor, William Rehnquist, is a little more accommodating on questions of press access. "Rehnquist seems a little less uptight about that stuff," says Mauro. "Burger was paranoid about leaks and any contact with the press."

Most of the debate about press access has centered on two issues: televising oral argument before the Court and disclosure about the justices' health. Support for cameras in the Court is strong among broadcast journalists and some print journalists, and it is substantial throughout the legal community. Advocates point out that an overwhelming majority of state courts have admitted cameras. Conservative Bruce Fein and liberal Alan Morrison agree that televised argument would be both educational and convenient for Court followers who can't be in Washington or gain access to the cramped courtroom if they're here.

The health issue was raised pointedly in the declining years of Justice William O. Douglas and erupted with increasing frequency in the 1980s and 1990s as several of the justices reached the age of 80. But the discussion wasn't confined to the octogenarians. The slurred speech of Rehnquist while on the bench was the subject of much speculation until it was revealed that he had been taking medication for back pain. Justice Sandra Day O'Connor prompted much gossip when she appeared to be wearing a wig following surgery for breast cancer in 1988, but she steadfastly refused to acknowledge questions about whether she had hair loss due to cancer treatments.

Another secrecy issue raised by Mauro concerns recusals, instances in which justices excuse themselves from taking part in an argument or voting on an opinion. Although these actions are assumed to be taken to avoid a conflict of interest—or the appearance of one—some justices never explain the reasons they recuse themselves. Some offer explanations infrequently, though never in writing.

Are these issues ever taken up directly with the justices? That's one of the mysteries about the Supreme Court press corps, for despite the "equally bad" treatment of the press dictated by Court custom, some justices do hold off-the-record lunches or chats with selected reporters. "In 22 years covering the Court," says Mauro, "I've only had one on-the-record conversation with a justice, and only about a dozen or 15 off-the-record conversations." Such meetings have a reputation of being interesting but not very substantive. The biennial lunches of Court regulars with the chief justice are "helpful in getting a sense of him and what his interests are," says the L.A. Times' Savage. "One of his (Rehnquist's) favorite topics is books he's working on, or others are working on. Everything from vacations, all kinds of topics. But not a lot of 'why did you decide this case that way,' and certainly none of 'how are you going to decide the next case?'"

Arberg notes that the lunches do in fact sometimes produce a change. Several years ago, reporters told the chief justice that they would like to be able to hear the announcement of opinions in the press room, so that they didn't have to go to the courtroom on deadline. The chief justice took the suggestion back to conference and as a result, speakers were installed in the press room for the announcement of opinions and orders.

The Enterprising Court Reporter

Court reporters and scholars agree that legal reporters don't distinguish themselves in the area known as enterprise. There is also considerable agreement on the reasons: Covering the Court involves so much reading and deadline reporting that little time is left for creative ideas. Editors don't consider court stories important enough to spend extra time and money on them. Laziness may even be a factor. "You have to get off your duff," says Mauro, "and some people don't want to do it."

"I suspect there's a whole lot of laziness in legal reporting, too," says Denniston. "People don't use their skills and aggressive energies as much as they should. . . . I don't like pack journalism, and you have a lot of it at the Court." But Denniston also blames news organizations for cutting back on space allowed for specialized reporting. He contends that that "is discouraging people from exploiting their expertise and opportunities, not only in law but everything else."

The debate over what constitutes enterprise reporting turned public and a little ugly in 1999 when the now-defunct Brill's Content magazine examined the issue in an article titled "May It Please the Court." The article noted that the scholarly aura of the Supreme Court press room frustrated some reporters enough to cut short their stint there. It also set tongues to wagging by drawing a sharp contrast between Mauro and New York Times reporter Linda Greenhouse because of their conflicting views on how narrowly the role of Court reporter should be drawn.

Greenhouse, who has covered the Court since 1981, was described as one who focuses her reporting and analysis narrowly on the Courts cases and decisions, while Mauro, who began reporting on the Court in 1979, was described as having a penchant for stories that "give insight into the justices as people, or for stories that put a human face on the Court."

The article recounted in detail how Mauro had exposed the justices' poor record in hiring minorities as clerks, and how The Times had ignored the story except to carry a brief Associated Press story and to criticize the Court in two editorials.

Mauro's exposé, albeit unusual for the Court's press corps, is a good example of enterprise reporting on the legal beat. Other examples might include the following.

IMPACT STORIES

Most experienced Court reporters take a stab at describing the potential impact of a Court opinion when it's handed down, but all too often the effort falls short of explaining to the average reader how it will affect his or her life, if at all. "If there's any deficiency I see in the Supreme Court press corps, and that includes me too," says Lyle Denniston, "it's that we're writing law stories mostly as law stories, and not as stories with direct human impact on real people." Even rarer is the instance in which a Court reporter revisits a decision months or years later to ask what happened to the original litigants, what the effect on relevant institutions was, and what new state or federal laws were spawned as a result of the decision.

An example of this kind of enterprise came from the Tribune's Greenburg in 1999 when she examined the effect of a 1998 Court ruling on same-sex discrimination. When the ruling in the case *Oncale vs. Sundowner Offshore Services Inc.* was announced, civil liberties groups were ecstatic. But a year later Greenburg reported that numerous lower courts were interpreting the ruling so narrowly that sex-discrimination claims were being smothered rather than expedited. She quoted the lawyer for the original plaintiff, oil-rig worker Joseph Oncale, lamenting that, ironically, he "may have set the cause of equal-employment rights back about 100 years."

ADVANCING ORAL ARGUMENT

Setting the stage for an argument is an opportunity not only to review the legal issues involved but also to explore the political, economic and social ramifications. Some of that information will be in the briefs, but it's also useful to talk to others who may be uninvolved but interested spectators.

HUMANIZING COURT STORIES

Press corps regulars often resist suggestions that they do People magazine stories about Supreme Court justices or the people who bring cases before them. Personal information about the justices is hard to come by, of course, but it has a lot of reader appeal, as do well-written stories about the personal trials and tribulations of carrying a case all the way to the highest court in the land.

THE CONFIRMATION PROCESS

The Senate's examination of a Supreme Court nominee is always a major story, but the reporting of it sometimes doesn't reflect that importance. National Public Radio's Nina Totenberg argues that the press gives short shrift to confirmation hearings for someone who may hold a critical job 25 to 30 years, when compared with the extensive coverage given a presidential candidate seeking a four-year term.

It takes hard digging to come up with a scoop on a nominee to the high court. Nominees frequently are lower court judges, which means they've probably led a fairly cloistered life in recent years. Most lawyers and bar association acquaintances are unlikely to bad-mouth them in anticipation of appearing before them. Long-standing groups like the ACLU, the National Association for the Advancement of Colored People Legal Defense and Educational Fund, and the Mexican-American Legal Defense and Educational Fund may provide more-candid appraisals.

Appeals court nominations can also touch off great controversy, and regional reporters must be alert for them. A prominent example of this came in 2002, when George W. Bush expended considerable political capital in a losing bid to place Charles Pickering, an Alabama federal district judge, on the U.S. Court of Appeals.

THE IMPACT OF JUDICIAL APPOINTMENTS

Appointments to the Supreme Court invite much speculation about philosophical swings and new alignments, as they should, but much less attention is paid to the impact a president has on the lower courts. Jimmy Carter, Ronald Reagan and Bill Clinton all had the opportunity to fill nearly half the federal judgeships at the district and appeals court levels. Carter appointed significant numbers of women and minorities, Reagan countered with significant numbers of conservatives, and Clinton countered that with an influx of liberal and moderate appointments, but few stories appeared assessing the legacy of these actions.

CONFERENCES

The annual meeting of the American Bar Association is often described by reporters as a gold mine for story ideas. Although senior Court reporters say they find it less essential, especially if they keep close tabs on cases pending before the Supreme Court, reporters newer to the beat can use the occasion to develop contacts and longer-range story projects.

FINANCIAL DISCLOSURE

The justices are required to file annual statements of their net worth, but—as with congressional disclosure forms—the information is too vague to permit a precise picture, because assets are listed by ranges of value. The enterprising reporter will scrutinize the reports nonetheless for evidence of stock trading, honoraria received, and so forth. Correlating these statements with justices' recusals in cases involving their holdings might produce interesting stories.

CASE STUDIES

You can pick one case in a lower court—preferably one that's a sure bet to go all the way to the Supreme Court and to be controversial—and follow it through the process, describing not only the process but also the issues and people involved.

PROFILES OF JUSTICES

It's not easy, but it is possible to profile a justice even if he or she won't agree to an interview. The Court press office keeps a list of former law clerks. Interviewing them is a prime place to start in trying to piece together a behind-the-scenes look at the justice. You can also use a justice's publication of a book as an excuse to ask for an interview in connection with writing a review. Several Court reporters did this in 2002, for example, when Justice O'Connor co-authored with her brother a memoir of growing up in eastern Arizona.

OTHER COURTS

The U.S. Court of Appeals for the District of Columbia Circuit

Although it has one of the most interesting caseloads, the U.S. Court of Appeals for the District of Columbia (www.cadc.uscourts.gov) gets little general press attention. Located in the same building as the U.S. District Court, the appeals court is the venue for most of the scores of petitions filed each year arising from decisions by the federal regulatory agencies. In fact, the federal government is a party to nearly three-fourths of the cases heard by the appeals court. Agencies such as the Nuclear Regulatory Commission and the Environmental Protection Agency are frequently challenged in this court.

The court's Web site contains a calendar of upcoming arguments and carries opinions that have been released. New petitions and briefs are available at the clerk's office and, as of 2002, the Court was contemplating electronic filing of petitions and briefs. Decisions are announced each Tuesday and Friday morning. There are no sourcebooks as such, but the Legal Times newspaper covers the court extensively enough to rank as a good resource. As with the Supreme Court, interest groups involved as litigants or amici usually make sure the press knows of significant arguments or pending decisions.

The U.S. Tax Court

The U.S. Tax Court (www.ustaxcourt.gov) is one of those out-of-the-way institutions in Washington that most reporters neither know about nor go near. Yet it can be the repository of great stories, especially for regional reporters.

The tax court, which is not part of the Internal Revenue Service, was set up in 1924 to handle cases in which taxpayers wanted to fight the IRS before paying a tax. It is a nonjury civil court with no criminal jurisdiction. Nineteen judges, who serve 15-year terms, travel the country hearing cases in some 80 cities. Another 14 special trial judges sit on small tax cases (concerning less than $50,000). The caseload is heavy, averaging about 20,000 suits a year. About 80 percent of the suits are filed by individuals and 20 percent by corporations.

There's not a lot of drama in tax court proceedings. In fact nearly nine in 10 cases are settled through negotiations before they go to trial. According to Court Clerk Charles Casazza, taxpayers tend to prevail in negotiated settlements, whereas the IRS more often comes out ahead in trials. But fascinating stories can be found in the cases, many involving ingenious schemes by which people tried to reduce or avoid their tax burden. Those schemes were especially prevalent before Congress eliminated a number of tax shelters in the 1986 tax reform bill. However, any case involving a celebrity or prominent local citizen or corporation is likely to make a good story. One bonus to tax court cases: Almost all of them include full copies of the tax returns in dispute— one of the rare instances when tax returns, with all their revealing details, enter the public record.

The tax court process works this way: If the IRS, upon completing an audit, decides to disallow a tax deduction, it sends a notice of deficiency to the taxpayer, who has 90 days to respond. If the taxpayer chooses to fight, he or she then files a petition with the court within those 90 days and pays a filing fee. The taxpayer also chooses from a list of cities where he or she would like the case to be heard. If the taxpayer elects to have the case designated a small tax case, and the amount involved is less than $50,000, he or she forfeits the right to appeal any decision by the tax court.

Looking for cases to write about at the tax court takes some work on your part, but it's a lot easier than it used to be. The court does not have a press office, and the court clerk does not deal with the problems of reporters. Opinions are posted online, but "stipulated decisions," in which an agreement is reached short of trial, are not. The court docket can be searched online by case number, name of individual or name of corporation.

The court calendar lists case docket numbers by the city where they will be heard, usually about five months in advance. By checking cities you're interested in, you may spot a familiar name. You can then ask for documents in the case, which are stored alphabetically in the file room.

You can also check the Commerce Clearing House Tax Court Reporter, which updates filings weekly with the case docket number, the name of the case, the year involved in the tax dispute, the amount involved, the lawyer representing the petitioner, and a brief discussion of the issues.

Unless you expect to cover the trial, which likely will be held outside Washington, your options are to do a spot story on the filing of the case or do an advance on the trial. If settlement is reached prior to trial, the reasons do not have to be publicly recorded. Court decisions are routinely announced by the court, and your best bet is to try to talk to the litigants and their lawyers.

The U.S. Court of Federal Claims

The U.S. Court of Federal Claims (www.uscfc.uscourts.gov) is the court where people who feel wronged by the government take their grievances: taxpayers seeking refunds (if the amount exceeds $10,000), government employees seeking back pay, government contractors charging breach of contract, and so forth. Oral arguments are heard by claims court judges, who serve for life, and decisions are available in the clerk's office. Like the tax court, the claims court is a good place for regional reporters to explore on a slow day.

The U.S. Court of Appeals for the Federal Circuit

Created to lighten the load of the rest of the appeals circuit, the U.S. Court of Appeals for the Federal Circuit (www.fedcir.gov) has exclusive jurisdiction over patent appeals and also hears appeals from the U.S. Court of Claims, the International Trade Commission and the U.S. Court of International Trade.

The U.S. Court of Appeals for the Armed Forces

As the court of last resort for military personnel convicted by court-martial, this court (www.armfor.uscourts.gov) is not a busy hangout for reporters, but it's one that reporters on the military or regional beat should be familiar with. Court personnel are helpful and seem eager to demonstrate that military justice is a fair and open process.

SELECTED RESOURCES

Guide to the U.S. Supreme Court. Published by Congressional Quarterly (www.cqpressbookstore.com), this massive book of more than a thousand pages is updated every 10 years or so, and is a valuable tool. Chock full of history about the Court, its members and its major decisions, the book is especially useful for studying Court precedents by subject area.

The Reporter and the Law. This complete step-by-step, nuts-and-bolts guide to legal reporting from the local courthouse to the Supreme Court was published by Hastings House and written by retired Baltimore Sun reporter Lyle Denniston, a 40-year veteran of legal writing. It includes an extensive glossary of legal terms.

Judicial Staff Directory. Published by Congressional Quarterly (www.jsd.cq.com), this guide lists all federal court judges and court staffs, provides maps of circuit and district court jurisdictions and, most important, includes biographies of judges and top staff members throughout the system.

U.S. Law Week. Published weekly by the Bureau of National Affairs (www.bna.com), U.S. Law Week is considered by most reporters to be the most complete regular guide to Supreme Court proceedings. Law Week gives a brief summary of every case filed with the Court and more extensive summaries of cases granted review. It also summarizes key oral argument, provides a running schedule of upcoming events and separately provides subscribers with copies of all opinions.

National Law Journal. The National Law Journal (www.nlj.com), published by American Lawyer Media, is known for its serious reporting and analysis of contemporary legal issues. Of particular interest for Washington reporters are annual previews of the next Supreme Court term, as well as summaries of Supreme Court action and a column called "Riding the Circuits," which reviews key decisions in all 13 appellate courts.

LEXIS/NEXIS. Access to either of these online computerized databases (www.LexisNexis.com) gives you quick entrée to almost every courthouse in America. Both provide full texts of opinions of all federal and state court cases, and most specialized court cases, going back to the founding of the court.

The Oyez Project. This project at Northwestern University (www.nwu.edu) contains a multimedia database of some 1,000 hours of audio materials, summaries of more than 1,000 Supreme Court decisions, biographical material on all justices and a virtual reality tour of the Supreme Court building.

Cornell University Law School Legal Information Institute. This Web site (www.supct.law.cornell.edu/supct) includes high court opinions, summaries of key decisions and a searchable archives.

Findlaw. The "Supreme Court Center" at this Web site (www.findlaw.com) includes orders, opinions, calendars, briefs, and so forth.

Preview. Published by the American Bar Association, Preview covers all cases and all issues before the Court, usually before they go to argument, and is written by legal experts. It also lists counsel on cases and any third-party attorneys and their phone numbers. Copies of Preview are kept in the press room.

State and Local Legal Center. A service of the U.S. Conference of Mayors (www.usmayors.org), this center is a pro bono operation set up to give state and local governments the kind of sophisticated help in preparing briefs that civil and constitutional rights litigants have long received from groups like the NAACP and the ACLU. The center, which produces about 25 amicus briefs a year, usually gets involved in cases in which the federal government is trying to preempt state or local authority. Supreme Court counsel for members such as the National Association of Counties are valuable sources for reporters advancing a case or reporting a decision.

National Association of Attorneys General. The association (www.naag.org) acts as a clearinghouse for the attorneys general in 50 states and five territories. It offers help in the form of briefs, moot courts to prepare AGs for argument before the high court, and annual seminars for AGs expecting to have cases before the high court. It also sends out newsletters and bulletins at least once a month.

Public interest groups. If you're a regular at the Court, you won't have to work hard to find interest group sources for Court stories; usually they'll seek you out. The granddaddy of public interest litigating groups is the ACLU (www.aclu.org), which has been around since 1920. It is a key source for reporters because it gets involved in about a fourth of all cases reviewed by the Supreme Court, either directly or as a friend of the Court. The ACLU also has a reputation for responding quickly to Court opinions, often within minutes.

The group's Washington office is across the street from the Supreme Court. Other interest groups with a heavy investment in Court activities include the NAACP Legal Defense and Educational Fund (www.naacpldf.org), which focuses on civil rights cases; the Southern Poverty Law Center (www.splcenter.org), which is active in civil rights cases; the Public Citizen Litigation Group (www.citizen.org), a Ralph Nader group whose director, Alan Morrison, is a frequent participant in argument before the Court and is a recognized constitutional law expert; and the Washington Legal Foundation (www.wlf.org), a comparative newcomer created by conservative lawyers seeking to counter the influence of liberal groups such as the ACLU. Many of the interest groups conduct annual seminars on the Court and publish newsletters and bulletins updating their litigation activity.

9 THE POLITICAL BEAT

The political beat has long been a plum assignment, with good reason: It's as simple as the police beat, but with more glamour. Some beats require an understanding of complex theories and concepts; the political beat requires an understanding of human nature.

For that reason, the best political writers are people who like politicians. That may seem obvious, but it's not. Increasingly in recent years, newcomers to the political beat have been intense young men and women who cover the mechanics of modern-day campaigns with great insight but betray an apparent distaste for many of the characters involved, including the candidates. These are people that retired political columnist Jack Germond describes as "salad-eaters," who seem to prefer dining together rather than with campaign advisers.

One result of this cultural shift has been a lot of clinical dissection of high-tech tactics and strategies, devoid of flesh and blood. Chances are, if you don't like trying to capture human emotions, and you feel more comfortable with scribes and scholars than with scoundrels and schemers, you'll never be a really good political writer.

Judy Keen, who has covered politics since the late 1980s for USA Today, says of the beat: "I just love the drama. I love the opportunity to watch. I like politicians and I think most reporters who cover politics have to." Keen says she agrees with Germond that "there's a sort of disdain in how we treat (politicians). And what we expect of them. And there's also a gotcha mentality, that you can make your professional reputation by ferreting out something negative about someone. I sense there's more relish taken in that kind of reporting than in good explanatory reporting or feature reporting about campaigns and what's at stake."

DEFINING THE BEAT

The beauty of the political beat, assuming you are on good terms with your editors and have any imagination at all, is that it has almost no limits. On any given day, the best political story in Washington may be a debate on the floor of the Senate, a new set of budget-deficit projections, a backstairs fight at the White House or a developing scandal at the Justice Department. You can put almost anything that happens in Washington into a political context, which means that you can even poach on other reporters' turf and usually get away with it.

Yet some political reporters have a purist attitude. If a story doesn't involve the president's latest approval rating or the latest projected gains and losses in the congressional elections, it's not worthy of their attention. That is the easy way out, for Washington is heavily populated with political "experts" who will comment on hidden meanings behind the latest numbers, ensuring that you can wrap up a 700-word analysis before 5 p.m.

"Horse race" stories—who's up, who's down, who's fading, who's got the Big Mo—are a legitimate part of political reporting. They're fun to do and they appeal to a wider audience than do most policy-oriented stories. But they also reflect the dark side of pack journalism. The focus of most of the political press corps in Washington is so narrow that vast areas go virtually uncovered.

Setting the Agenda

Every reporting beat has a select few who pretty much set the agenda, and the political beat is no different. Germond, who was a Washington bureau chief for Gannett and a Washington Star editor before becoming a television commentator and columnist for The Baltimore Sun, observes that "90 percent of the coverage of campaigns is derivative of what 10 percent produce." To some extent, that phenomenon is a function of visibility. A brilliant, original piece of reporting in a Seattle paper may never prompt a copycat version; any above-average story in The New York Times or The Washington Post will set members of the pack on the chase. Germond and his former columnist partner, Jules Witcover, were considered the best at charting the "inside baseball" of campaign tactics and strategy, on which the junkies of the political community—the press and politicians—thrive.

The Post's David Broder has long been in a class by himself as spotter of political trends and arbiter of political etiquette. Because he writes without obvious bias, he alone can shake up a national political campaign with one column.

But political writing is not a closed shop. Anyone with the determination to demonstrate sincerity can become a member. Judgments on who is serious on the political beat and who isn't are remarkably similar. Germond, guru to two generations of young reporters, makes a sharp distinction between campaign reporters and full-time political reporters. The former category includes scores of eager beavers who show up on campaign planes during the presidential cycle, then return to the relative obscurity of Capitol Hill or the labor beat. Political consultant William Carrick, a former Edward Kennedy aide who managed Richard Gephardt's 1988 presidential campaign, says he has an obvious prejudice for reporters he has known a long time and whose reporting he has followed. Beyond that, Carrick says he makes judgments based on how diligent a reporter is, how much of a quick study the reporter is, and whether the reporter does the story as promised—and has the clout to get it into print or on the air. Polling analyst Greg Schneiders, an adviser to several Democratic presidential candidates, as well as a former Senate and Carter White House aide, rates veteran political reporters as experts in their field. "They understand politics better than White House or congressional reporters understand their beats," says Schneiders.

Developing Sources

As on other beats, one key to success in covering politics lies in the number and quality of sources you have. Recasting the definitive work of the heavy hitters might allow the "derivative" journalists referred to by Germond to get by, but if you've set out to be a serious political writer, you'll have to cultivate your own source network—pollsters, media advisers, speech writers. The key is personal contact. You can't adequately develop sources by telephone; you need to get out and meet people, have coffee or breakfast or lunch with them. Without a Washington outlet, you are known only to the extent that you make yourself known.

Says Germond: "You have to build all your sources on a personal basis over a period of years. You can do that. You can get good sources, but it takes work and persistence and effort. You have to go to these guys' states and court them. . . . But any reporter working for any paper can build a network of sources that are reliable, and that he'll have access to, just by working at it."

The best time to develop sources is early. You need to establish your credibility during the political doldrums if you want to have your phone calls returned during the political high season. "The reporters who get their phone calls returned in even-numbered years are the ones who phone you and have lunch with you in the odd-numbered years," says pollster Peter Hart.

The quality of your source network is just as important as its size, if not more so. One perplexing trend among young political reporters is the reliance on political science professors as experts on campaign politics. Perhaps that tendency reflects insecurity in the reporter or in editors who think that a quote from anyone—anyone—gives a story credibility. Let's stipulate: Political science professors can be helpful in putting political trends into a historical context, and they usually are easy to reach by phone, but having studied a political experience is not the same thing as having lived it. Politicians or hired guns who have seen their best handiwork derided and rejected by the voters, have turned certain defeat into victory, have created the campaign ad that became an icon of the trade, or have spent endless hours on the phone trying to raise that last $50,000, not once but several times—these are the people who understand what politics is all about.

And you need to know more than just Washington-based campaign operatives. The perspective of experienced state and local political leaders and officeholders, and of their behind-the-scenes advisers, is as useful in presidential campaigns as it is obviously essential in reporting congressional and gubernatorial campaigns. Every state and major city has lawyers, businesspeople and public relations operatives who are tightly wired into one or both political parties. Cultivating these kinds of sources outside the Beltway is a vital part of establishing your credentials as a political writer.

Don't waste your time on sources who are no longer in the loop just because they're nice guys who like to talk to Washington reporters. On the other hand, protect without fail the confidentiality of sources whose judgment you've come to trust.

THE WASHINGTON POLITICAL SCENE

Political Consultants

Few recent trends have had as much impact on national politics and those who report it as the proliferation of political consultants. Along with lobbyists and the press corps, they constitute one of Washington's biggest growth industries.

Twenty-five years ago, perhaps a dozen pollsters, media advisers, strategists and public relations experts made up the fraternity of big-name political consultants. Today, scores of consultants have a national reputation, and hundreds more are trying to break into the big leagues. Specialists abound in every phase of campaigns, from negative-ad development to megabuck fund-raisers and focus-group surveys. Whereas consultants once were engaged primarily in presidential and big-state U.S. Senate and gubernatorial campaigns, now virtually every seriously contested congressional candidate has a consulting team, and many candidates for state and local offices are following suit.

One view in the political press corps is that the rise of consultants has been bad for politics but good for the press. The former is thought to be true because political candidates rely too much on what their handlers tell them rather than on their own instincts; the latter, because consultants give reporters so many avenues to good political information. Germond says he finds consultants more important than party activists "because they're going to be there the next time, and so will you. They're not just going to lie to you and put you in a jam because they know you're going to be there two and four years from now."

The value of consultants, once you discount their political biases, is simple: They have to know what is going on in a campaign. In the television era, the message and image of candidates are usually more important than their resumes or the size of their campaign steering committees. The primary responsibility of media consultants is to develop a coordinated message that extends from phone banks to the door-to-door script, stump speeches and paid media advertisements. But most consultants are also involved with the campaign manager, press secretary and pollster in other phases of campaign strategy, including planning, budgeting, designing research, polling and focus groups, and targeting the candidate's time. And it is the consultants who have to lead the response to a negative-ad attack, review the tracking polls, write and produce a response ad and get it on the air in less than 24 hours.

In short, the inside perspective of a media consultant can help you interpret evidence gathered on the campaign trail. The danger is in substituting a few quick interviews with consultants for a broad range of interviews with political activists, voters and candidates.

Political Parties

Discussing political consultants ahead of political parties reflects their relative value to you as resources. You can't ignore the party structures in Washington, yet you will sometimes find they are of limited use.

The Republican and Democratic parties each have four committees and associations, plus offshoots and affiliates, that you will want to become familiar with. All are involved to some extent in fund raising, candidate recruitment, services to incumbents and candidates, and so forth, and all promote a partisan agenda with varying degrees of fervor.

At the top of the list are the Democratic and Republican national committees, which meet twice a year to discuss rules, election strategies and party building; resolve state party disputes; and generally show the flag. For the party controlling the White House, these meetings frequently are little more than pep rallies for the president. For the out party, they become forums for propaganda assaults and promises of better days.

Much of what happens at national committee meetings is too esoteric to be of interest to the average reader, yet the meetings are a must stop on your agenda. To establish a precedent, you should go to all national committee meetings held in Washington and try to wring out a story. Then when the meetings are held in Miami or New Orleans or San Diego, you can refer your editor to the track record already set.

A more fruitful reason for going is to make and renew political contacts. National committee meetings bring together not only several hundred committee members, including state party chairs and vice chairs, but also an array of political consultants, fund-raisers, state party operatives and hangers-on. Also, at Democratic meetings, the Association of State Democratic Chairs usually holds a separate meeting that sometimes is as interesting as the meetings of the full national committee.

As a rule, the quality of help you'll get at the national committees—especially in the press offices—depends on the political stature and connections of the individual involved. National committee headquarters staffs tend to be uneven. It's obviously important that you become acquainted with each party's chairperson, and it's probably worth your time (though not always) to have breakfast or lunch with him or her two or three times a year, if you can swing it. In the long run, however, regular contact with the political director and the top press aide may prove more valuable. Committee field staffs and regional political directors are also good to know, for they usually are current on state and local political conditions.

The national committee staffs, working with their House campaign committee counterparts, are particularly useful concerning the decennial task of redrawing congressional district lines. Redistricting is one of the most thoroughly politicized processes you'll encounter as a reporter, and cultivating sources throughout both party structures is important in covering it. The four congressional campaign committees—the Democratic Senatorial Campaign Committee, the Democratic Congressional Campaign Committee, the National Republican Senatorial Committee and the National Republican Congressional Committee—are important contacts for doing stories about individual races and House and Senate overviews. The committees are officially composed of members of the Senate and the House—a handful on the Senate side, several dozen on the House side—but the important contacts are the staffs and, to a lesser extent, the chairs. The latter are judged on their ability to raise money, to recruit and support candidates and, when circumstances dictate, to deliver partisan television soundbites.

One difficulty for reporters is that most committee chairs serve only one term, and the top committee staff often changes with the chair. As a result, committee sources often move on to other things after one or two elections. Still, it's worth the effort to carefully cultivate at least one source on each staff.

The committees are routinely involved in all phases of House and Senate campaigns. They actively recruit candidates; school them and their managers on campaign techniques; introduce them to political action committees and fat cats; give them direct financial, logistical and research support; and so forth. Especially on the House side, the committees function also as political support systems for incumbents, providing polling data, media services, suggested campaign themes and research on potential opponents. Thus, beyond providing elementary information on campaign outlook, the committees can be sources on more-general questions: Which issues in Congress are best for raising money? Which issues are playing big in which regions of the country? What is the outlook for redistricting after the next census? Who are the parties' rising stars throughout the country?

The committees are also home to many of the technical advances of recent years. The House Republican committee, for example, has led the industry in state-of-the-art direct-mail fund raising and satellite-transmitted news releases and paid media.

At a minimum, the campaign committees are a first stop if you're doing one race or a roundup. They can provide news clips, suggest who to talk to in their party out in the states, and give you the lineup on campaign aides and consultants.

Because governors' races are also in the purview of many Washington-based political reporters, you should get to know the staffs of the Democratic and Republican governors' associations. Both associations maintain small staffs in Washington, and both meet twice a year in conjunction with the winter and summer meetings of the National Governors Association. In addition, the Republican Governors Association usually meets after each election. The chair position of each of the two groups rotates annually. The main purpose of each group is to help elect and re-elect their party's gubernatorial candidates. Though members frequently sound off at their own meetings, their partisanship is usually muted in meetings of the bipartisan NGA.

Covering governors' meetings is valuable for several reasons. For one thing, governors often become presidential candidates. (Four of the five presidents elected since 1976 were incumbent or ex-governors.) Thus, governors' conferences are good places to spot emerging national political figures and to cultivate their staffs. Second, governors frequently have the best political organization in a state; this can help you build the national network of sources you need. Third, because most gubernatorial elections have been shifted out of the presidential cycle, the gubernatorial outlook is sometimes the best political story of midterm elections, overshadowing congressional elections. Fourth, governors and the hard choices they have to make are often more interesting than congressional members and Washington issues. The aggressive political reporter will want to be knowledgeable about the states' side of the federal-state debate.

Interest Groups

Washington is crawling with interest groups whose collective goal is to influence in some way every legislative issue, every federal regulation, every presidential appointment, every political race. Some groups are so far out on the political fringe as to be irresponsible. Others seem to headed that way but are still sane. Some are driven solely by ideological zeal; others by the profits to be gained from gouging the gullible.

As a political reporter, you have to decide for yourself who is worth dealing with and who isn't. If you have ideological hangups of your own, being discriminating will be more difficult. If you enjoy covering politics because of the characters you meet, it will be easier.

One of the best forums for tracking Ronald Reagan's political odyssey in the 1970s was the annual meeting in Washington of the Conservative Political Action Conference, sponsored jointly by the American Conservative Union and Young Americans for Freedom. Reagan always made room on his schedule to speak to the group, and his appearance was always the highlight of the three-day meeting. Any inquiring reporter who spent a day or two at the conferences from 1974 on would have left with a new appreciation for the depth of Reagan's support among conservatives against all challengers. Yet some reporters dismissed the conferences as a gathering of kooks.

On the other end of the spectrum, annual meetings of Americans for Democratic Action, held in Washington, are useful forums for making contacts and keeping tabs on old-school liberals. Similarly, the annual legislative weekends of the Congressional Black Caucus afford one-stop shopping for the reporter trying to develop sources among the black political leadership. And any reporter who wants to stay in touch with feminist issues and leaders will attend meetings of the National Organization for Women and the National Women's Political Caucus.

Washington's political action committees can also be rich sources of political intelligence. One of the best examples is the National Committee for an Effective Congress. More than 50 years old, the NCEC supports only liberal or progressive candidates in marginal races against clearly conservative opponents, and it has a reputation as a shrewd handicapper. Dozens of other groups closely follow voting records and can provide political input on issues such as the environment, arms control, drug abuse, civil rights and crime. The trick in Washington is not in acquiring that kind of information but in making sure that it is accurate and balanced. (PACs are treated in more detail in Chapter 10.)

The largest interest group of all is organized labor. The 13 million members of the AFL-CIO and the 2.7 million members of the National Education Association together represent a formidable army whose leadership almost always favors the Democrats. Yet the internal strife that racked the Democratic Party at the height of the Vietnam War paralleled a decline in labor's membership and clout. Most of labor was appalled by George McGovern in 1972 and unmoved by Jimmy Carter in 1976. Perhaps as a reflection of that, coverage of labor as part of the political beat also declined. In 1984, labor saw in Walter Mondale's presidential candidacy a chance to reassert its clout, but its early endorsement only compounded the caricature of him as a captive of special interests. Four years later, labor held back, leaving local activists free to support whatever candidate could guarantee them a ticket to the Democratic national convention. Neither the AFL nor the NEA endorsed Michael Dukakis until after both party conventions. The result, ironically, was that labor emerged in the strongest position it had held in 20 years, at a time when its agenda on Capitol Hill was also gathering steam. It sustained a strong position through the Clinton campaigns of the 1990s and the Al Gore campaign in 2000.

But labor continues to get short shrift from the political press corps. Whatever the reason for that, a reporter cannot cover national politics well without developing sources in labor at the national, state and local levels. The NEA, for example, averages 5,000 members in every congressional district. You can't cover presidential primaries and caucuses confidently without good labor sources in Iowa, Illinois, Michigan, New York, Pennsylvania, Ohio and California, to name the most obvious. And you can't appreciate, much less report, what happens in the precincts of America from early October through Election Day without talking to local labor leaders and making on-site visits to phone banks, union halls and campaign offices.

You'll be ignoring a valuable resource if you don't get acquainted well enough to trade gossip with the national political directors of the more active unions such as NEA; United Auto Workers; Machinists; United Food and Commercial Workers; American Federation of State, County and Municipal Employees; Service Employees International; and the Communications Workers of America. Not only are they sounding boards for their union's rank and file, but they usually also have good channels into the hierarchy surrounding the Democratic presidential nominee.

Think Tanks

Occasionally a political reporter will need some authoritative research to add credibility to and otherwise fill in the gaps between a string of quotes and his or her own profound insights. There is a think tank in Washington for every such occasion. Turning to think tanks is getting dangerously close to academia, but, used sparingly, think tanks have their pluses. Whether the subject is welfare reform, congressional ethics, arms control, campaign finance, monetary policy or military spending, Washington think tanks can offer you a liberal, centrist, conservative or libertarian expert, usually backed up by several pounds of studies and computerized data. Some of the think tanks with better track records are the American Enterprise Institute, Brookings Institution, the Joint Center for Political and Economic Studies, the Heritage Foundation and the Urban Institute. Because think tanks often serve as a refuge for government officials in exile, making contacts can also prove beneficial when those officials return to government.

GETTING HOOKED ON POLLS

Public Opinion Polls

Few things in the past few decades have affected political coverage—mostly for the worse—as much as the increasing use of public opinion polls. By almost everyone's agreement in the polling profession, too many polls use questionable techniques and are in turn interpreted by ill-informed journalists for an equally unsophisticated public.

As a political writer, you may not have any say in whether your organization conducts polls, but you should have some say in how they and other polls are reported. At the least, you should set guidelines for yourself in writing about polls. You can get plenty of help from any number of political pollsters from both parties.

Polling analyst Schneiders, who has long criticized the way the media report and interpret polls, says that he thinks reporting of polls has generally improved in recent years. "I think the further away we've gotten from polls as a novelty, or as a stand-alone story, the more that they have become routine, ubiquitous and therefore more likely to be a part of a story, some small piece that sheds some additional light on something—the more we've moved in that direction—the better off we are."

Schneiders adds: "I think at one time it was for some journalists just an easy way to generate a story and build an entire story around a poll result. Now you don't see that."

As with other kinds of consultants, pollsters are used by reporters as instant experts in all manner of situations. The implication is that the word pollster connotes public opinion, even though the pollster may not have ever asked a question relevant to the situation. "More and more, in reaction to events," says pollster Hart, "we are plugged into stories (so reporters can) say, 'We talked to the public through the pollster.' The pollster doesn't have new data. The reporter knows he doesn't have data. But he also knows it fills part of the story out. You've got an advocate on one side, an advocate on the other side, and the political experts—the pollsters—so you've given all sides of the picture. The problem with pollsters, they're giving you their reaction as they look through their {old} data, and their judgment. But it is another voice, rather than a definitive voice."

Suffice it to say that pollsters are important sources, best used sparingly and intelligently. For example, pollsters who take state surveys frequently in one region of the country can give you a composite picture of trends in that region that is more useful to a thoughtful reporter than a string of horse-race numbers from one or more of those states. And they'll usually provide that picture even when they won't talk about the candidates' numbers.

Focus Groups

Political reporters are always looking for shortcuts in gauging the mood of the voters. One of the most popular techniques in recent years involves the use of focus groups. Newspapers such as The Wall Street Journal and The Washington Post have made focus groups a routine part of their political coverage, not only for exploring voter attitudes in the abstract but also for measuring reactions to major events such as conventions and presidential debates. Used by corporations for years to test ads and consumer products, focus groups are more interesting than polls because they add flesh and blood and emotions to cold survey data. But they must be treated cautiously because they are not scientific measures of anything—they are much too small a sample for that.

Typically, focus groups of 10 to 15 people are recruited by pollsters in shopping centers or in phone calls. If they qualify as registered voters and match the demographics sought, they are asked if they would be willing to attend a two-hour session for a fee, usually $25 to $50. During the taped session, a range of questions is raised and debated, as aides to the pollster view the proceedings from behind a one-way mirror and record facial expressions and other body language.

The most appealing aspect of focus groups is what's called the group dynamic, the give-and-take that prompts expressions that would rarely if ever be elicited by a pollster reading a questionnaire. It is also that aspect that generates sharp controversy. Media specialist Frank Greer, for example, says a focus group can be a "very valuable tool" that yields qualitative data on how people feel about the traits they're looking for in a candidate. "But it should never be used without quantitative data in a poll," Greer says. "In the dynamics of a group, you can get a kind of herd instinct going, and you can get a misreading that's dangerous. . . . It's an artificial environment, no question about it, they all become media experts."

Pollster Schneiders agrees, calling focus groups "useful and also very dangerous." Schneiders frequently asks group members to write down words or phrases in advance to describe their reactions to a person or event, so that each member is tied to something. "If you don't do that," he says, "the first person who speaks, particularly if they're articulate, can very well drive the rest of the group." Most people, he adds, don't make decisions about their support of candidates or issues in groups of 10 people in two-hour discussions. "So you get a focus-group artifact," Schneiders says, "a lot of opinions that didn't exist when they walked in the door."

Focus groups, Schneiders says, are best used in conjunction with quantitative research. "If you do the two together—you do the focus groups first, get whatever insights you can, get a better sense of the language people use, and the way they process information, and how they think about an issue, and then go do the quantitative, with all that as background—it's very attractive."

Hart, on the other hand, is an unabashed cheerleader for focus groups, describing them as "brilliant . . . marvelous tools" that give you voters who are talking and exchanging thoughts, with the time to cover a tremendous amount of information in a structured way.

The best advice for the political reporter is to use focus groups as one more aid in building a story, not as a replacement for old-fashioned street reporting. The shopping center that yields focus-group recruits will serve the reporter equally well as a place to interview 40 to 50 shoppers at random. Your survey won't be scientific, but neither will the people you interview feel any peer pressure, or any obligation to sound knowledgeable because they've been paid. You'll end up with tons of good quotes and, if you've asked reasonably objective questions in a reasonably objective manner, a pretty good sense of the mood of the community.

CONGRESSIONAL CAMPAIGNS

Whether you're the lead political writer, a Capitol Hill correspondent or a regional reporter charged with covering one or more congressional delegations, a key part of your beat should be documenting the biennial battle for control in the House and Senate. In presidential election years, congressional elections are sometimes overshadowed. In midterm elections, they sometimes get overplayed.

One of the biggest challenges for the press for many years was to find any suspense about the outcome. Democrats controlled the House for 40 years before losing to the Republicans in 1994. They controlled the Senate during most of the same period. Despite the advantage of having six-year terms, senators proportionately have more volatile re-election campaigns. With few exceptions, House members who survive their first re-election effort have effectively achieved tenure. Going into the fall campaign in 2002, fewer than two dozen House races were rated as too close to call. The reasons behind these and other trends are grist for any enterprising reporter.

The way to start, however, is to get a handle on the big picture, and that entails talking to the experts, beginning in the year before the election. Because of the need to raise money to finance costly television ads, House members and candidates now engage in virtual nonstop campaigning. Despite the six-year terms, pressures are only slightly less in the Senate, where campaign spending per race averages four or five times as much as in the House. A story by New York Times reporter Richard Berke in 2002 illustrated the pressure on challengers to raise money. He spent several hours observing a little-known candidate for the Democratic U.S. Senate nomination in Oregon trying to raise money by phone, a few hundred dollars at a time.

As was suggested earlier, the staffs of the four campaign committees on the Hill are a good first stop for background. They have a partisan point of view, of course, but if you compare all their assessments, you'll probably see some agreement on which races are marginal, meaning real contests. In the House, where all 435 seats are up, the number is likely to be somewhere between 25 and 50. In the Senate, where one-third of the 100 seats are up, it could range from 10 to 20. All you're trying to do at this point is to establish a baseline. Competitive races may shift several times before the election; lopsided races sometimes get tight.

A primary resource for keeping tabs on congressional races is the Hotline, the daily online publication that offers a separate edition on House races (described in detail at the end of this chapter).

Another good resource is the major interest groups in Washington. The U.S. Chamber of Commerce and the AFL-CIO keep close tabs on congressional races, as do the major PACs run by the NEA, the American Medical Association, the Realtors, and so on. Because most of their decisions on whom to support are based on hard-nosed political calculations, the endorsement lists of PACs are valuable intelligence for reporters.

Next, look for guidance and tips from experts in the media. Congressional Quarterly publishes a special report in February of election years (updated in October) that previews the House and Senate contests. These reports offer details about the local landscape in all competitive races. Another popular guide is the Cook Political Report, authored by Charles Cook, a former Democratic campaign committee staffer. The Almanac of American Politics and Politics in America provide background on individual districts and states.

Visit the Federal Election Commission Web site and study the early reports of PAC donations and money raised in marginal races. With this kind of background, you can call party leaders and pollsters in key states and ask intelligent questions.

But occasional "scorecards" do little to explain the forces at work in congressional elections. Whether you're covering one candidate or the big picture, you need to get beyond the bottom line of projected wins and losses. Some examples:

Incumbency. Holding office is variously estimated to be worth about a million dollars in a House election and twice that in the Senate. A story documenting that advantage—the franking privilege, the free media exposure, and so forth—helps put an election into context. Also, a story explaining the obstacles faced by a challenger makes good reading.

Presidential coattails. Trying to assess the impact the top of the ticket will have on congressional candidates is an intriguing (and sometimes humbling) exercise. In 1980, for example, no one expected Ronald Reagan to sweep 16 new Republicans into the Senate. Similarly, midterm congressional races can provide a referendum of sorts on the president's policies and performance, as happened in the recession year of 1982 when Republicans suffered at the polls, and as was forecast to happen in 2002 with George W. Bush riding high in the polls because of his response to terrorism. Are congressional candidates linking themselves with the White House or running away from it?

PAC money. Is special interest money more dominant than ever? Who are the big donors and recipients? How much of this money is coming from within a candidate's district or state, and how much from outside?

Issues. Which issues are playing big in which states or regions? Are phony issues being created with the introduction of certain amendments or roll-call votes in the House or Senate? Are voting "report cards," published by dozens of ideological and special interest groups in Washington, being used by challengers to bash incumbents?

The class story. A large turnover in seats in either house draws special attention. The Senate Republican class that was elected in 1980 on Reagan's coattails became the object of much scrutiny because many of its members were thought to be political lightweights. That proved to be correct; in 1986, seven of those 16 seats returned to the Democrats. On the other hand, the first post-Watergate election, in 1974, brought 75 mostly reform-minded new Democrats into the House, many of whom survived to become subcommittee chairs in the 1980s and virtually immune to challenge. Republicans who helped Newt Gingrich take over the House in 1994 became similarly entrenched in the late '90s.

Like pre-election stories, postelection stories should go beyond a simple analysis of which party did better at the polls and why. A switch in control of either chamber means massive changes, of course. But every election has a domino effect on some committees and subcommittees. What does the new lineup mean for new legislation or for legislation that has been in limbo because of a hostile chair, too few votes or a Senate filibuster? How are the newly elected members paying off their campaign debts? Are they being showered with money by PACs who supported their opponents before the votes were counted?

Perhaps your franchise is too narrow to do big-picture pieces; maybe you're expected to write only about, say, the Texas delegation. Most of the examples above still apply: Which members of your delegation were favorites of which PACs and—more important—why? Was legislation of crucial interest to your state helped or hurt by the election? Has your delegation lost or gained clout as a result of the election? How are its members paying off their debts?

PRESIDENTIAL CAMPAIGNS

There is a wrong way and a right way to cover presidential campaigns, and some large news organizations still get it wrong. Everybody wants to get in on the act. All too often, in the ensuing chaos, editors use presidential campaigns to play favorites in their newsrooms and Washington bureaus and, regrettably, to try out their own theories about political coverage.

They decide that the way to cover politics is to create instant experts on every phase of campaigns, from polling and fund raising to media and the issues. Then they assign other reporters to become experts on candidates, posting their favorite reporters with the apparent front-runners, of course. The chief political writer, with luck, gets to remain aloof from this chess game. By the time the campaign gets serious, the editors have a staff full of disillusioned reporters, those whose candidates have fallen by the wayside (along with their dreams of covering the White House) and all those other experts who still can't get their 30-inch stories in the newspaper.

The practice of assigning reporters to presidential candidates is perhaps the most egregious mistake made in political journalism, and yet it is repeated every four years at many of the nation's large newspapers and magazines. The problem is this: The moment a reporter is told that a candidate is "yours for the duration," he or she inevitably has a vested interest in that candidate's success. The long-term effect can be devastating both psychologically and physically. The point is, you don't need experts on candidates, you need experts on politics. What's more, assigning a reporter to a candidate full time is inhumane.

"You hear the same things over and over again," says Linda Feldmann, who covered the 1996 and 2000 campaigns for the Christian Science Monitor. "They're delivering their canned speeches at different stops along the way, and the trick is to stay awake—especially if you had baggage call at six in the morning after getting in at one o'clock the night before. The boredom factor, the exhaustion factor, is a real test of your physical stamina before you've even had any brilliant thoughts about how the campaign is going—whether the candidate is continuing to put his foot in his mouth, or whether he's getting over that problem."

Laying the Groundwork

The proper way to approach a presidential campaign is no different from the way you would approach a military invasion or a rocket trip to the moon: with careful planning. Every presidential campaign has phases that change little regardless of the candidates or the issues. Many stories can be planned and scheduled far in advance, regardless of the year or the size of the presidential field. In fact, probably 75 percent of the stories written in a presidential campaign are generic products that can be planned months, if not years, ahead.

The key to good planning lies in involving people with experience and a solid understanding of politics. You don't want to refight the last war; neither do you want to forget the lessons you learned from all the past wars. And remember, you are the one who should decide how the campaign will be covered, not the campaign aides.

One of the most consistent lessons of recent campaigns has been that they are an insider's game for at least the first half. Average folk simply don't connect with presidential politics until about the time the voting starts, and only then in the states that have been invaded by the media and political hordes. That suggests you start slowly and gradually expand your coverage.

The Pre-primary Phase

The marathon to succeed a president that often commences soon after inauguration is a legacy in part of the 1970s, when George McGovern and Jimmy Carter demonstrated that the darkest dark horse can be nominated, given the right issue or campaign style, enough stamina and enough true believers. Over time, this marathon has also come to reflect a rather benign conspiracy of several hundred political junkies who have no other purpose in life. It has a chicken-or-egg beginning: More and more politicians see presidential characteristics in themselves. A growing army of political consultants sees fame and fortune in encouraging such self-deception in the politicians. A corporal's guard of full-time political reporters, despairing at life without a weekly fix, stands ready to be romanced. Scores of other journalists gather on the fringes, convinced that the next campaign will be the one in which they will break into the big leagues. Would the candidates begin campaigning so early if the reporters weren't out there waiting for them? Would the reporters be out there waiting for them if candidates didn't start so early? Those are interesting questions for postelection seminars held on college campuses and at think tanks. They are also irrelevant to your task as a political reporter.

Presidential campaigns usually attract a mix of fresh faces and previous losers. You may be inclined to pay more attention to one candidacy than another just because you know the key players from an earlier campaign. But you ignore new faces at your peril. Several campaigns, especially the Democratic primaries of 1972, 1976, 1988 and 1992, and the Republican primary of 2000, showed that track records can mean little in presidential politics.

You need to get to know everyone you can in every fledgling presidential campaign. Don't assume they will come to you, unless you represent a key newspaper in an early primary or caucus state. Long-shot candidates are apt to target their early press contacts as part of the expectations game. They always want to be better organized than the press has reported.

The time for you to start is when they start, and they usually start no later than the midterm elections, and candidates for the 2004 Democratic nomination began far sooner than that. As part of your coverage of congressional and gubernatorial campaigns in the midterm, you should keep a sharp eye out for presidential tracks. Find out how many Republican Lincoln Day or Democratic Jefferson-Jackson Day dinners suspected candidates have finagled invitations to, how many campaign appearances they've slated for party colleagues, how many PACs and foundations they've set up for the ostensible purpose of helping others. Plan your travel schedule to intersect theirs—without tipping their staffs to your plans.

It's important for you to form some early judgments of your own about a likely presidential candidate without benefit of staff "spin." The best way to do this is first to research the candidate's public record and background thoroughly enough to memorize the highlights. Then quietly observe him or her on the stump and interview extensively in the audience afterward. Then go to the home state and talk to a wide range of political, business and civic leaders about their impressions of the candidate. Talk to his or her political associates in Congress or in the statehouses or wherever the candidate has made a mark. Next, sit down with the candidate's top political advisers and try to get their basic game plan for breaking out of the pack. Then sit down with the candidate and try to get a sense of why he or she entered the race.

You may or may not have written a line at this point, but that's not important. All this material will eventually fit into the detailed profile of the candidate that you'll want to write later. What's important now is that you have educated yourself about this candidate—and the half dozen other hopefuls—and you have left the clear impression with them and their top advisers that you are on a serious mission. These early contacts are extremely important and can determine whether you continue to have good access to the candidate after the media hordes arrive 12 to 15 months later.

You have to start writing about the campaign at some point, of course, but before you do, think about who you're writing for. Unless you work for The Washington Post or the National Journal, to use two obvious examples, most of your audience is not salivating for the latest tidbit about a race that will not take shape for another year. Indeed, your readers may be going through a midterm election that is making them more disgusted with politics than ever.

If you have an outlet in a state that has a budding presidential contender or hosts an early primary or caucus, interest may be a little higher. Otherwise, you have to accept that your story is of much more interest to you than to most of your audience.

"There are a few people who'll read good political coverage, but they're an elite," says Jack Germond. "You have to understand if you're writing politics that you're writing for a slice of a readership; you're not writing for most of your readers. You're writing for those who are interested a lot, and who are knowledgeable."

One compromise that will serve you and your audience is to develop your own presidential scorecard to debut soon after the midterm elections, perhaps pegged to New Year's Day of the pre-presidential year. If you are creative enough, promote it enough and update it regularly, it will generate interest in the campaign by itself. The beauty of the scorecard is that you can distill reams of information that would produce overkill if written as separate stories. Besides charting the entry (and withdrawal) of candidates, along with their campaign finance reports, the scorecard is a handy vehicle for summarizing and analyzing in a few paragraphs the status of each candidate's campaign.

The scorecard will in fact satisfy most voters' curiosity about the campaign until after Labor Day in the pre-presidential year, when the buildup to the first caucuses and primaries begins to attract the interest of television. In this last, intense phase of the pre-primary period, you should have a solid game plan that allows flexibility. It's standard procedure, for example, to produce your first round of in-depth profiles of the candidates and to identify the issues that are rising to the top on the campaign trail, as well as to explain the candidates' positions on important issues they may not be talking about.

It's also important to keep track of the money: how candidates are raising it, how they're spending it, how they'll do in earning federal matching funds. More candidates have failed because they ran out of money (usually because they weren't very good candidates) than for any other reason.

Other strategies and tactics prompt stories: negative campaign ads in the early states, endorsements, forums, debates and straw polls. It's important amid all these distractions not to lose sight of the candidates. What are they saying? What does it mean? Do voters understand their message? How are the candidates bearing up under the pressure of constant travel and political challenge? Is there something a little strange here?

Your task is to convey all of this clearly to the reader. You're not writing for your fellow reporters and political junkies; you're writing for schoolteachers and shoe clerks and CPAs and computer programmers who are just beginning to try to sort out what's going on. Your most timely early opportunity to help them do that comes with a presidential outlook story pegged to New Year's Day. You can play handicapper with the numbers and you can quote the experts, but this is the story that will demonstrate whether you understand what's going on or not. Avoid political jargon that means nothing to the average reader. Above all, don't confuse the reader.

The reality of presidential campaign coverage is that you don't always get to start as early as you would like. For a variety of reasons, most having to do with money, some news organizations decide to put off serious coverage until television gets into the act and makes it unavoidable. If you're dispatched to the campaign trail late in the pre-primary season, the first thing you need to do is to meet as many campaign aides as possible, as quickly as possible. Presumably you've been reading everything you can get your hands on for months. You've already figured out which journalists are doing the best early reporting, and you've followed their coverage closely. You've studied the backgrounds of the candidates, and you know who the key people around them are, even if you've never met them. You've got your own list of stories you want to do as soon as you are turned loose. For a true political junkie, in this day and age, there's no such thing as going into a campaign blind.

The Primary Season

By the time the primaries and caucuses begin in late January or early February, much of the fun of covering a presidential campaign is over for print journalists. With the arrival of television crews, campaigns become a blur of photo opportunities and inane press conferences, a battle of TV ads and expectations, upon all of which the voters have the audacity to intrude briefly every week or so. Secret Service protection restricts reporters' access to candidates. The losers get grouchy and start blaming the press for their inadequacies. The press demands to know when the losers will get out and stop cluttering up the picture.

The pack mentality seems to flower at this period of the cycle, as hundreds of frenzied reporters invade Iowa and New Hampshire and other early states. It is not a scene conducive to good journalism, and very little good journalism results. All you can do at this point is to try to keep your cool and remember that the race has a long way to go.

Getting away from the hordes will help you keep your perspective. If the venue is Iowa or New Hampshire, spend as much time as you can outside the cities of Des Moines and Manchester and Concord. If you have the latitude, jump ahead for a few days to a state or region that votes three or four weeks later. In any event, figuring out who is going to win a caucus or primary is not as important as understanding why a candidate is doing well or doing poorly—and explaining that to the reader. In the 1988 campaign, Democrat Bruce Babbitt became, in the memorable words of Jack Germond, the "pet rock" of the political press corps. For several weeks before the Iowa caucuses, Babbitt was the beneficiary of dozens of glowing articles about how he was taking courageous stands on numerous issues. The interesting thing about it, almost entirely ignored by the press, was that all of that favorable press coverage had zero impact on the voters. But Babbitt fared rather poorly compared to the loving attention lavished on Republican John McCain in the 2000 presidential primary campaign. Reporters dazzled by McCain's strategy of giving them unlimited access swooned about the Arizona senator to a degree never seen in modern-day politics.

The challenge to you as a chronicler of this constantly moving battlefield is to assimilate, week after week, all that is going on. How does the exit of a candidate change the dynamics of the race for others? What do primary exit polls tell you about the efficacy of an issue or about possible pitfalls ahead for one candidate or one party? What does the latest delegate count mean for voters in the late states who wonder if they will be courted or taken for granted? Are negative campaign ads being used, and to what effect?

Reducing answers to these and other questions to weekly overviews is the staple of good primary coverage, but they should be supplemented with more narrowly focused pieces. When a candidate drops out, that campaign deserves a careful post-mortem. In 1988 the two candidates whose campaigns were built exclusively on issues, Republican Pete du Pont and Democrat Bruce Babbitt, were among the first to bite the dust. A similar fate befell Democrat Bill Bradley in the 2000 presidential primary. What did that say about the voters? Periodic updates on issues should also be done—not long, dull tomes but bright, tightly written pieces that explain which issues are important in the campaign and why.

As the field of candidates thins, it's appropriate to do updated profiles of the front-runners. Don't assume your readers remember what you wrote the previous fall. Recap the biographical highlights, then move on to assess the candidate in the context of campaign performance. All of this will help you lay the groundwork for that most overhyped of all modern-day political orgies, the national conventions.

The Conventions

Because conventions in the modern era have become carefully choreographed television productions, devoid of any suspense except contrived suspense, they can be frustrating for the thousands of print reporters trying to justify their existence there. Traditionally, reporting at conventions is on two levels: coverage of delegations on a state or regional basis, and coverage of events, issues and personalities on a national basis. Either approach requires planning if you're going to be able to churn out regular stories that don't strain credibility. For national reporters, the contacts that you've made in the nominees' camps during two years of wining and dining and schmoozing should pay off. Regional reporters will have a much harder time of it.

It's not unusual, for example, for Washington-based reporters to be assigned to cover delegations from one or more states where they've never worked, or where their contacts have grown cold. Because this arrangement is so common, it's worth some treatment here. If you're going to a convention for the first time, or if you're assigned to cover a delegation where your contacts are minimal, you can do several things:

• Get to know the delegates. The national and state parties have their names weeks before the conventions start. Call them up and talk to them. If you have the time, prepare a short questionnaire and mail it to them. Find out which delegates were with the likely nominee early—they may have more clout at the convention. Find out in which direction uncommitted or unpledged delegates are leaning (if any semblance of a contest remains) and how they're being courted. Find out which delegates are on the platform, rules and credentials committees, and cultivate them for use when floor fights erupt.

• Find out who else from your audience's region is going to the convention—business leaders, party fat cats, issue activists—and whether they have an official function there. Find out what all the locals' plans are for parties, social events, and so forth.

• Review coverage of the state convention for clues to the makeup of the delegation and internal feuds that may continue at the national convention.

With this background, and especially with the benefit of a delegation questionnaire, you can do several pre-convention stories, ranging from soft to hard:

• The cost of attending. Among the delegates and alternates may be hardship cases, or some delegates may have held bake sales or other fund-raisers in order to attend.

• Delegate profiles. The oldest, the youngest, the veteran of most conventions, and so forth often make good stories.

• Delegation politics. Choose topics such as who the delegates favor for vice president, if that's still in question; which delegates are going to the convention with a personal agenda; how the delegation lines up on pending platform or rules fights.

Stories you can do once the convention is under way are unlimited. Working the delegates at their morning caucuses and on the floor later should produce logistics stories (for example, the horror stories encountered by delegates getting from their hotel to the convention hall), as well as offbeat stories about the strange behavior that alcohol and distance from home often evoke. You'll want to track your delegation's participation in floor fights, report reactions to the keynote speech, look for local angles in the platform debate, monitor any continuing political feuds in the delegation, report the breakdown on major roll-call votes, and be prepared to gather reactions to any unexpected development.

You should also keep a sharp eye out for state and local figures who may be holding fund-raisers or otherwise using the convention to warm up for a future political campaign. Likewise look for emerging presidential hopefuls who may be romancing your delegates.

After the balloting and acceptance speeches, a number of stories should be routine: What was the reaction to the vice presidential choice and to the acceptance speeches by both nominees? More important, how will the ticket play in your delegation's state? To do this story right, you'll need to talk to state political leaders of both parties. You should arrange in advance to do that.

National reporters have a fairly standard agenda for approaching a convention: a reprise of how the likely nominee put it all together; perhaps another profile of him or her; a speculative piece on who the running mate might be, if that's unknown; a convention curtain raiser that explains the objectives of the party and the nominee; as well as any glitches, such as floor fights, to look for.

An endless number of sidebars can be done about the platform, the nominee's convention team, the ambitions of the keynote speaker and other high-profile figures—if you have the time. You probably won't, but your input can be helpful to others in your news organization.

The conventions should offer you, as a political writer, the opportunity to stretch your mandate a little, to be creative, perhaps to wax historical. The nuts and bolts are simple. You know who the delegates are for, by and large. You've written about the likely nominee ad nauseam. You know what the platform is apt to say once the shouting has subsided. You know that every utterance from the rostrum has been scripted down to the last punctuation mark. Before you get too cynical, however, keep these things in mind as you try to put events on the television screen into perspective:

• Images are important, both large and small: an embattled George McGovern delivering an acceptance speech at 3 a.m. in 1972; Jimmy Carter chasing Edward Kennedy around the stage in Madison Square Garden in 1980, trying to raise his hand in salute; nervous Democrats in 1988 patronizing Jesse Jackson in Atlanta. Pat Buchanan urging the GOP to revert to the Stone Age in a 1992 convention speech in Houston. Al Gore embracing his wife with a made-for-TV kiss that lasted much too long at the 2000 Democratic convention. Such impressions remain long after the balloons drop.

• Acceptance speeches are important. They are the first chance the nominee has to set the tone and message of his or her fall campaign before a prime-time TV audience on all networks. Michael Dukakis and George Bush both used them advantageously in 1988; in 1984, Walter Mondale managed to overshadow earlier good speeches by Mario Cuomo, Jesse Jackson and Geraldine Ferraro by promising to raise taxes.

• One party or the other will sometimes botch the vice presidential selection process. From the Thomas Eagleton fiasco in 1972 to the Gerald Ford "co-presidency" in 1980, from Mondale's special interest pandering in 1984 to George Bush's 1988 choice of Dan Quayle in splendid isolation, presidential nominees seem to get jinxed the moment they face their first key political test. The 2000 election was one of those rare cases when both party nominees appeared to have boosted their ticket with their vice presidential choice.

The General Election

You usually have two to three weeks after the second convention to prepare for the fall campaign. There will be a lot of ballyhoo in this period about how much of a boost the two parties received from their conventions and how much staying power it may have. Given the recent history of vice presidential choices, there may also be a lingering firestorm over one of the running mates. You'll want to take all these factors and a lot more into account as you prepare a Labor Day kickoff piece that synthesizes all the political intelligence you've gathered for two long years.

Your Labor Day piece should describe a road map that will take one of the two party nominees to the White House in January. The two routes on the map will wind through many states, with footnotes explaining why each is an important pit stop, what kind of reception the two candidates will likely get as they pass through, and why. Other footnotes and legends will explain prevailing conditions regionally and nationally, and whether forecasters are predicting changes. Finally, an important footnote will describe the candidates' physical and mental conditions, their track records, the reputation of their pit crews, the readiness of their backup drivers. Once you've done this, you're ready to hit the road yourself. The preferred place to be on Labor Day is with the presidential nominee of the challenging party. After a couple of days with that candidate, you'll want to cross over and travel with the nominee of the incumbent party. A couple of days later, you'll want to get away from both candidates and strike out on your own.

If you're fortunate enough to be able to plan your own schedule, you'll ride campaign planes only often enough and long enough to catch the mood of the candidates and their traveling staff. You'll probably be seeing them at debates and at other rendezvous' on the campaign trail, and besides, you have too many other things to do.

No single approach works best for covering the blitz from Labor Day to Election Day, but if you're the lead political writer, it's important that you have the broadest possible reach. Here is one agenda that works:

The key-state tour. First identify a half dozen to a dozen states that both campaigns consider crucial. Visit each state for a couple of days, talk to the political hierarchy as well as to common folk, and write a story that explains what the election is all about through the eyes of that state. R.W. Apple of The New York Times has done this to great effect in several presidential elections.

The candidate hits. Try to spend a couple of days a month traveling with each of the presidential and vice presidential candidates. This provides a spot check on performance, new material and campaign mood, as well as a chance to exchange gossip with traveling aides.

The debates. Given the extent to which debates have become orchestrated party productions, their potential as watershed campaign events has waned. But you still have to take them seriously. Avoid the debate site, with its partisan cheering squads and "spin patrols," and either watch the debate alone or with a group of voters in someone's living room. If your organization has the wherewithal, consider convening a focus group of your own. Also, if you can get away with it, wait at least a day before you write a line about the debate.

The mood of the voters. It's old-fashioned in the era of focus groups and polls, but interviewing voters door-to-door or at shopping centers is still a valuable experience in the heat of a presidential campaign. The Washington Post's David Broder does it with regularity. You can get sophisticated about it and have a pollster select a precinct with certain demographics and voting history, or you can wing it. One compromise is to stake out a grocery store that draws from a variety of neighborhoods. In three or four hours, you'll have a notebook full of revealing quotes. If you're any good at this kind of interviewing, the biggest problem you'll have is getting people to stop talking. (Also, watch out for nosy proprietors who don't permit soliciting within 50 miles of their establishments.) Another option is to develop a list of interviewees in a community or neighborhood and return each election year to assess their mood. This allows you to assemble a cross section of voters with an array of occupations and interests. How you do it is less important than doing it.

The candidate's impact. Most of the hoopla surrounding presidential campaigning is designed to get the candidate on the evening news locally and nationally, as well as to generate enthusiasm among local supporters. One of the most revealing stories you can do is to measure the impact of one campaign stop. Select from the candidate's travel schedule a town or city in a closely contested area. Get there a couple of days before the candidate to assess the advance work done by the campaigners and to evaluate the level of support. Don't tell anyone you're coming. Scrutinize the skill with which the visit is handled, the media coverage that is generated, the crowd turnout, and so forth. After the visit, spend a day talking to political and community leaders, campaign aides, interest groups and average voters. You then should be able to sit down and write a fascinating behind-the-scenes account of one brief slice of a presidential campaign—and its impact. The value of this kind of reporting is that it gets you beyond the staged events that normally comprise a campaign stop.

"You have to remember who it is you're seeing (at campaign stops)," says The Monitor's Linda Feldmann. "Let's say you go to an event in an airport hangar. The local Republican Party, say, will rally the people . . . so these are people who are already active or committed. You could have an entire room full of cheering people. It doesn't mean the guy has a prayer. If they put out the calls and no one shows up, that's obviously very telling. But just because you have a room full of cheering people doesn't mean anything."

Feature stories. Campaign coverage doesn't have to be dull just because the candidates are. One of the most interesting and enjoyable stories you can do is to profile a day in the life of a presidential candidate, from the moment he wakes up, to what he eats for breakfast, to who he meets—everything that happens until he turns out the light that night. You'll need the help and cooperation of his staff, obviously, and some careful planning, but an inside look at the hectic pace and "Animal House" character of life on a campaign plane can be revealing and fun to write.

The issues. The horse-race-versus-issues approach to campaign coverage has been argued ad nauseum, but the argument is off the mark. Responsible journalism requires that you cover both. People want to know who is ahead and who is behind. But you also have an obligation to help voters make up their own minds about the candidates, which is a different matter. An occasional review of the issues—which ones are rising, which are fading—is in order. You may want to treat one issue in depth, if you've discovered in your travels that it's cutting hard in one state or region. As a campaign expert, you must also say if the candidates are avoiding certain issues or if they're wildly distorting an opponent's stand through negative TV ads.

Qualities of leadership. Charting where the nominees stand on the issues is not enough, however. How prepared—and qualified—are they to hold the presidency? Jack Germond notes that while the press does a good job of outlining differences on issues, they do not adequately explore the qualities of the candidates and the top people around them. "There was nothing in the 2000 campaign—primaries or general—to tell you which of the candidates would be good in responding to a crisis like 9/11," says Germond. "You had no way of knowing."

Candidate interviews. These interviews are not the most important thing on your agenda, and in the era of television dominance they are more difficult to arrange than they used to be. But you should push for your own sit-down with each presidential nominee. Consider teaming up with other reporters who aren't competitors. If you get an interview, it's apt to be short and on the run—on the campaign plane, in the back of a limousine, in an airport holding room—which is all the more reason that you need to be well prepared. This is the time when those early contacts, back when no one took the candidate seriously, should pay off.

You can choose from an endless variety of other compelling stories about voter registration, the clash of TV ads, the impact of third-party candidates, the role of surrogate campaigners, and so on. Among those, TV ads may be the most important story. Increasingly, TV ads are designed to generate news coverage, especially by television, which understands the medium. It's your responsibility to dissect those ads and expose false charges.

You should try to assess the campaign in a perspective piece every two or three weeks during the first half of the fall campaign, and every week during the last month. To do this, you not only need to absorb everything around you as you travel but also need to monitor closely the nightly network news coverage, the campaign TV ads and the constant stream of national and key-state polls. You also need to make regular checks with your political contacts around the country and in Washington.

The most important stories you will write come just before and just after Election Day. Your election preview piece may require you to go out on a limb, but you're the expert. You're expected to know by this point which campaign game plan worked and why, if the race is not really close, or which factors will make the difference on Tuesday, if the race is too close to call. You can play with electoral college numbers, polling numbers, gut instincts or the predictions of futurist Faith Popcorn, but you've got to put your money where your mouth is.

In writing postelection analyses, you will have the benefit of hindsight. You will find no dearth of help, some of it unsolicited. Exit polls will help you understand voting patterns enough to compose a perspective on why one candidate won and the other lost. But before you can assess the long-term impact on the political landscape—relations with Congress, policy making, political realignment, the power balance in Washington and in the parties—you'll need to seek out the wisdom of current political pros as well as old-timers with a longer view of history. Do it right and you can take that long-awaited vacation with the knowledge that you contributed something to the process.

THE COMPLETE POLITICAL WRITER

The difference between a campaign reporter and a political reporter is that life for the latter doesn't end a few days after a presidential election—it only slows down for a while. The full-time political reporter is constantly on the prowl for political stories and new political faces. When both Washington and the nation are your beat, that's a lot of ground to cover.

An important part of your job is to make subjective judgments about emerging politicians who may have a national future. Their personality, their demonstrated political skills, the size of their state—any or all of those factors may put them on your watch list.

To cover the big picture requires the flexibility to travel frequently. Conferences of governors, state legislators and mayors are must stops. Developing sources around the country requires personal contact. Some of the best political towns are also some of the most pleasant places to visit: Austin, Boston, Atlanta, Chicago, Des Moines, Nashville, Madison.

Midterm elections are an important part of the big picture. Not only do key Senate and gubernatorial races provide a lot of spice, showcase the latest campaign techniques and produce new presidential farm-league players, but they also provide a checkpoint on the health of the president and the two political parties. And you don't have to go by the campaign calendar: A few days in the country with a senator or representative on recess any year will give you valuable perspective.

But there's plenty going on in Washington, too. Most presidential and congressional actions have political ramifications that cry out for analysis. The president's State of the Union address is a political statement. The president's budget is a political document. The White House staff is a political team. Every presidential news conference has a political motive. Veto fights are political battles. The maneuvering for advantage in the next redistricting is a political mission.

The trick is to be ever skeptical, without becoming cynical. A reputation for hard-nosed perseverance, seriousness of purpose and fairness will serve you well. A reputation for cheap shots, sloppy reporting and favoritism will do you in.

"The worst thing a political reporter can be is judgmental," says Jack Germond. "It suggests you think the political press has a social purpose, and I don't believe that. Our function is to report the political process with as much detail and analysis as possible, but not with the idea that we're going to improve it."

SELECTED RESOURCES

No standard resource list exists for political reporters. Washington has a glut of political newsletters and groups that churn out political commentary disguised as bipartisan analysis. Little of it is of any use to the working reporter. In fact, the best resources are shoe leather and a telephone. If you want to be sure of what's going on, it's best to find out firsthand. But some publications can be helpful along the way, including these:

The Hotline. Begun as the Presidential Campaign Hotline in 1987, the online political gossip sheet has evolved into what Editor in Chief Chuck Todd calls "the trade publication for the industry of politics." With a readership of 25,000 (half in government, one-fourth lobbyists and one-fourth in the media), the Hotline is the place political junkies of all stripes intersect. There are now five separate editions of the Hotline, including one that focuses solely on U.S. House races. Reporters read the Hotline not only to keep up with political tidbits from around the country but also to see what their colleagues are writing— and to see if their own contributions were used. Todd says he is constantly lobbied by both political operatives and journalists to include items—and encourages it.

Almanac of American Politics. Published by National Journal, the Almanac is the closest thing to a bible that many political reporters will ever hold. Updated every two years, the Almanac is indispensable for providing background on recent political history at the state and congressional district levels. It includes demographic data, as well as data on campaign contributions and expenditures, election results in recent years, and interest group ratings on the senator or representative.

Politics in America. This competitor of the Almanac is published by Congressional Quarterly. It contains much the same information as the Almanac does, but it breaks out separate profiles of each congressional district to accompany its very readable portraits of the members.

Congressional Quarterly. CQ's Weekly Report is required reading for those who cover the Hill. Political writers will want to review it quickly to keep up with Hill issues and will study it in more detail in election years. Its coverage of House and Senate primaries is particularly valuable, and the special reports on congressional elections in February and October should go into your bag of traveling files.

National Journal. The Journal is heavier on government than on politics but is nonetheless useful for the political subjects it does tackle. Few questions are left unanswered when the Journal finishes a political trend piece. The publication also includes an assortment of political columns of varying quality, as well as a "People" section that is helpful for keeping tabs on who is moving where in politics.

Cook Political Report. After years of struggling financially, Charles Cook's newsletter was purchased by National Journal and now flourishes as a top political handicapper. The report is chock full of good analysis and easy-to-read campaign data. Cook also does a weekly column that's available at no charge via e-mail, another example of how the Internet has made reporting easier. Despite his former association with various Democratic causes, Cook is regarded as an objective analyst.

In addition to the two parties' national and congressional campaign committees described earlier in this chapter, several institutions provide studies and data of interest:

Federal Election Commission. Now computerized and online, the public records of the FEC are an essential resource if you're trying to understand the dominant role that money plays in both congressional and presidential campaigns. Reports on how candidates, campaign committees and PACs are raising money, as well as how they're spending it, are kept here in files that are retrievable in seconds.

The Center for Responsive Politics. The center is one of those good-government outfits that hard-bitten political reporters spurn until some scandal sends them in search of a fast quote. The center was established to analyze ways in which Congress might operate better, but political reporters will find most useful its studies on PACs, campaign spending, congressional ethics and loopholes that allow campaign spenders to circumvent federal election laws.

PoliticalMoneyLine. This online database, operated by former FEC staffers Tony Raymond and Kent Cooper, offers a wealth of information on campaign donors, political action committees, and so forth, similar to that provided by the Center for Responsive Politics.

Committee for the Study of the American Electorate. The executive director of this committee, Curtis Gans, has made a career out of analyzing voter turnout, trying to figure out why it has been on a downward trend for most of the past 40 years. Not surprisingly, Gans gets the most attention just before and after Election Day, and his biennial reports should provoke more story ideas than they do.

Common Cause. You don't have to accept the increasingly political agenda of this "citizens' lobby" to appreciate the work it does on campaign finance. If nothing else, its reports on the amazing coincidences involving PAC contributions and votes in Congress should prompt bloodhound responses in the press corps.

10 THE MONEY BEAT

Government and politics, it turns out, is a big business—so much so that The Hill, a Washington newspaper focusing on coverage of Congress, calls it the "Influence Industry." Just how big is this uniquely Washington enterprise? According to records of the Federal Election Commission, the congressional elections of 2000 cost more than $1 billion to stage, and presidential candidates raised and spent in excess of $500 million, including more than $165 million in federal funds paid to presidential contenders and their parties. On top of that, the national political parties raised and spent another $300 million. But even though campaign finance gets the lion's share of attention from reporters, it's not the only operation of the influence industry, and perhaps not even the largest. The other major part of the industry is lobbying designed to shape the direction and details of federal policy on everything from how many cows can graze federal lands to arms sales to South Korea. Based on reports lobbyists are required to file by federal law, the Center for Responsive Politics estimates that businesses, labor organizations, foreign countries and other interest groups "invest" nearly $1.5 billion a year in their lobbying efforts. Even the estimated 20,000 Washington lobbyists have a lobby—the American League of Lobbyists. It's likely that the actual lobbying tab is somewhat higher than the reports show because some "lobbyists" are not required to register or file reports. When you add up all the parts, total "revenues" of this large, and rapidly growing, influence industry amount to well over $3 billion annually in an election year (it goes down somewhat in odd-numbered years). A corporation that recorded $3 billion in annual sales would have been large enough in 2001 to slip into the Fortune 500 list of America's largest companies. The bottom line is that this industry is too big and too important to be ignored by Washington reporters.

The good news is that changes in disclosure laws, and the availability of campaign finance and lobbying data online, have made access to information much easier than ever. The bad news is that in many Washington newsrooms,

Quick links to campaign finance resources on the Web

Federal Election Commission (http://www.fec.gov)	The starting place for any campaign finance question
Investigative Reporters and Editors (http://www.campaignfinance.org)	A wide selection of federal and state data, plus tips on covering campaign finance
PoliticalMoneyLine (http://www.politicalmoneyline.com)	Operated by Tony Raymond. Probably the best-known campaign finance site—check out the lobbying information, as well
Center for Responsive Politics (http://www.opensecrets.org)	This is one of the most popular Web sites among journalists. See the FEC data sliced and diced endlessly
American University Campaign Finance Website (http://www1.soc.american.edu/campfin)	A site maintained by Wendell Cochran since 1996. The most popular feature is the ability to download data from specific House districts and states
Common Cause (http://www.commoncause.org/laundromat/)	Search the soft money database, among other features

the connections between money and government are not routinely and systematically covered. Few news organizations in the capital have created "money" beats. While he was with the Associated Press in the early 1990s, Jim Drinkard, now a national correspondent at USA Today, was one of the first Washington reporters to cover campaign finance and lobbying as a beat. And even he was skeptical at first about the wisdom of the assignment. "When I was asked to write about special interests and lobbies, I said, 'Gee, I don't know. How would you write about that?'" Soon enough, he found that he had located a rich—mostly untapped—vein of information that could produce interesting and important stories, and often he had the mine to himself. One of Drinkard's most important insights was his discovery that campaign finance activity and lobbying are pieces of a complex mosaic, not separate operations. But he also learned that to draw a complete picture of the intersection of money and government, he needed to learn a new vocabulary and to develop sources in a community that, for the most part, would just as soon operate in silence.

Tony Raymond, who runs PoliticalMoneyLine.com, a Web site that tracks campaign spending and lobbying activities, says: "D.C. lobbyists call the shots. They decide how the money (given to campaigns) gets spent." James Albertine, who operates his own lobbying firm and recently served as president of the American League of Lobbyists, concurs: "You have to be involved in a big way in helping them make those decisions. If they don't take your advice on something as fundamental as where to spend their money, then why do you have them on board?"

Although the trail between campaign finance and lobbying often converges, reporters will find that they need to learn the ins and outs of covering each separately. So, we will look at them as separate entities and offer tips on ways to cover each of these complex areas.

CAMPAIGN FINANCE

Perhaps the three most famous words in modern journalism are contained in the parking garage advice imparted by "Deep Throat" to Bob Woodward during the Watergate investigation: "Follow the money." As a reaction to Watergate, Congress created the Federal Election Commission in 1974 and put into place a reasonably comprehensive—if somewhat hard-to-follow—disclosure system that requires candidates, political action committees and others involved in the money game to report who gives them money and how they spend it. Of course, many politicians didn't much cotton to the idea that reporters and others would be able to watch the flow of money through campaigns. Rep. George Hansen, an Idaho Republican, complained during the debate that, "If we pass this, reporters will cover all our peccadilloes." Ironically, Hansen later became the first member of Congress to be convicted for failing to file proper ethics disclosure forms, which were required under another law designed to bring openness to government.

Almost everyone who has pondered campaign finance issues has concluded that the political compromise that created the FEC—a six-member board that is by law evenly divided between Democrats and Republicans—resulted in an agency that rarely has been able to deal effectively with major issues. Certainly, the existence of the commission did not lead to a reduction in the amount of money being raised and spent by candidates to run their campaigns for federal offices. In that sense, the FEC has established a disappointing record in the eyes of many who advocate limiting campaign outlays as a means of achieving political reform. In fact, many blame the agency's rules and reluctance to act for opening the gaping "soft-money" loophole, clearing the way for unlimited contributions from corporations, labor unions and wealthy individuals. Eventually, the FEC ruled that such contributions had to be disclosed, but concluded that as long as the money wasn't used in federal elections it couldn't be banned. After more than a decade of political theater, marked by often-bitter partisan wrangling, Congress acted in 2002 to close the loophole, though the new law is being challenged on constitutional grounds. The FEC also had difficulty dealing with such issues as personal use of campaign contributions and enforcing the election laws restricting "coordination" between parties and candidates.

But whatever shortcomings the FEC might demonstrate as an enforcement agency, it has received generally good marks when it comes to openness and disclosure. "The FEC traditionally has been helpful to reporters, especially with explanations of arcane and complicated matters," says Derek Willis of Congressional Quarterly. "I've found the press shop to be reliable and informative. Best of all, most of them are veterans of the agency, which is a great advantage for reporters seeking clarification or illumination."

In addition to doing a good job answering questions, the FEC has adopted an attitude toward openness that is remarkable in modern Washington. For example, for years the FEC has added evening and weekend hours at its Washington office just before and after major filing dates—something repeated in few, if any, other federal agencies. Officials in the agency's public disclosure section usually are generous with their time and answer reporters' questions and requests for information with little hesitation. In fact, journalists treat the public disclosure office as if it was a giant data library with open stacks—anyone is free to poke into any file or file cabinet and to use a variety of computer terminals or copy machines. The FEC also was fairly quick to move to make its files available electronically, first via dial-up modem and then the Internet. If you need a hard copy of any FEC filing, you can get it through the FEC's Web site because the agency now scans all paper records. More recently, the FEC acted to require electronic filings from candidates for the House and the presidency (the Senate continues outside this requirement) and political action committees.

The availability of campaign files on the Internet has led to the creation of a cottage industry dedicated to making FEC data even more accessible to journalists and the public. (Several of those sites are listed in the table in this chapter.) In fact, according to a recent survey done by Professor Albert May for the Institute for Politics, Democracy and the Internet at George Washington University, one of those Web sites, opensecrets.org, run by the Center for Responsive Politics, is the most popular of all Internet sites among political journalists in Washington and around the nation.

Even though the campaign finance reports and figures are readily available, reporters still need to master a range of intricate details. "Reporters need to spend a little more time knowing what is in the law," Willis says. That will be especially important for the 2004 elections, which will be the first conducted under the 2002 amendments to the campaign finance laws.

When it comes to knowing the system, reporters need to understand the law's reporting requirements—who is required to file, what are candidates and committees required to file, what are the deadlines? The FEC's Web site is a good source for detailed information about what the law demands in the way of disclosure.

The campaign finance files contain a vast storehouse of untold, but important stories. At the least, newspapers and broadcast stations should report the summaries of what was raised and spent in every congressional race and by presidential candidates. Some of the stories journalists take for granted are more problematical. For example, a staple of campaign finance coverage is the story that starts: "Political action committees representing (fill in the blank) gave $(fill in the blank) to Rep. (Fill N. Blank), a member of the House (fill in the blank) Committee just (days, weeks, months, years) before the panel voted (for, against) a measure the industry (favors, opposes), according to Federal Election Commission records." A typical second paragraph: "A spokesman for FillBlank denied the congressman's vote was related to the contributions. 'We just serve our constituents' best interests,' she said." A computer could be programmed to write these dull, uninspired stories and likely will be one day soon. These stories inevitably leave the impression that Rep. Fill N. Blank is in the pocket of whatever industry it was that gave the money. They also usually leave out the unfortunate truth that proving such an allegation, at least on the basis of one gift and one vote, is virtually impossible. Simply put, it usually isn't possible to know whether the gift bought the vote or the vote bought the gift.

James Thurber, director of the Center for Congressional and Presidential Studies at American University, says the press has "picked up uncritically the line . . . that money buys votes, which is bullshit in my opinion." He continues: "It goes both ways. A congressman doesn't help his constituents because he's receiving money from them—he's receiving money from them because he's helped them. The relationship is much more complex. He'd still help his constituents—the wheat farmers, the dairy farmers—whether or not they gave him money or whether or not he accepted money."

What's more, the stories almost never mention that in the context of a $1-million-plus campaign, one contribution, even of $2,000 or $10,000, is fairly small potatoes. In an attempt to get around this fact, journalists and public interest groups aggregate donations from an "industry," but don't acknowledge that most industries are made up of a collection of factions that usually are business rivals, not allies. For example, stories about the contributions from the telecommunications industry regarding telecommunications legislation ought to point out at least that, among other things, the telephone and cable companies are at odds and that the long-distance and local phone providers barely agree on the time of day. If such competing interests are combined as "an industry," how is the reader to know which group really is trying to influence the member? Or do they imply that the member is able to be in more than one pocket at once? None of this questioning is meant to discount the reality that money sometimes does buy action or inaction. Reporters should aggressively look for connections between contributions and political results, but they also need to be careful of claiming too much.

In addition, the tone of campaign finance coverage usually makes it sound as if contributions were solely a "supply-side" phenomenon. The reality is quite different. Modern campaigns cost a lot of money, and candidates spend considerable amounts of money and time identifying and soliciting likely contributors. Corporations, labor unions, lobbying groups and others often feel intimidated by requests for contributions from legislators who make decisions about issues of importance to their business or membership. James Albertine says his Washington lobbying firm receives hundreds of solicitations for contributions every year and that "they aren't subtle at all." Independent lobbyist Howard Marlowe says some of his clients are unwilling participants. "It's gotten out of hand, but the pressure is on lobbyists to respond. If you walk into a member's office, and they've never seen you before, they're going to have your card in their hand. The card isn't so they can send you a Christmas card, I assure you. The card is to make sure they hit you up for the next fund-raiser." The money chase is so prevalent that fund-raising expenses are a big chunk of the cost of many campaigns and journalists would do well to look at this "demand-side" of the campaign finance equation in more depth. At least a few journalists have given token amounts to campaigns (don't do this with company money, it's against the law) in order to get on mailing lists for candidate and party solicitations.

Willis, who covers money and politics for Congressional Quarterly, also sees another part of campaign finance that needs more attention: how campaigns use the thousands, or millions, of dollars they raise. "Donations are important. But expenditures tell what a campaign is doing, what they are trying to accomplish," Willis says. There are other good reasons to watch where the money goes. Everything we know about letting politicians spend money without controls should tell us that there are great, unreported stories in those records. The lack of reporting on the flow of dollars out of campaigns is especially a problem in the case of presidential campaigns, where the major candidates and parties each spend more than $70 million in public money. As one example, diligent reporting of campaign spending might have unearthed a payoff the Clinton campaign made in a sexual harassment case in 1992. It took an understaffed FEC three years to uncover the payment and declare it an improper use of campaign dollars. In 1996, a journalism student at American University discovered that about half the money spent by a member of Congress from Connecticut went to his wife as payment for a variety of jobs with the campaign. The story became an issue in the race and the incumbent lost his seat, at least partly as a result. In many ways, journalists would do well to treat campaigns as small businesses and look at such questions as: Who are the vendors? Who is on the staff? How much is the staff paid? Who owns the building? Who does the printing? How many cars are leased? What is the rent?

Another story to follow closely will be the implementation of the 2002 reforms, which take effect for the 2004 cycle. The new law passed after years of debate in the spring of 2002, but by midsummer, The Washington Post and other news organizations were reporting ways in which political parties and other groups were maneuvering to find ways to raise money inside the new law's strictures. "The money isn't going to disappear," says CQ's Willis. "It's going to go somewhere." One place the soft money almost certainly will go is to state and local political parties, which means reporters trying to understand the flow of campaign dollars will have to get more familiar with the patchwork quilt of disclosure and other rules in the 50 states.

In addition, it now appears that after years in which the so-called "soft money" was the dominant feature of the political money landscape in Washington, the new law will again place a premium on "hard money," especially from political action committees. This should spur increased and improved coverage of the 4,000-plus PACs that represent large corporations, trade unions and virtually every interest group you can name. Journalists could construct ways and means of assessing the power and effectiveness of PACs that go beyond simply reporting the amount of money these organizations give to support or oppose candidates. What share of their funds do PACs give to winners? Do they give early or late in an election cycle? The aim of these measures would be to get a better handle on the actual power of such groups as the National Rifle Association, the AFL-CIO and other large interest groups. Similarly, little has been written about how PACs are administered. Again, it would be useful to tell the public who runs the leading PACs and how the committees go about making decisions on whom to support and or oppose. In other words, it would be helpful to take the view that PACs are such important players in public policy that they should be covered like a public institution.

LOBBYING

Along with reporters and political consultants, lobbyists have been a major growth industry in Washington since the mid-'70s. No one knows how many there are or even how to define precisely what a lobbyist is. The best guide to lobbyists, a book called "Washington Representatives," lists about 20,000 names, but not all of those are registered lobbyists and not all lobbyists are registered, although changes in registration laws in 1995 have forced more disclosure.

Lobbyists are paid—most of them quite handsomely—to do a lot of things, but most important, they're paid to know what's going on. That's reason enough for any reporter on any beat in Washington to want to get to know as many lobbyists as possible. Few experienced Washington journalists can conceive of covering a major piece of legislation as it wends it way through Congress and the executive branch without depending heavily on lobbyists, who often know the ins-and-outs of complex bills much more intimately than congressional staffers or members of Congress. Lobbyists usually can explain the consequences of legislative proposals—at least from their particular perspective—better than almost anyone else.

This information comes at Washington from all directions and from folks of all political stripes. Perhaps the most powerful lobby in Washington is AARP, formerly known as the American Association of Retired Persons. What gives the AARP such power? Numbers. AARP will sign up anybody over the age of 50 as a member, and it now claims a membership of 35 million—that's one in eight Americans. The group has been, not surprisingly, especially vocal about such issues as prescription drug benefits and Social Security. No politician wants to be cast as being on the side opposed to Grandma. But you might make an argument about power for many other groups. The AFL-CIO swings a big stick, especially among Democratic constituencies, as does the National Education Association, which represents teachers. The National Rifle Association, one of the most strident political combatants, isn't afraid to put its substantial money where its mouth is. The National Federation of Independent Business brags on its Web site that it is "America's most powerful small business lobbying organization."

In truth, virtually every corporation, small business, trade association, labor union and organized interest group in the country has someone—and often a team—in Washington looking out for its interests. Lobbying isn't just for business, either. Governments are big players as well. The White House has lobbyists, as do the federal agencies, though, technically, federal law prohibits agencies from lobbying Congress. Lobbyists work for the nation's governors, and many state legislatures, cities and universities.

Although it might appear to be a modern invention, lobbying always has been a feature of the American political system (indeed, probably every political system). The name comes from folks who would hang out, literally, in the lobbies of government offices waiting for a chance to make their pitches. But there is no question that in recent years, the Washington influence industry has had substantial growth—and it's a major reason why the Washington area economy tends to fend off economic problems easier than other regions of the country. There is no single explanation for this growth. However, one driving factor is the increasing size and complexity of the federal government— annual federal budgets top $2 trillion. And as the government has gotten more deeply involved in more areas of the economy, more companies and more interest groups have a stake on decisions made in Congress and the bureaucracy. As an offshoot of that, members of Congress and their staffs, faced with ever-more complex legislative proposals and the demands of raising ever-greater sums of money to finance re-election campaigns, turn increasingly to lobbyists for information and financial support.

Some younger reporters new to Washington tend to view lobbyists as shady characters. It's a strange attitude, because lobbyists are no different from people in any other professions or trades. Some are sleazeballs, to be sure, but the vast majority are upstanding citizens doing a job that is as American as apple pie.

"We're all lobbyists, by virtue of the Constitution," argues Howard Marlowe, a former president of the American League of Lobbyists and head of his own K Street lobbying firm. Marlowe is referring to the First Amendment guarantee of the right to petition the government. James Albertine, who represents a variety of corporate and other clients through his firm, adds, "It's a constitutionally protected enterprise. The Constitution encourages you to participate in the government and to contribute to the overall knowledge of the government officials so that they actually make decisions based in reality."

Albertine knows, though he doesn't like, the image his trade has with the public. He says that much of that view is based on the fact that lobbyists and others seeking to influence Congress and the administration have access to money. Still, he says, "The overall notion that lobbying equals corruption of some sort I believe is incorrect." Of course, it doesn't help much when one of the more prominent practitioners—James Lake, who had deep ties to the Republican Party—is convicted of illegal campaign contributions.

It's no secret that much of the clout of many lobbyists comes not from "real world" experience—running a company or a union or anything else—but from knowing the ways of Washington. The most popular routes for becoming a lobbyist run from Capitol Hill and the White House to the plush office towers that line K Street in downtown Washington. Typically, a lawyer or political operative will spend five to 10 years on a congressional member's staff or committee. Legislative directors, committee staff directors and top aides to committee chairs or congressional leaders are best positioned to trade their know-how and know-who for big bucks. Lobbydom is also a big lure for retired or defeated members of Congress; more than 125 former lawmakers have hung out their shingles as lobbyists, according to the Center for Responsive Politics. Ex-members have one unique advantage—access to the House and Senate floors, though few blatantly flaunt that privilege. Likewise, service on the White House staff in a top- or midlevel post confers instant marketability as long as the president is in office, although in recent years rules have been tightened in an effort to restrict the lobbying efforts of administration officials in the time just after they leave office. Those worried about falling out of favor can join one of the many bipartisan lobbying firms cropping up in Washington. Almost anyone who has worked at a decision-making level in the executive branch has something to sell.

The lobbyists' routes are not all one-way streets. "It's a huge revolving door," says Albertine, who himself spent time on Capitol Hill staffs before moving to the world of government relations. The revolving door in Washington often takes lobbyists back into the government, sometimes several times and usually to more prestigious positions than before. That, in turn, increases their value as lobbyists during the next interim in the private sector. There also is no substitute for longevity: The longer you are in town, the more people you know, the more fights you have seen. "This is not the kind of business where you can come in from Hazelton, Pa., and hang up a shingle and say 'Here I am hire me,'" Albertine says. "It requires relationships, institutional knowledge, people that really know where the bodies are buried."

The most successful lobbyists are those who learn from experience and are willing to be innovative. Take, for example, Anne Wexler. Wexler was a Connecticut housewife in the late '60s when she got caught up in the antiwar movement, plunged into the presidential campaign of Eugene McCarthy, and never slowed down. After working first for Edmund Muskie and then George McGovern in the 1972 presidential campaign, followed by a stint as associate publisher of Rolling Stone magazine, Wexler joined the 1976 campaign of Jimmy Carter, served as a leader of his transition team and ended up at the Commerce Department as an assistant secretary. After little more than a year, Wexler was moved to the White House, where she headed the public liaison office, generating grassroots support for programs such as the SALT II Treaty.

After Carter's defeat in 1980, Wexler, with two other Carter White House staffers, set up her own lobbying firm and began courting clients. She then teamed with a Reagan family adviser, Nancy Reynolds, giving the firm a bipartisan cast. Wexler enhanced that image in 1989 by hiring Craig Fuller, former chief of staff to Vice President Bush. In the late 1990s, after Republicans took over the House of Representatives, the Wexler Group hired longtime Pennsylvania Republican Rep. Robert Walker. Now the firm is known as Wexler & Walker. Today the shop represents a blue-chip list of major corporations and associations.

What Lobbyists Do

The image of lobbying as cigar-smoking characters wining and dining and discreetly passing envelopes of cash to favored lawmakers is at least a quarter century out of date. Cash contributions were outlawed in 1971. But it's still often tough to get a table at Washington's expense account restaurants, many of which aren't far off the K Street corridor. Today, however, more time and effort go into researching and simplifying information for members of Congress and their staffs, distilling the advocacy message, drafting legislation and amendments, rounding up cosponsors and votes, stirring up the grass roots, analyzing the impact and pitfalls of legislation for a member of Congress, helping to find re-election support, and similar tasks. It all boils down to advocating a cause.

A few companies, notably Microsoft, have tried to avoid playing the influence game; but they usually find the strategy doesn't pay off. When Microsoft ran into antitrust problems in the mid-1990s, one of its responses was to create an active Washington presence. However, simply having a team in the capital doesn't mean a company or an industry will necessarily get what it wants. Albertine admits his connections, his information and, even, to an extent, the money his clients control, provide him with the access he needs. But he says that often it's not that easy. "I walk out and someone else walks in who might have a very different perspective." And, sometimes, every lobbyist runs into a client who just can't be helped, like the CEO of a firm Albertine represented who told a senator, in all seriousness, "it's good to see that even ugly people can get elected."

Lobbying Techniques

Convincing congressional members (and, increasingly, officials in the executive branch agencies), of course, is the name of the game—and the task that preoccupies much of a lobbyist's time. But simply presenting the "facts" and a client's position is rarely enough. Lawmakers want to be sure that it's politically safe to take a stand.

Most major lobbying battles these days are fought simultaneously in at least three arenas:

- Coalitions of lobbying groups formed in Washington
- Grassroots campaigns waged outside Washington but controlled and directed from Washington
- The fund-raising circuit, which increasingly is concentrated in Washington because of the presence of lobbyists and their political action committees.

Coalitions, which have become a specialty for some lobbyist-organizers, are popular because they allow many groups with at least one common interest to leverage their collective clout at a reduced cost. They are sometimes forged quickly to react to pending legislation; others are long-term pacts designed to guard against legislation that may slowly be gaining acceptance. They usually have nice, appealing names. Typically, a coalition begins with a few phone calls. A meeting is set up. A mission statement is drafted. A steering committee is formed, with committee members paying higher dues or providing staff help. A poll may be commissioned to explore voter attitudes, with the results showered on the media. Meetings with members of Congress and key aides are set up. A plan for a grassroots component of the campaign is adopted.

Increasingly, these grassroots efforts are tied to the Internet. Coalitions build elaborate Web pages (many with links that will generate an e-mail message to a particular member of Congress). E-mail lists and alerts keep members up to date and give them the means to respond en masse and immediately. A reporter covering a particular issue might do well to seek out these Web pages as one way to stay on top of fast-moving issues. As an example, take a look at the Home Recording Rights Coalition, which has sprung up to argue against the entertainment industry's attempt to prohibit, or at least severely restrict, digital copying of movies, records and other materials. Its allies are the Consumer Electronics Association and other groups with a stake in making sure recording equipment stays available. There are profiles of coalition members (many of whom appear to be, unsurprisingly, folks who sell VCRs and other recording equipment). The Web site makes no bones about what the group does in Washington: "The HRRC staff at the Washington headquarters is responsible for keeping an eye on developments in government which could affect consumers, retailers, professional servicers, and manufacturers of consumer electronics and computer products. And it's our job to keep you informed of them." Anyone can join, for free, and get a periodic newsletter, along with e-mail alerts and updates. There also is a link to send an e-mail to Congress. Drinkard, who covers money and national politics for USA Today, calls these efforts not grass roots, but "AstroTurf roots," indicating there's a chance they sprang from Washington and not the countryside.

Many of the grassroots lobbying techniques were pioneered by Gary Nordlinger, who perfected them in a quarter century of campaigns for issues and candidates. Nordlinger Associates frequently is mentioned as being among the best political consultants in the business. One of the earliest stories about Nordlinger's exploits has attained the level of legend. It happened two decades ago while he was lobbying against a particular feature of a Social Security reform package. His strategy involved targeting the swing members on the House Ways and Means Committee, which had jurisdiction over the legislation. Among other tactics, Nordlinger sent research assistants to the House garages to watch the parking spaces of the targeted members to see what time they got to work. The assistants logged the times for several days and then, using flashlights, checked the needles on the members' car radio dials to find out which stations they listened to while driving in. Then the assistants bought three ads on those stations to run in the hour before the members arrived at work. "They thought the airwaves were just saturated with this stuff," Nordlinger says. Then Nordlinger had associates do the same kind of sleuthing at hometown airports where the members had left their cars and bought radio ads to run over those stations over the weekend.

Nordlinger's firm also bought an ad in the Washington edition of Time magazine at a modest cost of about $2,000 and had copies of it mailed to every member of Congress with the note, "Of course you saw our advertisement in Time magazine." The members assumed it was a national ad.

Then Nordlinger and company held teleconferences in 13 cities with high concentrations of federal employees. In each city, they had employees write letters to their representative by hand and then collected, stamped and delivered them to the post office. The upshot was that Nordlinger's coalition spent about $130,000 on a grassroots effort that was widely reported to be a $4 million campaign.

Using Lobbyists as Sources

What do the internal workings of lobbyists and PACs have to do with reporting in Washington? Quite a bit, if you want to write knowledgeably about what's going on here. Few things happen in Washington by accident. Bureaucrats and regulators in the bowels of the executive branch usually don't flip a coin to decide how they will rule on a dispute that may cost an industry millions of dollars. Usually, one side of the issue has out-lobbied the other. And not many members of Congress get out of bed each morning inspired by a new and novel idea for legislation to sponsor.

Few important issues are so free of controversy that they sail through Congress and across the president's desk without opposition. Almost every bill introduced and every regulation proposed has a lobbyist's fingerprints on it somewhere. And once it's made public, an army of lobbyists is apt to form to take exception. That's the way the system works, and that's why it often takes years to change a law or regulation.

For reporters, it all goes back to the basic imperative of covering Washington: Find out the real agenda. You can do this by developing sources in the lobbying community who will tell you what's really going on. It won't be easy. Many lobbyists are uncommunicative, especially if they don't know you. Some have agreements with their clients that they simply won't discuss their business with the press, although they will sometimes introduce a reporter to a client. "Most lobbyists try to operate under the radar screen," says Dennis Beal, a former Senate Budget Committee staff member who has his own lobbying firm. "Suspicion is the first thing that would hit a lobbyist's mind when a reporter calls them." Much of that feeling arises from the nature of much of the coverage about lobbying and lobbyists. Beal thinks that lobbyists, as well as reporters, could benefit from a closer relationship. Reporters would get information they need to write better stories and lobbyists would get an opportunity to "develop some pressure on the matter. If you've got somebody out there writing about what you're for and writing about it a positive way it can help you." Beal cautions, though, that it can't be a one-way street. "A smart lobbyist knows if you're going to talk with reporters about things you want to talk to them about, you'd better talk to them about the things you want to avoid."

One way reporters can build stronger relations with lobbyists is to keep track of past contacts. Most lobbyists in Washington used to do something else. Good sources from previous beats, whether it was the White House or Congress or a federal agency, may be key lobbyists on an issue you're now writing about. With the influx of political operatives into big-bucks lobbying firms, political writers can find old and trusted sources all over Washington. You should monitor the new lobbyist registrations as they are reported by the clerk of the House and the secretary of the Senate. Make a note of familiar names and put them in your Palm Pilot. Another tack is to look for cracks in the lobbying coalitions that usually form for and against major legislation. Odds are you'll find someone in the coalition who isn't happy with the coalition's game plan and is ready to give a behind-the-scenes account that assigns blame for pending defeat. Lobbyists on the losing side in almost any battle are often approachable.

A little legwork at the ground level can pay dividends. If you attend hearings on legislation at the subcommittee level, you're apt to see many more lobbyists than reporters. This is a good time to get acquainted, demonstrate serious interest in the subject matter, trade business cards and make follow-up calls.

Finally, you can ingratiate yourself with lobbyists by checking out your facts with them any time you're going to mention one of their clients. That's a basic tenet of good reporting, of course, but it's sometimes overlooked in Washington. Even the most uncommunicative lobbyists will appreciate that, and it may make them more willing to talk in the future.

Tracking Lobbyists and Their Money

Trying to figure out who is lobbying whom on what issue can be a time-consuming exercise. Trying to demonstrate a connection between legislative actions and financial contributions made by lobbyists is both time consuming and risky. Yet both are part of good reporting.

The federal act under which lobbyists are required to register was toughened considerably in 1995 and again in 1998. Among other things, the law now requires more disclosure and forces more folks who engage in lobbying to register and report their activities. The 1995 amendments require anyone who spends 20 percent of his or her time lobbying or makes more than $10,000 in any six-month period from lobbying activities to report. PoliticalMoneyLine.com makes the registrations available online. The same organization also offers, on a subscription basis, information about clients, fees and other lobbying details. The Center for Responsive Politics also has that information on its free Web site (www.crp.org), although on a less timely basis than PoliticalMoneyLine.

The bottom line: Washington is a swirl of conflicting agendas, high-stakes battles, monied interests and hardball players. The role of money increases in direct proportion to the cost of getting re-elected. You can't cover Washington intelligently without being ever mindful of this, and ever suspicious. You're not going to uncover many scandals. Few things are cast so black-and-white; most questionable activity by lobbyists and their targets involves subtle shades of gray. You'll miss it all if you're not willing to take the time to develop the sources that will enable you to understand the nuances.

11 INVESTIGATIVE REPORTING

The groundbreaking 1960s television series about the police in New York City, "Naked City," ended each episode with the tag line: "There are eight million stories in the Naked City. This has been one of them." In many ways that captures both the promise and the challenge of doing investigative reporting in Washington: The city and its institutions hold so many potentially great stories it is hard to know where to begin. The truth is, with so many stories available, it hardly matters where you look or where you start. But, unfortunately, too few Washington journalists have the time or the inclination to take advantage of the surfeit of stories and resources available to an enterprising investigative reporter. Edward Pound, who has done investigative reporting for The Wall Street Journal, The New York Times and USA Today and now is an investigative reporter with U.S. News and World Report, gives this glum assessment: "I think that the state of investigative reporting in Washington is not all that good."

Brant Houston, executive director of Investigative Reporters and Editors, gives several explanations for why there might not be a focus on investigative reporting in the capital.

> One, there is so much news that you have to dedicate someone to do the longer projects.
> Two, if a journalist loses his energy, it's easy to rely on press conferences and releases.
> Three, sometimes journalists in D.C. are seduced by the trappings of power and access to the powerful and lose their aggressiveness.

The promise of prizes shouldn't be a big motivator for journalists, but they certainly are one way to measure the impact of a story. And in the realm of investigative journalism, perhaps more than in other arenas, prizes seem to have a special significance. The recent track record for Washington-based reporters isn't strong, in that regard. For example, few of the Pulitzer Prizes given in the investigative reporting category have been given to Washington-based journalists writing about Washington-related topics. From 1985-1999, no Washington reporter won an investigative Pulitzer. In 2000, the Associated Press won an investigative Pulitzer for uncovering a long-suppressed story about a massacre by the U.S. military during the Korean War. And in 2001 the Los Angeles Times, one of the few newspapers with a full-time Washington-based investigative team, won the investigative Pulitzer for coverage of the Food and Drug Administration's drug approval policy. In fact, few have been given for any investigation related to Washington subjects. The Seattle Times won the 1996 Pulitzer for coverage of problems in Native American housing programs, but the work was done by a team based in Seattle. To be fair, several Washington-related stories or stories done by Washington-based reporters that many would consider at least partly "investigative" won Pulitzers in other categories. But the last time any reporting Pulitzer went to a story that focused on Congress was 1960.

There's a saying in journalism that all good reporters are investigative reporters. True, but that doesn't mean that all good reporters are good investigative reporters. To do it right requires a certain disposition characterized by patience, perseverance and stubbornness that few reporters are born with or ever acquire. The first thing you need is the mindset that all this work—and there is no getting around it, good investigative reporting is time consuming, painstaking and mentally and physically challenging—will be worth the effort.

Don Muhm, the retired farm editor of The Des Moines Register, liked to say as he mined piles of obscure documents about federal agriculture programs from his Iowa vantage point, "Big programs, big stories." Muhm also understood that it wasn't the programs, but the people whom they touched—for good or for ill—that made the stories worth the digging. Pound, who has been doing investigative reporting for nearly 40 years, says: "You need to have a sense of outrage. You need to feel that when things are wrong, somebody has got to get out there and try to expose it and get it out to the public. Persistence and focus are also extremely important. You can't lose sight of that. You need to be focused on this job and you need to have an ability to stay with this story. The key to investigative reporting is not to give up."

Getting the necessary stick-to-it-iveness might be more difficult in Washington, where legions of politicians, consultants, PR people, think tanks and other spinmeisters are clamoring for attention and holding out the lure of easy, done-by-dinner stories. It also can be hard to justify to editors hundreds of miles away; they see other papers and broadcast outlets with stories from their Washington reporters and wonder why their person doesn't have the same thing (or, anything, for that matter, given the time solid investigative projects can consume). Alan Levin of USA Today says that freeing time is a problem, even at a large organization and even though he is where his editors can see him and know what he is up to. "It's hard in this city to sit back for a month and work on a project, because you will end up missing so many other things."

One thing you need to be prepared for when you enter the world of investigative journalism is the amount of paper that's involved. Unlike much reporting, particularly relating to politics and government, in which public statements and quotes from sources usually are sufficient to build stories on, investigative pieces derive their credibility from evidence. Simply put, the more, the better. And frequently that evidence is well concealed, often by people with the means and motives to make sure it never sees the light of day. Says the Los Angeles Times' Rick Serrano: "Something different about investigative reporting is that reporters (need) documents, paper, videotape or audiotape—some kind of concrete record that you could hold. And once you get that there is a great sense of accomplishment, because you know you've basically got the story."

That doesn't mean that people aren't important sources in investigative reporting; they are. Many of the best investigations come from tips, though you'd do well to ask yourself why a source might give you a particular piece of information. What you hope for is that the tipster knows enough to point you in the right direction and toward sources—both paper and human—that can help keep you moving toward the story.

But there can be too much reliance on tips and trades with sources. Charles Lewis, formerly a senior producer for "60 Minutes" and now head of the Center for Public Integrity, denigrates much of what he passes for investigative journalism in Washington as "the illusion of investigative reporting." By that he means reporters merely latch onto a probe being done by a congressional committee or the General Accounting Office or the Justice Department and write about developments, rather than finding and developing their own stories. Pound agrees: "In Washington what passes for investigative reporting is someone picking up the phone and calling a federal source on an investigation and them leaking some information to you and you write a story about a federal investigation." Instead, he says: "I would say there needs to be a lot more original investigative reporting where you bring to the public stories that they wouldn't otherwise get because of your reporting. . . . I think there are examples like Watergate that are extraordinary; but what a lot of reporters do out here is chase the same story and they are not doing original reporting such as issues that the public doesn't know anything about."

For example, reporting of the Clinton-Lewinsky scandal wouldn't qualify as original reporting in the eyes of many investigative journalists. Peter Eisler, a member of the special projects staff at USA Today, says:

> Frankly I didn't consider the impeachment story to be an investigative story at all. That was a quote story, it was working sources, it was covering a federal investigation, in this case an independent counsel investigation, and it was trying to get material that was coming out of the independent counsel's office and also the Hill based on investigations that were going on

by Hill staffers. There wasn't a lot of original investigative reporting that I saw surrounding the impeachment story. It was more well-sourced reporters who were breaking stories, getting news out there that had actually been dug up either by congressional investigators or by investigators working for the independent counsel's office. It was not original reporting in the way that the original information is being dug up and generated by the reporters themselves.

In many ways, practicing the craft in Washington is not much different from reporting elsewhere. The people-versus-paper approach to investigative reporting is debated here, as it is beyond the Beltway, but most of the best practitioners here, as elsewhere, blend the two. If there's a slight edge, it probably goes to people because Washington is a town of networks within networks within networks, as noted by U.S. News and World Report's Pound: "People are more important here because connections—who you know, whether you know the right lawyers in town, the right investigators—that's more important in Washington than records."

There are few full-time investigative reporters in Washington, but many reporters do fine investigative reporting as part of their beats at the Pentagon, the Environmental Protection Agency, the Department of Housing and Urban Development, or wherever. The universal grumble is that they don't have more time to uncover all those things federal bureaucrats and politicians are working so hard to keep hidden.

Being based in Washington as an investigative reporter has many advantages and few disadvantages. The purpose of this chapter is to outline those advantages briefly, not to provide a primer on investigative techniques. Presumably you learned the basics of researching documents and constructing paper trails long before your employer agreed to finance your mission here.

Perhaps the biggest disadvantage to investigative reporting here is the never-ending obfuscation encountered. Federal officials are much more accomplished at lying than, say, your garden-variety local medical examiner or courthouse clerk.

Scott Higham, whose Washington Post team won the 2002 Pulitzer for its compelling investigation of abuses in the city's child welfare programs, says: "The most frustrating thing is when people (who) are in positions of power lie to the public and lie to the press and try to hide information that the public is entitled to see. . . . That is part of the landscape because a lot of the times you are looking into things that people don't want you to know. When you realize that people are lying to you, you realize that there is something for you to be looking into because they wouldn't be lying otherwise."

When he first came to Washington from Chicago nearly a quarter century ago, where he was an investigative reporter for the Sun-Times, Pound noticed the difference: "At the higher level of federal agencies, they are trying to manipulate you and they do have agendas. If you think otherwise, you're stupid—you haven't been here long enough. There are a lot of agendas here, and you should never lose sight of that when you're working on a story. In Washington, I really think you have to look at things cold. . . . There is a lot of crap to put up with here, a lot of phony posturing."

The good news is that Pound finds "overwhelming advantages" to being based here. First, Washington is a city awash in paper. Government agencies, congressional panels, advisory committees, task forces and presidential commissions are daily grinding out official reports to be embargoed, classified, declassified, sanitized, advertised and pulverized. The most interesting ones are the ones not yet released, of course, but the bulk of all reports go unread, no matter their status.

Washington also *is* a city of investigators, and we're not just talking about the FBI. The General Accounting Office investigates more than a thousand different subjects in an average year. The Justice Department and special prosecutors investigate sleaze in the executive branch, and House and Senate ethics committees investigate sleaze on Capitol Hill. Inspectors general look for waste and mismanagement in the bureaucracy. Congressional oversight committees investigate programmatic abuse wherever they can get a whiff of it.

With all this investigating going on, it shouldn't be hard for an aggressive reporter to tap into a good story if he or she can develop the right sources. Pound, for example, relies heavily on two groups of contacts—congressional staffers and Washington lawyers. "The Hill is the place to start," he says, "because everything goes through the Hill sooner or later . . . and then lawyers, because this is a lawyer's town. There's a zillion of them, and they're into everything. For young reporters, I'd say get to know lawyers involved in criminal cases and civil cases."

Working the Hill right is a balancing act that can require trade-offs. Investigators for oversight committees, once they're cultivated, are frequently willing to give reporters a scoop or steer them to other sources who can help them break a story. There's an unspoken quid pro quo, however: They usually expect some publicity for their boss, the subcommittee chair, or whomever.

Pound says he has "absolutely no qualms" about asking Hill staffers to help him ferret out information, as long as no laws are broken. As for the quid pro quo, he says:

> It's not quite that refined, but I don't think it's an unreasonable conclusion for anyone to make. As long as it's honest brokering, I don't see anything wrong with it. I think most investigative reporters look at it that way. But you can't look aside from the fact that these committees provide reporters with a lot of valuable information. It's incumbent upon you as a reporter to check the information out like you'd do anywhere else. Be satisfied that you're getting good information.

But there is nearly universal awareness that simply passing along information from other people's investigations often isn't enough. Reporters need to be able to spot the openings left by Hill and agency probes to go deeper and do more original work. For that, you will need to be able to get into the nooks and crannies of the government, looking for those telltale documents and records that can support your case.

Pound says he now makes extensive use of the Internet to supply him with background information and documents—on a recent story he turned up 2,500 cases. He also says reporters must have a "knowledge of the records that are available in this country and how to get at those records. By that I mean government records, private records, tax records. Understand the record systems, how to use FOIA, the Freedom of Information Act, how to research government records."

USING THE FREEDOM OF INFORMATION ACT

The law can't make any source talk to you. But when it comes to getting documents, journalists (and the public at large) do have some legal levers to pull. One of the most commonly used tools in Washington, and elsewhere, is the federal Freedom of Information Act. Reporters disagree about the value of the FOIA, but most of them in Washington, whatever their beat, use it at one time or another. Enacted in 1966 and amended several times, the law has become an accepted and routine part of news gathering in Washington. Surprisingly, reporters are not the biggest users of the FOIA. Lawyers, corporations and prison inmates file more FOIA requests each year than the press. (Lawyers are looking for evidence to bolster their cases, the corporations usually are trying to spy on their competitors, and the convicts are trying to figure out who did them in.) One huge caveat about the law: It only covers executive branch agencies. Congress has conveniently exempted itself from forced disclosures. And the judicial branch isn't covered because of separation-of-powers issues.

The value of the FOIA to reporters over the years has tended to reflect the current administration's attitude toward it. The Clinton administration took some steps to open up access, including supporting some amendments to make it easier to get documents in electronic form and starting a move to get many federal documents onto the Internet. The Clinton Justice Department also instituted a process that would permit requests to be filed for "expedited review" in particularly newsworthy cases. But the Bush administration— particularly after the attacks of Sept. 11, 2001—has tried exceptionally hard in the minds of many FOI observers to crack down on the flow of information. Jane Kirtley, now the Silha professor of media ethics and law at the University of Minnesota and former executive director of the Reporters Committee for

Freedom of the Press, says the administration, led by Attorney General John Ashcroft, has given federal agencies the signal that withholding information is all right, maybe even encouraged. Ashcroft, in a memo a month after the attacks, pledged Justice Department support for agencies that are sued over refusing to give up documents. In a column for American Journalism Review, Kirtley wrote: "Even the most obtuse government-records custodian couldn't mistake the message: When in doubt, don't give it out. Instead of upholding the presumption of disclosure that is indispensable to FOIA, Ashcroft's memo (outlining administration policy) guts it, ensuring that decision makers can do their work without fearing public scrutiny of the process" (Kirtley, 62).

You don't have to be a lawyer to compose an FOIA request. You don't even have to be a legal junkie. Today, many large news organizations have stored sample FOIA request letters on their in-house computer networks. Every government agency of any size has an FOIA office staffed by people who do nothing but answer questions and route FOIA requests to the appropriate offices. And you may not need to file a request in the first place. Bob Woodward, assistant managing editor for The Washington Post and perhaps the most famous investigative journalist of modern times, says journalists should be forceful in seeking access to documents, including filing FOIA requests and appeals and lawsuits, when needed. But, he says, too many reporters forget that the most important words for reporters are, "Can you help me?" Woodward, who estimates he has filed only about 100 "serious" FOIA requests in his 30 years as a reporter and author, still regards the formal letter to an agency as more of a last resort approach. At the least, you need to talk with the press offices and FOIA officials and others at the agency to see whether the information is available without a request. Negotiation often works better than confrontation. Much information is routinely available and any material released through a previous FOIA request should be provided without an additional request. If you hit a stone wall in the negotiations, then it's time for a more hard-edged approach, though you should be prepared to hunker down for what can be an extremely long haul; sometimes it takes months or years to get the material you're seeking.

Before you do anything, get familiar with the Freedom of Information law. One place to start is the Reporters Committee for Freedom of the Press (www.rcfp.org). The committee has a hot line for reporters seeking advice, but even better is the committee's handy guide called How to Use the Federal FOI Act, available for $5. The handbook, complete with sample forms, spells out step-by-step how to file, appeal and litigate an FOIA request, and when and how to ask for expedited review of your request. It explains the nine exemptions under which your request may be denied. (It also explains what is protected by the federal Privacy Act and how to use that law if you want to find out what the government has on you. Privacy claims have become an increasingly popular way for agencies to get around releasing information they wish to protect.) The committee will help you find a lawyer if you want to sue an agency over an FOIA dispute, and it maintains an extensive library of material on access and other media-law issues.

Before you vow to go all the way to the Supreme Court, however, consider all your options and make sure your bosses are prepared for the time and costs of pursuing a full-blown FOIA case. Tony Mauro, who covers the Supreme Court for The American Lawyer magazine and is considered an expert on media-law issues, provides these 10 informal tips for using the FOIA:

1. Work the phones. See if the information is readily available without an FOIA request. Find out everything you can about the document needed, the form number, dates, and so forth.

2. Be specific. Usually, the more specific the request you make, the quicker you will get it. But don't be so specific that the agency can get away with not sending you an important document.

3. Don't assume the information you're seeking is private. You would be surprised how much information is available at the FBI and the IRS that you might think is private. Be imaginative.

4. Request help. Many federal agencies have a big and public-minded bureaucracy that deals with FOIA requests. Such bureaucracies will sometimes help you fashion a request so that it will have a better chance for success.

5. Try the horizontal approach. Instead of making an FOIA request with one agency, look closely at the object of your search. If it's a business, it may have to file many forms with many different agencies. Talk to someone at a competing or similar business to learn what kinds of forms it has to file, and then request them all for the business you're studying.

6. Move quickly. Because making an FOIA request entails waiting beyond tomorrow's newspaper, it's easily forgotten. Make the request before you forget it.

7. Make filings a routine. To help yourself move quickly, set up a letter in your word processor that includes all the boilerplate language but lets you plug in the specifics.

8. Talk up the FOIA. At meetings with staff and editors, promote the FOIA as a reporting tool that's as handy as a backward city directory.

9. Be patient. Keep in mind that, depending on what information you get, the story that comes out of an FOIA request might be just as newsworthy six months or a year from now as it will be tomorrow.

10. Don't take no for an answer. Some agencies refuse requests routinely, just as an opening strategy. The appeals process on the state and federal levels can often turn a no into a yes.

Mauro is one of the most innovative users of the FOIA in Washington. He routinely requests the FBI files of famous people when they die, sometimes with fascinating results. In the file of Supreme Court Justice Potter Stewart, for example, he found that former FBI director J. Edgar Hoover had once vetoed Stewart's application to be an FBI agent because Stewart's mother was a member of the League of Women Voters. Mauro also uses the FOIA to pursue leads suggested by spot stories. A request to see the details of a Justice Department settlement with families of the astronauts killed in the Challenger shuttle accident disclosed that the government had first tried to "zero out" the families—give them nothing.

SOURCES AND RESOURCES

Congressional Investigative Arms

As a first step, find out what the General Accounting Office, the Congressional Budget Office and the Congressional Research Service have done in the area you're probing. All of them publish indexes of past reports. As arms of Congress, these agencies tend to be more open with reporters than agencies in the executive branch. They usually won't talk about investigations in progress (members of Congress want to get the publicity of releasing their reports), but afterward they may give you tips on where else to look for information.

The GAO is perhaps the most respected and useful of the congressional investigators. Except for the two top officials, who are appointed to long terms, all GAO employees are careerists—lawyers, auditors, economists, computer experts and specialists in areas ranging from defense to health and agriculture. At any given time, the GAO has about a thousand investigations under way; there is almost no area of government policy and spending that GAO hasn't looked into.

Congressional Oversight Panels

Many major standing committees in both houses have oversight and investigations subcommittees. Developing sources on these committee staffs is a long-term objective of any investigative reporter. In the short run, you're equally interested in the public hearing records they accumulate. These books are chock full of testimony, correspondence, witness lists and related documents that can give you leads to pursue.

Investigative Reporters and Editors

Although the office of IRE (www.ire.org) is located at the University of Missouri in Columbia, it provides a number of services that make the

$50-a-year membership a bargain for any investigator and make it a good place for a Washington-based reporter to contact early. Actually, it is hard to imagine that any reporter wouldn't be well served to join IRE. IRE maintains a repository of several thousand top investigative pieces from reporters across the country. With one phone call, you can get citations on investigations similar to what you're doing, and even have copies faxed or e-mailed to you.

IRE's focus in recent years has been on training, particularly in the area of computer-assisted reporting, which has been a real boon for investigative reporters trying to make sense of mountains of federal data. IRE also has used money raised through grants to acquire and maintain databases on a variety of federal topics, ranging from aircraft safety to federal contracts to drug effectiveness to campaign finance. The organization also holds national and regional conferences and makes most of the handouts and tipsheets available from its Web site.

Reports of Inspectors General

The Office of Inspector General was created during the Carter administration and has received mixed reviews. All the cabinet departments and most large agencies now have IGs. Most IGs maintain hot lines for reporting fraud and abuse. Their primary job is to ensure that their agencies are spending funds the way Congress intended. They make regular agencywide reports to Congress each year and make separate reports when they undertake special investigations. They also are required to report, every six months, a list of the reports and audits they issued in the previous six months. Some IGs take on the role of agency protector-in-chief, but others have been willing to go far out on limbs to find, ferret out and report egregious examples of waste, fraud and abuse. When she reported for Gannett News Service, Chris Collins developed a beat around IG reports and broke stories on issues ranging from the deteriorating roof of the Kennedy Center to thefts of Native American art objects from Interior Department offices in the West. Whatever an IG's track record, IG reports should be sought out by reporters, preferably in the drafting stages, before they're massaged and officially released.

The National Security Archive

Reporters delving into national security or foreign policy investigations have an important and relatively new resource in the National Security Archive. Founded by Scott Armstrong, a former investigative reporter for The Washington Post and co-author with Bob Woodward of "The Brethren," the archive, now housed at George Washington University, is collecting an unmatched library of materials concerning the contemporary history of national security and foreign policy initiatives. The archive also assists reporters in using the FOIA. Armstrong says, "Secrecy in this government is used to protect the United States national security from its five major enemies: Congress, the press, the American public, the major hostile nations, and its allies."

The National Archives

Not to be confused with the National Security Archive, the National Archives is the official repository of federal government records dating back to 1775. The archives also operates the 10 presidential libraries open as of 2002 and oversees the collection of Richard Nixon's and Bill Clinton's papers. Most available information at the archives is more than 30 years old. That's not true at the presidential libraries, however, and former Investigative Reporters and Editors director Steve Weinberg rates librarians there as among the most helpful people in the world.

Federal Disclosure Reports

For probing an elected official or high-ranking appointee, a lobbyist or the corporation a lobbyist represents, or a potential major political contributor, numerous disclosure forms are easily accessible to reporters. You can start at the Federal Election Commission, where computer searches will quickly tell you if a person or political committee contributed to a federal candidate or received payment from one. A little manipulation with the computer will also reveal if a congressional member or candidate is particularly beholden to one source of money or special interest group. (For more information on covering campaign finance, see Chapter 10.) Some careful cross-checking should indicate the proximity of a particular committee vote, public hearing or bill sponsorship to a campaign fund-raiser or large contribution.

You can move next to the Hill, where regularly published reports of the House clerk and the secretary of the Senate will tell you how members of Congress or committees spent their money, including staff salaries and expenditures on overseas junkets. Reports of the junkets themselves are filed with the same offices. Lobbyists must file registration forms with the House clerk and the secretary of the Senate, stating for whom and for what issues they're working, but the law is so fuzzy that some lobbyists ignore it. Lobbyists must also file disclosure forms detailing their lobbying activities at the House and Senate, and those who lobby for foreign governments or corporations must publicly disclose the details to the Justice Department. (More information about these resources is in Chapter 10.)

Perhaps the most useful document to be found on the Hill is the personal financial disclosure form filed each May by members of Congress, official candidates for Congress and senior staff members. Although most assets and liabilities are reported in ranges, such as $15,001 to $50,000, the reports can tip you to potential conflicts of interests in investments. They also document gifts and reimbursements. Senior executive branch and legislative branch officials, including Supreme Court justices, also are required to file disclosure statements.

Legal and Regulatory Documents

Whether you're tracking an individual, an organization or a business, there may be court or regulatory documents that will help you. The U.S. Tax Court is a venue for sometimes arcane and sometimes juicy feuds between the Internal Revenue Service and wealthy individuals or corporations. The U.S. Court of Appeals for the District of Columbia Circuit hears a lot of disputes in which federal regulations are being challenged. The U.S. Court of Federal Claims hears grievances against the government involving back pay, breach of contract and taxes paid under protest. The U.S. Court of Appeals for the Federal Circuit considers patent appeals, and the U.S. Court of Appeals for the Armed Forces may be a place to check if your subject has a military background.

One shortcut here is to wangle a search through LEXIS or WESTLAW, two computer databases that carry opinions from virtually every federal, state and specialized court case in America in which there was a reported decision. Finding the opinion is just the starting point, of course. To get the underlying documents of a case—exhibits, transcripts, depositions, interrogatories—you have to go to the court where the case is being heard.

For regulatory disputes that haven't yet reached litigation, there are many places to look for documents. Most regulatory agencies maintain public documents rooms that may provide details on financial distress (the Securities and Exchange Commission), union disputes (the National Labor Relations Board), accident histories (the Occupational Safety and Health Administration), and so forth. Much of this information now also is available through the agency sites on the World Wide Web. The easiest way to access these is through the federally maintained gateway, Firstgov (www.firstgov.gov).

Private Watchdog Groups

There are many self-appointed investigators in Washington, and some have pretty good track records for documenting abuses. Common Cause is a good source on lobbying, campaign finance irregularities and government ethics in general. Several groups founded by Ralph Nader produce interesting material on regulatory abuses and inadequacies in the areas of health, environment, auto safety, nuclear power, and so on. Numerous environmental watchdog groups and defense critics like the Project on Government Oversight and the Union of Concerned Scientists have proved to be useful to investigative reporters. They can sometimes lead you to whistle-blowers that you can develop on your own as sources. The caveat is that all of them have an ax to grind.

Reading and Reference Books

If you're a joiner or a First Amendment junkie, several publications will keep you up to date on investigative techniques and the problems encountered by investigative reporters. Among the best are quarterlies published by Investigative Reporters and Editors (IRE Journal) and the Reporters Committee for Freedom of the Press (News Media and the Law). The Society of Professional Journalists publishes an annual report that covers the waterfront on media-law issues. Washington lawyer Harry Hammitt publishes a newsletter, Access Reports (www.accessreports.com), which closely tracks Freedom of Information Act issues in the courts and the federal agencies.

As for reference works, Washington offers directories of varying and sometimes marginal utility. Experienced reporters will know where to look. They don't need a directory to tell them to look in the Code of Federal Regulations for a firsthand account of what a federal regulation says. They'll know to check the Congressional Information Service index or the Library of Congress's computers to track the history of a piece of legislation.

Washington has no indispensable publications for investigative reporters, but three come close. The United States Government Manual is the best single book published for quick reference to who does what in the bureaucracy. The Federal Register, published each weekday, and the Congressional Record, published each day Congress is in session, are the two best resources for story ideas and keeping up with what's going on in the bureaucracy and on the Hill. If you read both of them every day, you'll know more about what's going on in Washington than 95 percent of the people who work here.

REFERENCES

Kirtley, Jane, "Hiding Behind National Security," *American Journalism Review*, Vol. 24, No. 1, January/February 2002, p. 62.

12 COVERING WASHINGTON AS A FOREIGN CORRESPONDENT

For many foreign newcomers, Washington can be a new and refreshing journalistic experience because of the comparative openness of the government and the American people. Indeed, foreign correspondents in Washington can sometimes learn more about their own country in the United States than they can at home, thanks to our more open approach to news.

Leo Wieland, who spent 18 years in Washington reporting for the Frankfurter Allgemeine before being posted to Madrid in 2002, says: "What I came to like here early on was the fact that somebody working for the American government does not consider giving out information a personal favor. It's part of his duty—what he or she is paid for. That is particularly refreshing for a European who more often than not comes from a society that traditionally is not only bureaucratic, but where the old-fashioned attitude is, first we don't want to tell you anything and, second, if we do, you have to be eternally grateful."

Karin Henriksson, correspondent for Stockholm's Svenska Dagbladet, says Americans in general are easier to deal with than, for example, the French. "America is very easy to work in for a journalist because Americans are very outgoing and Americans have a high regard for the media and the importance of the media. In that sense, it's been more rewarding to work in the U.S. than in a lot of countries where I've been."

Philip Tazi, correspondent for the Cameroon Herald, says he finds U.S. society to be "unusually open." People don't get paranoid when you come up to ask them questions, he says. "People just seem delighted to share their views with you. I found American government institutions to be very, very open." That presented a sharp contrast for Tazi, who grew up in Cameroon, but has also lived in France and Canada. "I don't think the appreciation for information has really gained the same importance in Africa as it has gained in other cultures," he says. "Journalists are seen in Africa as parasites, not just by the political leadership, but also by the people."

Despite the openness of the government, frustrations abound for the more than 1,000 foreign correspondents registered with the State Department's

Foreign Press Center, especially those trying to get their feet on the ground. The leading complaint is getting access, particularly to elected officials, who feel little compunction to talk to journalists whose readers or viewers don't vote in U.S. elections. "As a foreign journalist, you're very far down on the list in Washington," says Henriksson. "But that's not necessarily true for the United States outside Washington and New York. It's easier to get in touch with people outside those areas."

"That's the biggest problem," says Taipei Times correspondent Charles Snyder, "the fact that we don't have a constituency, aside from the occasional congressmen who are particularly interested in the area you're into. If you're The New York Times or The Washington Post or Wall Street Journal or television reporters, you have a much greater entrée to these people than if you're a reporter without a domestic constituency."

"Congress is the part that requires the most effort," says Leo Wieland. "You have to work pretty hard on your contacts there, because the mindset is, are you writing for somebody who's voting for us? And if the answer is no, the interest is flagging."

Wieland tells a story of trying repeatedly without success to get an in interview with Indiana Sen. Richard Lugar when Lugar was chairman of the Senate Foreign Relations Committee. He finally wrote a profile of Lugar without benefit of an interview, and an Indiana constituent of Lugar's somehow got hold of the profile in the Frankfurt paper and sent it to Lugar. "He (Lugar) then wrote me a letter and said 'thank you,' and that I'd always be welcome to see him. So that's the angle: If somebody who is actually a voter tells him, things are looking up."

GETTING STARTED

If Congress is problematic, there are some basic steps to take when arriving in Washington that will make the transition smoother. In fact, if you can arrange it, an ideal first step is to take part in the U.S. State Department's international visitors' exchange program, which includes a month of travel around the country and meetings in Washington.

Lee Siew Hua of the Straits Times of Singapore took part in the program when she moved to D.C. in 1997 and calls it "a fantastic preparation." In addition to extensive travel, she met with midlevel and senior officials at the State Department, the Commerce Department and the U.S. Trade Representative's office, as well as policy analysts at several think tanks.

Without benefit of that experience, the basic formula for getting started is this: Get to know as many reporters as you can (they've been in the same boat and will be sympathetic), meet as many government officials as you can, be patient, be prepared to be frustrated and turn to the State Department's Foreign Press Center for help.

The Foreign Press Center, located in the National Press Building, is an important starting place for foreign journalists; indeed, for many, it serves as office and home away from home. It offers one-stop shopping: an FPC press credential, work tools and meeting facilities, media briefings, press tours and—most critical—help in getting interviews with government officials and access to places like the White House and State Department. Work at the FPC is divided among a half-dozen or so desk officers representing various regions of the world, and the Center has branch offices in New York City and Los Angeles.

"We obviously encourage people to join the center so we can include them in our program, and I think most do," says center director Peter Kovach. "I'm sure the vast majority of foreign correspondents in the United States are members because they know we can help them. We get their messages to authoritative sources and we help them in a lot of ways. We help them to better understand the United States, to report more accurately and ultimately to promote a deeper appreciation of the United States and its foreign policy overseas."

The FPC has about 15 computer terminals connected to the Internet, a briefing room that will accommodate as many as 100, and a conference room for background briefings by invitation.

The first step at the FPC is to register for a press credential. It's not compulsory to register, but FPC credentials give you a leg up if you're going to apply for credentials at other places, such as the White House and State Department. The FPC acts as clearing agency for reporters who want to go to the White House, for example, and don't have a White House pass.

"The reality," says George Newman, FPC desk officer for Africa and Northern Europe, "is you can't get White House or State Department or Pentagon credentials unless you cover those places at least two or three times a week. They're not going to give you a credential if you show up just once a month for a briefing. Congress (press gallery) credentials are a little easier. We encourage people to get those if we think they have a reasonable chance of getting them."

"A one-man bureau from a third-world country, these passes really aren't going to do them a lot of good," says Newman. "At the same time, there are occasions you can get there without a pass if you have our credential and, in the case of the White House, our specific clearance requests."

One of the most important ongoing functions of the FPC is helping foreign correspondents gain access to important sources around town. "We do that a fair amount," says Newman. "We also work on behalf of people who are parachuting in for stories—there were an awful lot of those after Sept. 11 (terrorist attacks), as you can imagine." The FPC staff not only runs interference with government officials, it will also help make arrangements for you to see experts at think tanks and universities around Washington.

FPC Director Kovach acknowledges that there are limits to what the center can do, and says correspondents sometimes have unrealistic expectations.

"The president and the vice president aren't going to be available everyday," says Kovach. "What we do try to point out is that, just because you know those big names, it doesn't mean that (a) you're going to get to interview them, or (b) that they're the best source on what the topic is. Often it's the officers at the expert level that advise the top leaders who sometimes give the best interviews. It's that expert level that we tend to push, though we do get cabinet-level officials here and we get some very senior people to brief."

The FPC's press briefings are open to anyone who is a foreign journalist—nationality is determined by the news organization, not the citizenship of the journalist. A typical week might include a briefing by a foreign head of state, an assistant secretary of state and an official of the National Security Council. Some briefings are broadcast on the American Embassy television network and on the FPC Web site and transcripts are available there afterward. Briefings are usually held on the record or on background.

Media tours are another popular feature. The FPC in Washington or one of the branch offices makes all the arrangements and provides for local transportation at tour sites. Other expenses are borne by reporters. In 2001–2002, tours included visits to the site of the Olympics in Salt Lake City, a tour of the reconstruction site at the Pentagon, and a visit to upstate New York to observe the Oneida Indian Nation and a concentration of refugees around Utica.

The FPC Web site is a resource gold mine for foreign journalists. It includes details on how to obtain press credentials (including a downloadable application), transcripts of media briefings, a long list of government reports, details on upcoming media tours, and links to a vast array of Web sites: think tanks, universities, government agencies and organizations of interest, such as the International Center for Foreign Journalists.

RESOURCES

As the links on the FPC Web site illustrate, there is no shortage of expertise available at the drop of a phone call or e-mail. The city is loaded with think tanks staffed by policy experts, many of them past (and future) government officials.

"What makes Washington a very fascinating place is the number of specialists you find here," says Cameroon's Tazi. "I just don't know if you can find them anywhere else in the world." Tazi is partial to Johns Hopkins University's School of Advanced International Studies. "You can always call someone there for a certain point of view." Tazi also gives Georgetown and Howard universities high marks for their willingness to provide experts for interviews.

Wieland of Frankfurter Allgemeine says he made extensive use over the years of the Brookings Institution, the Carnegie Foundation, the American Enterprise Institute and the Heritage Foundation. "They're good at what they do," Wieland says. "They present their experts, their bios and phone numbers, and you get your phone calls returned, usually, and these people are very knowledgeable. If you do not get a quick answer from the government, or at the Congress, you still have a lot of expertise available from that quarter."

Lee Siew Hua of the Straits Times favors Brookings, Heritage ("It's very media-friendly"), AEI, and sometimes uses the Center for Strategic and International Studies, the Carnegie Endowment and the Asia Society. She says she also finds forums on international issues at the National Press Club to be helpful.

The enterprising foreign correspondent will quickly discover treasure troves of information in the government that will provide grist for stories and analysis. Wieland, for example, found the Census Bureau to be a "wonderful source" for someone trying to report and interpret ethnic and social change in the United States for a foreign audience. Like many of his colleagues, Wieland also learned that one of the best ways to understand the United States and develop sources is to report outside Washington. "I found local governments fairly easy to talk to," says Wieland, "even better if a German company had a presence in the area." For example, Wieland traveled to Alabama and South Carolina after Mercedes-Benz and BMW built manufacturing plants in those states. "That kind of angle was very helpful," Wieland says. "It helped me establish contacts to use on other stories."

ADVICE

What advice would foreign press corps veterans give newcomers? Generally, they say: Be realistic about the fact that it takes time to get established. "I'd start with a sort of negative advice," says Sweden's Henriksson. "You have to think a little more creatively than starting to call Congressman so-and-so's office. Maybe you try to use your local church or school as a place to start, for a first vantage point for your reporting. I'd also say, leave Washington, get a feel for what a big country this is . . . and how many groups there are."

Echoes Wieland: "Be open-minded. Get to know the country first. Leave behind all the European notions that they know all about this country even before they arrived, at home."

Lee Siew Hua says she spent a lot of time during her first two years in Washington attending congressional hearings. "They help you catch the tone, the emphasis and the highlights of an issue," she says. They are also a great place to make contacts, she adds. She also goes to receptions and schedules as many lunches as she can with diplomats, scholars and congressional aides. "It's amazing how important one lunch could be," she says. "After just one meal, people become friendly with you and you can call and talk to them without having to see them face to face. After one meeting, it becomes much more personal."

"The most important advice is that you've got to be conversant in this language, in issues that are important to you," says Michio Hayashi of Tokyo's Yomiuri Shimbun, who was posted earlier in New Delhi. "If you are not conversant or fluent in the language, they don't respect you. If you're not familiar and knowledgeable in issues about which you talk to those experts or government officials, without adequate knowledge and ability to make arguments and ask questions properly, they won't respect you. Washington is a place where all that matters is who you know."

13 RESOURCES

"Washington is like one big file cabinet." That comment by retired Gannett News Service chief correspondent William Ringle describes the greatest single advantage of working here as a journalist: There are few places on the globe where the tools of the trade are so readily available.

"It's not knowing something—it's knowing where to go to get it," says investigative reporter Seymour Hersh. "There's nothing you can't get sophisticated on here in a couple of hours if you know how to do it." Although you may have difficulty reaching contacts and developing sources, there's no excuse for asking unintelligent questions once you get to them.

Perhaps nothing in modern history has changed the mechanics of reporting and improved the access to information more than the creation of the Internet. Reports; press releases; studies; polls; and transcripts that you used to have to retrieve by mail, fax, special delivery or a trip to the bowels of some federal office building are now available instantly at Web sites or by e-mail. While it may have made some reporters lazier—and has certainly reduced the amount of personal interaction between reporters and sources—it has also freed up time for enterprising reporters to work more productively and creatively.

"It's made the job tremendously easier," says Larry Lipman, who covers Washington for The Palm Beach Post in the Cox bureau. "I think reporters rely on the Internet as a constant tool, so much that it's almost unimaginable that we were able to do the job before the Internet . . . it's just a wealth of information at your fingertips."

In a survey conducted for this book by co-author Cochran, more than 90 percent of some 300 responding Washington journalists said they found the Internet to be either "indispensable" or "very useful" in their reporting.

While most journalists are no doubt veterans at using the Web, it bears repeating that reporters need to be certain about the authenticity of information they find there.

Jonathan Dube, technology editor of MSNBC.com, has compiled an "Internet IQ Checklist for Journalists," republished on Poynter.org, that is a handy reference. Dube says there are five steps you should take to assess information quality before relying on anything found online:

- Authority: Who wrote it, why, and what are their credentials? Who published it and why? With whom are the author and publisher affiliated?
- Objectivity: What opinions or biases, if any, are expressed? Is there a sponsor that might have influenced the content? Is the site a mask for advertising or an agenda? Could it be satire or a hoax?
- Timeliness: When was it produced and last updated? Is it up to date?
- Sourcing: What is the source of the information and is it reliable?
- Verification: Find at least one other reputable source, preferably not online, that provides similar information.

If you can't determine even one of these, says Dube, "then you probably shouldn't rely on the information."

Many of Washington's resources are well known and are still routinely used by reporters, Internet notwithstanding. The House and Senate press galleries, for example, have the basic publications, reference works and press services necessary for covering Capitol Hill. Serious Washington reporters start their day with a thorough reading of The Washington Post. Many then scan the Congressional Record and Federal Register for the official account of what's going on in the bureaucracy and on the Hill. Those interested in in-depth treatment of Congress read Congressional Quarterly religiously, and for analysis of politics and the government at large, reporters follow the National Journal. Although beat reporters are routinely alerted to events by e-mail, they also check the wire service daybooks for news conferences and newsmaker forums, and CQ's Congressional Monitor or National Journal's Congress Daily for a rundown on committee hearings.

Those are the basics; they barely scratch the surface of what's available for reporters who get beyond handout journalism. Many additional resources related to particular beats have been described previously in this book. What follows is a sort of catchall group snapshot of resources mentioned most often by reporters.

THINK TANKS AND RESEARCH GROUPS

The thinking and commenting business is thriving in Washington, and the old-timers in the think-tank business are getting squeezed on all sides. Veterans such as the American Enterprise Institute and the Urban Institute now have competition from think tanks that reflect virtually every shade of the political spectrum, though few are considered to be openly partisan.

Most think tanks do pretty much the same things: They produce studies and analyses that they hope will attract attention and influence public policy; they sponsor seminars and retreats that allow their big contributors to hobnob with high government officials; and they serve as a temporary home for scholars and professionals who are in exile from one administration and awaiting the call of the next, and whose major interim purpose is to get quoted in the press and invited to appear on television as experts.

There's a self-serving quality in all this, but that shouldn't stop reporters from using think tanks as regular sources, for two reasons: They do a lot of interesting research, and today's think-tank scholar may be next year's—or last year's—assistant secretary of defense. Either way, he or she knows a lot about what's going on inside the government and therefore has a double value to you as a source. Most of the major tanks produce annual guides to their experts, as well as brochures that describe major studies under way.

Four think tanks dominate the Washington scene, and a fifth gets special mention because of its unique mission.

1. Brookings Institution (www.brook.edu). Brookings is the oldest and most venerable of the group, long identified with Democrats and moderately liberal thinking. It is a prolific publisher of studies and books and is known for its expertise in economics and foreign policy.

2. American Enterprise Institute (www.aei.org). This moderately conservative think tank survived a rocky management and financial period in the mid-1980s to become a leaner but still highly visible outpost for moderate Republicans and conservative Democrats. The institute is strong in social, economic and foreign policy studies but is perhaps best known for its public opinion mavens.

3. Urban Institute (www.urban.org). First created with federal funds to analyze urban issues for President Lyndon Johnson, the Urban Institute is unique in that it still depends on government contracts for much of its financing. This means that some institute researchers have to market themselves to stay employed. Despite that, the institute has a reputation among reporters for generally objective and thoughtful research in areas far beyond urban concerns. There are nine major policy centers at the institute.

4. Heritage Foundation (www.heritage.org). There has never been—and never will be—a think tank that matches the capacity of Heritage to churn out paper. Although it's the youngest of the big-four think tanks, it has also been the most innovative since its birth in 1973 and is never at a loss for new ways to promote its unabashedly conservative views. The Heritage has its own syndicate of conservative newspaper columns, and throughout its existence the foundation has produced quick-hit analyses of issues for members of Congress and a steady diet of seminars, lectures and debates. It also has created a special data analysis unit that will do custom work for journalists on a particular federal database.

5. Joint Center for Political and Economic Studies (www.jointcenter.org). Although it doesn't have the resources or the visibility of the big four, the Joint Center is a popular source for reporters covering politics and social issues. The center seeks support from both political parties to conduct research into the attitudes of blacks on a wide range of issues. The center is best known for its annual National Directory of African American Organizations and its monthly magazine Focus.

Numerous other research groups are located in Washington. Among them, the CATO Institute (www.cato.org) is known for its libertarian agenda; the Center for Strategic and International Studies (www.csis.org) is used a lot for its expertise on foreign policy and national security issues, as is the Johns Hopkins Paul H. Nitze School of Advanced International Studies (www.sais-jhu.edu); the Free Congress Foundation (www.freecongress.org) is a source for conservative dogma on social issues; and the Institute for Policy Studies (www.ips-dc.org) will give you the left-wing line on human rights and the underclass. The Washington Institute for Near East Policy (www.washingtoninstitute.org) provides pro-Israeli expertise on Middle East questions; the Worldwatch Institute (www.worldwatch.org) is a respected source for research on how population growth, weather and the abuses of man are threatening the globe. The Center for Immigration Studies (www.cis.org) touts a "pro-immigrant, low-immigration vision" and provides research and policy analysis on the impact immigration is having on the United States.

LIBRARIES, ARCHIVES AND RECORDS ROOMS

For reporters old-fashioned enough to enjoy rooting around in libraries, Washington is a dreamland, starting with the granddaddy of them all, the Library of Congress. But dozens, if not hundreds, of libraries in the Washington area are open to reporters, including most libraries operated by federal departments and agencies. Among those are some of the most specialized repositories in the country. In addition, most federal agencies maintain public documents rooms where you can inspect and copy all open files on agency business. The following libraries are among the favorites of Washington reporters.

The Library of Congress (www.loc.gov)

In addition to all its other resources available to the public, the Library of Congress provides a reference service for reporters who are accredited to the congressional press galleries. The service is intended to respond to simple requests, such as verification of a quote or biographical fact, and does not engage in extended research. Reporters can also obtain materials produced for members of Congress by the library's Congressional Research Service. Technically, the requesting congressional member is supposed to give approval for the release, but reporters who develop sources among the scores of researchers at the CRS can usually get materials without going through that formality. The CRS gets more than a thousand requests a day from Congress for research, books, editorials, and so on; about 90 percent of its product is never published anywhere. Almost any subject you would ever write about has been studied by the CRS at one time, so it's a good place to start your research. CRS reports are not available on the LOC Web site.

The library's Web site will also connect you to the congressional Web site THOMAS (thomas.loc.gov), which lets you track bills and public laws, roll-call votes, committee reports, committee schedules, and so on.

The Senate Library

The Senate Library has one of the most helpful staffs on the Hill. The only caution: Service to members of Congress and their staffs takes precedence over reporters' requests. Open weekdays and also at night and on weekends when the Senate is in session, the library has an excellent reading room and an exhaustive collection of reference books in several nooks and crannies on the third floor and attic on the Senate side of the Capitol. Library staff can answer general reference questions.

The National Press Club's Eric Friedheim Library (npc.press.org/library)

The Eric Friedheim Library, in the National Press Building, is open to members of the press club, but nonmembers who are accredited to the congressional press galleries can use it for an $80-a-year fee. The location alone makes that an attractive offer. The library maintains a Web site that is rich in resource links, and offers computer and Internet access and a research service.

Firstgov (www.firstgov.gov)

This Web site, run by the General Services Administration, is the official government gateway and is aimed at consumers more than journalists. Created in the Clinton administration and expanded under the second Bush administration, it links you to various federal and state government Web sites by subject area. It also includes links to a wide array of government phone directories.

Fedstats (www.fedstats.gov)

FedStats is a nifty stop for data-gatherers. It provides access to official statistics collected and published by more than 70 federal agencies.

The National Archives (www.nara.gov)

The National Archives is the official repository of federal government records dating back to 1775. The 10 presidential libraries open as of 2002, plus the collection of Richard Nixon's and Bill Clinton's papers, are managed by the archives. Government rules and a lack of declassification staff mean that most available information at the archives is more than 30 years old. Congressional investigative records not made public previously, for example, are closed for 50 years.

Records at the presidential libraries may be more easily obtained, depending on whether the former president claims that they are personal, and depending on reviews by White House national security specialists and by agencies where the material originated. The bulk of the 44 million Nixon papers, which have been the focus of numerous legal proceedings, are yet to be made public. These kinds of presidential papers are a logical resource for reporters profiling members of Congress or any prominent figure who might have had dealings with the White House.

The National Security Archive (www.gwu.edu/~nsarchiv)

The National Security Archive, at George Washington University, is a library conceived by Scott Armstrong, a former investigative reporter for The Washington Post and co-author of "The Brethren." It contains a unique collection of unclassified or declassified documents, oral histories, congressional reports and court records designed to illuminate and resolve contradictions in the contemporary history of national security and foreign policy initiatives. Its resources are available to all journalists.

The Library of Medicine (www.nlm.nih.gov)

The Library of Medicine is an example of a specialized library that can make life a lot easier for the diligent researcher. Part of the National Institutes of Health, the library is located in Bethesda, Md., and houses more than four million books, journals, manuscripts and other items. Its Web site provides access to MEDLINE, a searchable database of more than 11 million medical articles, as well as MEDLINEPlus, a guide to health information for consumers.

The Federal Election Commission (www.fec.gov)

Old-timers in Washington can remember when searching campaign finance records meant traipsing down to the FEC and groping your way through paper documents lined up in banks of file cabinets. Then for many years, the same search meant going to the FEC public records room and logging on to their computers. The Internet now means you can do all that from your own computer in your office. The FEC Web site provides access to databases on campaign contributions and expenditures, as well as background on campaign laws, election results, election calendars, and so forth.

NEWSLETTERS AND TRADE PRESS

One of the best aids in following a beat in Washington is to monitor the newsletters and magazines that cover relevant agencies for a specialized clientele, primarily the industry being regulated or otherwise affected by the agency or program. The trade press is a booming industry—newsletters are launched almost weekly in Washington, and others fall by the wayside. Adoption of any major piece of legislation is guaranteed to spawn at least one and perhaps several newsletters that examine the smallest nuances of the law and the regulations adopted to put it in place.

Lobbyists and bureaucrats feel more comfortable talking to trade press reporters precisely because those reporters are specialists who understand what they're covering and what questions to ask. Not surprisingly, lobbyists and bureaucrats use newsletters to leak stuff and send messages. Although big-time print reporters sometimes thumb their noses at the trade press, the better ones acknowledge the value of newsletters as sources not only for tips and insider gossip but also for authoritative reporting on complex subjects. The magazine Aviation Week and Space Technology, for example, is considered virtually indispensable by reporters who follow the aeronautics industry.

Two of the major publishers of specialty reports in Washington are the Bureau of National Affairs (www.bna.com) and McGraw-Hill (www.mcgraw-hill.com). Between them, they put out more than 200 publications and Web services covering everything from affirmative action to water pollution. BNA, founded in 1929, now sprawls across three adjacent buildings in Northwest Washington.

About half of BNA's subscribers are lawyers, and the rest of the audience includes large numbers of human resource officers and regulators concerned about government action in the areas of environment, health and safety.

OTHER PUBLICATIONS

The list could be long, but only a few other publications are frequently mentioned by reporters. Anyone who follows Congress, for example, will want to read the Capitol Hill newspapers Roll Call (www.rollcall.com) and The Hill (www.hillnews.com). They have a gossipy small-town flavor but occasionally contain hard-hitting pieces.

GOVERNMENT WATCHDOGS

Almost any beat in Washington eventually will take you into the realm of government hanky-panky. You don't have to be Seymour Hersh or Jack Anderson to uncover a conflict of interest deep in the bowels of the Department of Housing and Urban Development. Chapter 11 deals with investigative reporting in Washington, but here's a quick review of taxpayer-supported resources that can help you develop background for any special project.

1. The General Accounting Office (www.gao.gov). The GAO is one of the most underused resources in Washington. It performs more than a thousand investigations every year, the vast majority of them requested by members or committees of Congress, and provides testimony to Congress hundreds of times a year. Many of its investigators like to talk to the press and can sometimes give you leads that will take you beyond the reach of their investigations. Get to know them.

2. Inspectors General (www.ignet.gov). The IGs in all the cabinet departments and federal agencies are political appointees and not known for being palsy-walsy with reporters, but that doesn't mean you shouldn't read their reports, try to interview them if they've shown any signs of independence and try to cultivate sources on their staffs. Their reports can be a fabulous source of stories.

3. The Congressional Budget Office (www.cbo.gov). As part of the budget reform movement in the mid-1970s, the CBO was created by Congress to counter the too-rosy economic and budget projections emanating from the White House Office of Management and Budget. But CBO does far more than analyze the president's budget and issue projections. It also churns out numerous studies a year, examining policy in the areas of health, the economy, trade, agriculture, education and national security.

CONGRESSIONAL STAFFS

Pick a subject to write about and rest assured that there's a lawyer or investigator or legislative aide on Capitol Hill who knows a great deal about it and, more important, can steer you toward bureaucrats and lobbyists who know even more. In addition, congressional staff members can point you toward hearing records and other documents that provide background and new leads. Remember: Congress gets involved in everything sooner or later.

SPECIAL INTEREST GROUPS

Many of Washington's hundreds of lobbying and private watchdog groups refer to themselves as public interest groups. That designation seems to presume that their interests as an organization always dovetail precisely with those of the public at large. It is more accurate to say that their interests occasionally coincide with those of a majority of Americans, but their interests may just as often reflect only a minority view. Special interest groups inevitably have an ax to grind, but that's what the American system of government is all about.

The presence in Washington of so many pleaders makes a reporter's job all the more interesting—or should. Whatever they're called, whether they represent business barons, narrow ideological agendas, or broad and pristine public policy objectives, lobbying groups are great resources for the press. Cultivating them can be a tedious game, but one that almost certainly will pay dividends over time.

Every significant cause in America is represented by someone in Washington, and often by a small army. In any given administration, some groups are in the ascendancy, others in decline. Regardless of their health, many of these groups continue to churn out annual "report cards" on members of Congress and maintain PACs that they hope will buy congressional access, if not votes.

A reporter trying to chart all the potential sources of influence in any Washington battle—be it a piece of legislation, a controversial regulation, a big budget item or a presidential nomination—has many places to look. Among the most obvious are the following.

Trade Associations and Lobbying Coalitions

Described in detail in Chapter 10, trade associations play a powerful role as protectors of their industries and professions. Their officials are generally more open with the press than individual lobbyists are, but their value as sources is often less. One of the fads of recent years in Washington lobbydom is to create ad hoc coalitions on behalf of one bill that cut across industries and sometimes even ideologies. The idea is that such tentative alliances can produce the image of a widespread outpouring of public demand. One component of this strategy is to organize and unleash grassroots sentiment in the form of telephone calls, letters and e-mails to members of Congress. The members, of course, can spot an orchestrated campaign a mile away, but it still makes them take notice.

Political Parties

The Democratic (www.democrats.org) and Republican national committees (www.rnc.org), as well as the two parties' campaign committees in the House (www.dccc.org and www.nrcc.org) and Senate (www.dscc.org and www.nrsc.org), often are drawn into major confrontations when the political reputation of the president or the opposition leadership is on the line. The committees not only help orchestrate the party line in the media but also conduct polls and arrange paid advertising to promote the cause. These staffs and their chairs are excellent sources for political, congressional and White House reporters.

State and Local Organizations

Governors, mayors, county governments, state legislatures and even universities maintain large stables of lobbyists in Washington to guard the federal money pipeline and to prospect for new "pork." Many of them do budget and legislative analyses that are useful to regional reporters. Particularly helpful are the National Governors Association (www.nga.org), the National Association of Counties (www.naco.org) and the National Conference of State Legislatures (www.ncsl.org).

Self-Appointed Watchdogs

Self-appointed watchdogs come in all sizes and flavors. The industrial-strength version is represented by consumer advocate Ralph Nader and the group Common Cause. Nader's empire, called Public Citizen (www.citizen.org), has seven divisions: Auto Safety, Congress Watch, the Health Research Group, Critical Mass Energy and Environmental Program, The Litigation Group, Global Trade Watch, and Buyers Up, a group-buying organization that encourages a smarter consumer in the marketplace. Common Cause (www.commoncause.org), which began as a crusade for government accountability and ethics, has increasingly branched out into more-contentious issues such as arms control and defense spending. But it has made its biggest mark with reporters for its tireless pursuit of campaign finance abuses.

In the defense area are groups that sport a lower profile. You'll find such watchdogs as the Center for Defense Information (www.cdi.org), a moderately liberal critic of much big-ticket Pentagon spending; the Project on Government Oversight (www.pogo.org), the successor to the Project on Military Procurement, an outlet for defense whistle-blowers that drives the Pentagon brass into apoplexy; and the Union of Concerned Scientists (www.ucsusa.org), which has done a lot of work on missile defense, among other issues. The Center for Strategic and Budgetary Assessments (www.csbaonline.org), formerly called the Defense Budget Project, has a solid reputation among reporters seeking perspective on the Pentagon budget, and the National Taxpayers' Union (www.ntu.org) is a good source for budget horror stories of all shades and colors.

REFERENCE BOOKS AND DIRECTORIES

Trying to figure out who might have the information you're seeking is a constant part of reporting in Washington. Fortunately, the city abounds in books that explain how things work, where people work and which groups are trying to influence what issues. One of the best aids in maintaining a well-stocked library is the annual catalog of publications offered by Congressional Quarterly. There is no exclusive list, of course, but, assuming you have access to the Congressional Record, the Federal Register, Congressional Quarterly and National Journal, the following resources will serve nicely as a basic reference library for any Washington correspondent.

Start with the phone books for the District of Columbia, northern Virginia and suburban Maryland. You'd be surprised how many reporters look in the phone book last, when they ought to look there first. Until you've built your own Rolodex, you'll be able to find most of the offices and organizations you need to reach in phone books. Federal agencies have their own phone books, too, and you'll want to obtain those if your beat requires close coverage of them.

Then add these essentials:

The United States Government Manual (www.access.gpo.gov/nara), the best basic guide to federal agencies and their powers, responsibilities and key personnel.

Washington Information Directory, published annually by Congressional Quarterly (www.cqpressbookstore.com). Not only is this directory crammed with organization charts and specialized lists of key personnel, such as government Freedom of Information officers, it also breaks down Washington into

17 subject categories (education and culture, law and justice, and science and space, for example) and then lists both government and private groups with jurisdiction or interest in each subject area.

The Capitol Source, a phone book published by National Journal (nationaljournal.com). The Source divides Washington into four groups: government, corporate, professional and media—with numerous subgroups, such as law firms, political consultants, trade and professional associations, and so forth.

Public Interest Profiles, compiled by the Foundation for Public Affairs and published by Congressional Quarterly (www.cqpressbookstore.com). This helpful book provides snapshots of more than 200 Washington organizations (including think tanks, which consider themselves to be public interest advocates), all grouped according to subject.

Several other books facilitate coverage of the federal bureaucracy:

The Federal Directory (www.carrollpub.com), a phone book published and updated bimonthly by Carroll Publishing Company. It lists alphabetically and by organization all top and midlevel bureaucrats in Washington.

The Federal Staff Directory (fsd.cq.com), published annually by Congressional Staff Directory, Limited. It contains the names and titles of the top 28,000 officials in the executive branch, along with 2,400 biographies of key executives.

The Federal Regulatory Directory, published biennially by Congressional Quarterly. It (www.cqpressbookstore.com) explains the functions of each regulatory agency and lists its top officials.

The following books are helpful for covering Congress:

The Congressional Directory, published by the Government Printing Office (www.access.gpo.gov). The official bible of Hill staffers and members, it also includes directories of the executive and judicial branches.

The Congressional Yellow Book, published by the Monitor Publishing Company (www.leadershipdirectories.com), and the Congressional Staff Directory (fsd.cq.com), published by Congressional Staff Directory, Limited. Both are useful guides to Hill staff; the latter also includes biographies of key staffers. Another good addition to the field is the Almanac of the Unelected. Published by Bernan Associates (www.bernan.com), it profiles the top 600 or so staff members on the Hill.

The Almanac of American Politics, published by National Journal (nationaljournal.com), and *Politics in America*, published by Congressional Quarterly (www.cqpressbookstore.com). Both contain comprehensive profiles of the members of Congress, and political guides to their states and districts.

A valuable supplement to them is Congressional Quarterly's Congressional Districts in the 1990s, which provides massive census data.

A good book for historical perspective on Congress and how it works is the massive Guide to Congress (www.cqpressbookstore.com). Vital Statistics on Congress, by Norman Ornstein, Thomas Mann and Michael Malbin, is a useful compendium of data on congressional voting alignments, budgeting, campaign finance, and so forth, and is published by the American Enterprise Institute (www.aei.org). No bookshelf in the congressional field is complete without regularly updated volumes on House and Senate spending. The Report of the House Clerk, issued quarterly, and the Report of the Secretary of the Senate, issued semiannually, list the expenditures of every member of Congress and every committee, including staff salaries by name.

Reporters interested in the courts in Washington will want two basic works, the Guide to the U.S. Supreme Court (www.cqpressbookstore.com), published by Congressional Quarterly, and the Judicial Staff Directory (www.jsd.cq.com), published by Congressional Staff Directory, Limited. The Guide is an excellent layperson's resource for studying precedents. The Staff Directory lists all federal judges and top staff members in Washington and across the country.

Finally, reporters who follow the influence-peddling activities of Washington's lobbyists and PACs should start with two publications: Washington Representatives, a directory of some 20,000 Washington lobbyists that is published by Columbia Books (www.columbiabooks.com), and the Almanac of Federal PACs, published by Amward Publications (www.politicalresources.com) and compiled and edited by Ed Zuckerman.

INDEX